Bredon

In summertime
The bells they s...
Round both the shi...
In steeples far and near,
A happy noise to hear.

Here of a Sunday morning
My love and I would lie,
And see the coloured counties,
And hear the larks so high
About us in the sky.

The bells would ring to call her
In valleys miles away:
'Coe to church, good people;
Good people, come and pray.'
But here my love would stay.

And I would turn and answer
Among the springing thyme,
'Oh, peal upon our wedding,
And we will hear the chime,
And come to church in time.'

But when the snows at Christmas
On Bredon top were strown,
My love rose up so early
And stole out unbeknown
And went to church alone.

They tolled the one bell only,
Groom there was none to see,
The mourners followed after,
And so to church went she,
And would not wait for me.

The bells they sound on Bredon,
And still the steeples hum,
'Come all to church, good people,'
Oh, noisy bells, be dumb;
I hear you, I will come.

A E Houseman 1859-1936

Colin Carruther, Iona Gallery, Woodstock

3

I have a close relationship with all the areas for which I have produced guidebooks. As with siblings, these relationships differ in style and intensity, and develop over time. None of the other regions is quite as close to me as the Cotswolds…my regional twin, if you like.

Until moving to North Devon, the Cotswolds were my base for 30 years. For 20 of those years I lived and ran Goldeneye in Cheltenham. I walked, drove and cycled around the area - researching, writing and photographing for Goldeneye maps and guides. I played cricket in many of the towns and villages, and sampled many a brew in the local hostelries. I eventually married a Cotswold girl and our wedding took place in Gloucester Cathedral, a privilege rarely granted to those outside the Church. It so happened that Caroline's grandfather had been Vicar of Guiting Power for 25 years and had collapsed and died on the Altar of the Cathedral while taking a service. An unique event that gave us entry to the inner circle. My parents and father-in-law still live in the Cotswolds providing me with a base there. My proof reader Mike Taffinder was brought up in Bibury and educated in Cheltenham. David Cox my cartographer has lived in West Oxfordshire all his life. Chris Dyer, my book designer, lived in the South Cotswolds for many years whilst working for James Dyson. Our Cotswold credentials are significant and deeply ingrained and this guidebook represents the sum of our collective years in the Cotswolds and all the knowledge and opinions that that engenders.

Having worked on Cotswolds Mapguides over the years, it has been a long-standing ambition to produce a book on this scale and my intention is that it be practical and easy-to-use, clear to navigate, fun to read and a pleasure to turn the page, and one that will encourage you to delve beyond the surface of the region. There aren't enough pages in this edition to fit in everything and so future editions of the book will grow and develop - in parallel, I hope, with your relationship with the region. For this is more than a simple guidebook - it is meant to be a souvenir and an object to treasure.

As well as photography, I have included contemporary and traditional paintings to provide a different perspective. The touring maps offer an immense amount of detail, not necessarily common to guidebooks, and this has saved me a lot of unnecessary descriptive prose. But the major difference of this guidebook compared to many others on the market (who first commission a writer, then gather the images from various picture libraries) is that I have researched and written it, and taken 90% of the photography. Repeated visits to chosen sites at different times of the day or year, in differing lights and weather, have given me a greater insight into my subject, and helped create an intense labour of love. Goldeneye's small enthusiastic team works closely together on each guidebook. And they build up an undiluted passion for each region as well as for the guidebooks as a series. So, thank you Chris (book designer), Dave (cartographer) and Caroline (sub editor) for sharing this incredible journey.

I realise that for many this may be your first time in the Cotswolds and so I want you to be made aware of the best the region has to offer. It is home to some remarkable hotels and restaurants and some luxurious inns and B&Bs. I believe I have illustrated the finest. Not all are excessively pricey but the top hotels are not cheap. They offer an experience that will live with you forever and are thus worthy of a special occasion. It is worth noting that many serve afternoon tea to all comers so you can experience at least a taste of their luxury. If you prefer to lead the simple life you can always try one of the campsites listed - these are independent sites geared up for those wishing to sleep under (the stars or) canvas.

William Fricker *Buckland Barton, June 2009*

The Maytime Inn, Asthall

CONTENTS

What and where is the region known as the Cotswolds? To those who know it, this may seem like a silly question. However, it is a place that manifests itself in many different ways to different people. Even down to the area they would define as the Cotswolds on a map. To some fashionistas, and magazine editors, the Cotswolds bears comparison to the New York Hamptons and Tuscany. Whilst to others the name is synonymous with wool and hunting, stone walls and majestic churches.

The Cotswolds region is perched on the central section of a ridge of oolitic limestone. The geological structure has thus had a profound and lasting effect on the landscape, and 'look' of the area. The oolitic limestone that forms these hills has the appearance of thousands of tiny balls, like fish roe, and is between 200 and 175 million years old.

This ridge has been tilted on its side and is drained by streams and river valleys that lead off in a south-easterly direction to feed the Thames basin. On the western edge the scarp is steep in places with outcrops of rounded hills, notably Cam Long Down and Bredon Hill, and makes for fine walking country and pleasing views across to the Malvern Hills and Wales.

Linguistically, the Cotswolds derived their name from two Saxon words: 'Cote' - sheep fold, and 'Wold' - bare hill. This references the importance of sheep in the development of the area. And it is to the Cotswold Lion sheep that one must look for the origin of wealth and endeavour that brought prosperity to this region.

Neolithic Man found refuge on these hills from the swamps of the Severn and Thames flood plains. The Celtic Dobunni tribe established hill forts where they farmed, bartered their crafts and founded coinage before the Romans arrived. They were not a warlike tribe like their neighbours the Silurians (Welsh) and eased into a compatible relationship with the conquering Romans to build Corinium Dobunnorum (Cirencester) into the second largest Roman settlement in Britain with a populace of 12,000 inhabitants.

The Saxon farmer laid the foundations of prosperity for the medieval wool merchants, and it was these merchants who built the great 'Wool' churches and manor houses.

Henry VIII's Dissolution of the Monasteries in the C16 saw the destruction of the Abbeys at Cirencester, Winchcombe, Hailes and Malmesbury. The first and last battles of the English Civil War, 1641-1651, saw skirmishes at Edgehill, Lansdowne (Bath) and Stow-On-The-Wold.

In the more peaceful C18, Bath and Cheltenham epitomised the elegance, hedonism and splendour of the Georgian era.

The landscape is rich in imagery: dry-stone walls divide the vast, sweeping sheep pastures and lazy, winding, trout streams meander through the rich pastureland. And, scattered across this landscape, you will come across quaint hamlets undisturbed by coach, sightseer or time itself. All this makes for an idyllic scene rarely bettered in England.

In recent times this region's closeness to London has attracted wealthy residents and an increase in second homes being bought by out-of-towners. This development brings with it all the associated benefits and disadvantages. Now the region attracts glitzy minor celebrities with their hangers on in tow and the seemingly necessary trumpet and fanfare. This has meant an increase of high-class restaurants and pubs which is of benefit to all. And, of course, any money spent in the area ensures that the great historic buildings are being brought back to their original glory and maintained for future generations - for which I for one am very grateful.

A Day at Cheltenham Races

Antique Trail: Tetbury to Burford to Stow

Asparagus at the Plough Inn, Ford

Bore Breakfast, Old Passage Inn, Arlingham

Christmas Carol Concert & Evensong, Gloucester Cathedral

Climb Broadway Tower to view the 13 counties

Collect conkers in Cirencester Park

Cycle (or drive) down the Coln Valley

Day's shopping spree in Bath and or Cheltenham

Enjoy a play at the Royal Shakespeare Theatre, Stratford

Enter the weird and wonderful world of Charles Paget-Wade at Snowshill Manor

Follow the 'Wool' Trail starting at the Cotswold Woollen Weavers to Cotswold Farm Park to one of the many 'Wool' churches

Follow the Arts & Crafts Movement Trail: Kelmscott Manor to Sapperton Church to Cheltenham Art Gallery to Arts & Crafts Guild, Chipping Campden

Mess about on the river in a punt (or rowing boat) at Bath or Stratford

Moreton Show

Pamper yourself at the Roman Baths

Prescott Hill Climb

Sheep shearing, Cotswold Farm Park

Take a week off and infuse yourself with music at one or all of the Bath, Cheltenham and Three Choirs festivals

The first snowdrops at the Rococo Garden, Painswick

The snowdrops (all ninety one varieties) at Colesbourne Park

Three Counties Show, Malvern

Visit five "Wool" churches in a day

Visit spooky Woodchester Mansion

Visit the Roman Villa at Chedworth followed by a walk and picnic in the woods

Walk a section of the Cotswold Way

Walk from Lower to Upper Slaughter

Walk the ridge of the Malvern Hills in the steps of Edward Elgar

Walk to the top of Bredon Hill and listen for the skylark

Watch a Polo match at the Beaufort or Cirencester Polo Clubs

Wake boarding or wind surfing, Cotswold Water Park

Westonbirt Arboretum in the Autumn and Spring

WHICH VILLAGE TO VISIT

The Cotswolds are noted for their wealth of beautiful villages. Cotswold villages are often grouped under the same name, for example Upper and Lower Slaughter, Little and Great Tew, Duntisbourne Leer, Middle Duntisbourne and Dunstisbourne Abbots. And, if so named, it is well worth visiting the collective for they are never too far apart, and often connected by footpaths. The reason for your visit may be to explore the church, or perhaps to visit the village pub and, as luck would have it, it is often the case that the two are found right next door to each other. This is a personal selection.

1. Bibury
William Morris described Bibury as one of the prettiest villages in England.

2. Bisley
Home of the writer Jilly Cooper. Noted for the Well Dressing on Ascension Day and its stone cottages.

3. Bourton-On-The-Water
One of the most popular beauty spots, but is best avoided on a busy bank holiday.

4. Broadway
'The Painted Lady of the Cotswolds' is a term often used to describe this beautiful village.

5. Burford
A fine introduction to the area for there are splendid inns and pretty hidden cottages.

6. Castle Combe
One of the prettiest and most visited of English villages lies sheltered in a hidden valley.

7. Chipping Campden
If you choose to visit just one Cotswold village make sure it's this one.

8. The Duntisbournes
A group of hamlets dotted along a beautiful wooded valley. The Dunt Brook flows through each hamlet.

9. Great Tew
A sensationally beautiful village lined with ironstone cottages covered in thatch or stone tiles.

10. Guiting Power
An estate village untouched by time and the ubiquitous property developer.

11. Painswick
Its description as 'The Queen of the Cotswolds' is justified. The churchyard is famous for its 99 yews.

12. Stanton
A charming village with houses of honey-coloured stone. The Mount Inn is a welcome refuge.

13. Stanway
This village is dominated by the outstanding Manor House and one of the country's finest tithe barns.

14. Upper & Lower Slaughter
One of the most popular of the twin villages. Famous for the Old Mill and the three classy hotels.

WHERE TO STAY

Lygon Arms, Broadway

This is a selection of our favourite hotels, B&Bs and campsites to make choosing your place of stay an easy and quick process. The selection has been rigorous and determined by the professional care and attention to detail one would expect from only the very best. The odd, quirky house can be fun, too. B&Bs rarely provide evening sustenance but the owners will happily advise you of the best places to eat in the locale. The English Country House Hotel is well represented here, too. Nowhere in the British Isles has a region such an abundance of sophisticated and stylish hotels, from the traditional to the state of the art Spa. I suggest you view the venues' websites to find one that suits your budget, style and expectation. Sleep well and bon appetit. This is a judicious selection of some of the establishments listed in the book.

Boutique Hotels

Cotswolds88Hotel, Kemps Lane, Painswick. 01452 813688
www.cotswolds88hotel.com

Cotswold House Hotel, The Square, Chipping Campden.
01386 840330 www.cotswoldhouse.com

Spa Country House Hotels

Barnsley House. 01285 740000 www.barnsleyhouse.com

Calcot Manor, Tetbury. 01666 890391 www.calcotmanor.co.uk

Cowley Manor. 01242 870900 www.cowleymanor.com

Lygon Arms, High Street, Broadway. 01386 852255
www.barcelo-hotels.co.uk/lygonarms

Country House Hotels

Bay Tree Hotel, Sheep Street, Burford. 01993 822791
www.cotswold-inns-hotels.co.uk/baytree

Buckland Manor Hotel, Nr Broadway. 01386 852626
www.bucklandmanor.co.uk

Feathers Hotel, Market Street, Woodstock. 01993 811251
www.woodstockarms.co.uk

Greenway, Shurdington. 01242 862352
www.thegreenway.co.uk

Lords of the Manor, Upper Slaughter. 01451 820243
www.lordsofthemanor.com

Lower Slaughter Manor. 01451 820456
www.lowerslaughter.com

Mill House Hotel, Station Road, Kingham. 01608 658188
www.millhousehotel.co.uk

Rectory, Crudwell. 01666 577194 www.therectoryhotel.com

Small Hotels

Corse Lawn Hotel, Nr Tewkesbury. 01452 780771
www.corselawn.com

Cottage in The Wood, Holywell Road, Malvern. 01684 588860
www.cottageinthewood.co.uk

Dial House, Bourton-On-The-Water. 01451 822244
www.dialhousehotel.com

Evesham Hotel, Cooper's Lane, Evesham. 01386 765566
www.eveshamhotel.com

Fosse Manor Hotel, Stow-On-The-Wold. 01451 830354
www.fossemanor.co.uk

Grapevine Hotel, Stow-On-The-Wold. 01451 830354
www.fossemanor.co.uk

New Inn, Coln St Aldwyn. 01285 750651 www.new-inn.co.uk

Noel Arms Hotel, High Street. Chipping Campden.
01386 840317 www.noelarmshotel.com

Swan Hotel, Bibury. 01285 740695
www.cotswold-inns-hotels.co.uk

The Inn at Fossebridge. 01285 720721
www.fossebridgeinn.co.uk

Washbourne Court, Lower Slaughter. 01451 822143
www.washbournecourt.co.uk

Inns With Rooms

Churchill Arms, Paxford. 01386 594000
www.thechurchillarms.com

Ebrington Arms, Ebrington. 01386 593223
www.theebringtonarms.co.uk

Falkland Arms, Great Tew. 01608 683653
www.falklandarms.org.uk

Fox Inn, Lower Oddington. 01451 870555 www.foxinn.net

Howard Arms, Ilmington. 01608 682226
www.howardarms.com

Kings Arms, Stow-On-The-Wold. 01451 830364
www.thekingsarmsstow.co.uk

Kings Head Inn, Bledington. 01608 658365
www.thekingsheadinn.net

Lamb Inn, Sheep Street, Burford. 01993 823155
www.cotswold-inns-hotels.co.uk/lamb

Maytime, Asthall. 01993 822068 www.themaytime.com

Sign of the Angel, Church Street, Lacock. 01249 730230
www.lacock.co.uk

Wheatsheaf, Northleach. 01451 860244
www.cotswoldswheatsheaf.com

White Hart, Winchcombe. 01242 602359
www.wineandsausage.co.uk

Wild Duck at Ewen. 01285 770310 www.thewildduckinn.co.uk

Luxurious B&Bs

Bradford Old Windmill, 4 Mason's Lane, Bradford-on-Avon.
01225 866842 www.bradfordoldwindmill.co.uk

Cardynham House, Tibbiwell Street, Painswick. 01452 814006
www.cardynham.co.uk

Mill Hay House, Broadway. 01386 852498 www.millhay.co.uk

No.12 Park Street, Cirencester. 01285 640232
www.no12cirencester.co.uk

Thirty Two, Imperial Square, Cheltenham. 01242 771110
www.thirtytwoltd.com

Country House B&B

Barton House, Barton-on-the-Heath. 01608 674303

Blanche House, Turkdean. 01451 861176
www.blanchehousebandb.co.uk

Clapton Manor, Clapton-on-the-Hill. 01451 810202
www.claptonmanor.co.uk

Lords of the Manor, Upper Slaughter ss

Isbourne Manor, Winchcombe. 01242 602281
www.isbourne-manor.co.uk

Ivydene House, Uckinghall. 01684 592453
www.ivydenehouse.net

Malt House, Broad Campden. 01386 840295
www.malt-house.co.uk

Rectory Farmhouse, Lower Swell. 01451 832351

Winstone Glebe B&B, Winstone. 01285 821451
www.winstoneglebe.com

Guest Accommodation (B&B)

Hanover House, Cheltenham. 01242 541297
www.hanoverhouse.org

Talboys House, Church Street, Tetbury.   01666 503597
www.talboyshouse.com

Lacock Pottery, 1 The Tanyard, Lacock. 01249 730266
www.lacockbedandbreakfast.com

No.107 Gloucester Street, Cirencester. 01285 657861

Country Cottage B&B

Nation House B&B, 3 George Street, Bisley. 01452 770197

Thatch Cottage, Folly Lane, Lacock. 01249 730398
www.thatchcottagelacock.com

True Heart, The Street, Frampton-on-Severn. 01452 740504
www.thetrueheart.co.uk

Farmhouse and Barn B&Bs

Barn B&B, Pensham. 01386 555270
www.pensham-barn.co.uk

Blackwell Grange. 01608 682357 www.blackwellgrange.co.uk

Brooklands Farm, Ewen. 01285 770487

Cross O' Th' Hill Farm, Clifford Road, Stratford-upon-Avon.
01789 204738   www.cross-o-th-hill-farm.com

Deerhurst B&B. 01684 293358 www.deerhurstbandb.co.uk

Rectory Farm, Salford. 01608 643209 www.rectoryfarm.info

Salford Farm House, Salford Priors. 01386 870000
www.salfordfarmhouse.co.uk

Snowshill Hill Estate. 01386 853959

Sudeley Hill Farm, Winchcombe. 01242 602344

Westward, Nr Winchcombe. 01242 604372
www.westward-sudeley.co.uk

Whalley Farm House, Whittington. 01242 820213
www.whalleyfarm.co.uk

Self-Catering

Frampton Court (The Orangery), Frampton-on-Severn. 01452
740698 www.framptoncourtestate.co.uk

Upper Court, Kemerton. 01386 725351
www.uppercourt.co.uk

Rustic Camping

Far Peak Camping, Northleach. 01285 720858
www.farpeakcamping.co.uk

Folly Farm Campsite, Notgrove. 01451 820285
www.cotswoldcamping.net

Long Compton Camping, Mill Farm. 01608 684663

Thistledown Environment Centre (organic campsite),
Nympsfield. 01453 860420 www.thistledown.org.uk

WHERE TO EAT & DRINK

Trouble House, Tetbury ss

Selecting an inn or restaurant can make or break a romantic weekend. It may also determine where you decide to stay. Luckily, you have an amazing choice. The Cotswolds has an over supply of food emporia, from the humble tearoom to the swanky restaurant and a vast selection of pubs from the now ubiquitous gastro-pub to traditional hostelries steeped in history and character. The area also has three fine breweries namely Donningtons, Hook Norton Brewery and the Uley Brewery. Specialist cider houses have fallen by the wayside. The English Country House Hotel is well represented here, too, and they all have prestigious restaurants and (often) a more laid-back brasserie or bistro for informal dining. So bottoms up and bon appetit, again. This is a judicious selection of some of the establishments listed in the book.

Cafés, Bistros & Delis

Blades Coffee Shop, The Old Prison, Northleach.

Blue Zucchini Brasserie, 7-9 Church Street, Tetbury. 01666 505 852

Broadway deli, 16 High Street, Broadway. 01386 853040

Hampers Food & Wine Company, Oxford Street, Woodstock. 01993 811535 www.hampersfoodandwine.co.uk

Hamptons Deli, High Street, Chipping Sodbury

Hobbs House, 4 George Street, Nailsworth. 01453 839396 www.hobbshousebakery.co.uk

Lakeside Brasserie, Spring Lake, Cotswold Water Park.

Made By Bob, Corn Hall, Cirencester. www.foodmadebybob.com

New Brewery Arts, Brewery Court, Cirencester. 01285 657181 www.newbreweryarts.org.uk

Olive Tree, 28 George Street. Nailsworth. 01453 834802 www.theolivetree-nailsworth.com

Quayles, 1 Long Street, Tetbury. 01666 505151 www.quayles.co.uk

Rectory Kitchen, Off Black Jack Street, Cirencester. 01285 644700 www.therectorykitchen.com

Williams Kitchen, 3 Fountain Street, Nailsworth. 01453 835507 www.fishandseafood.co.uk

Ethnic Restaurants

Chef Imperial, High Street, Woodstock. 01993 813593

La Galleria Ristorante Italiano, 2 Market Place, Woodstock. 01993 813381 www.la-galleria.co.uk

La Passione, Chipping Sodbury 01454 326444

Mayflower Chinese Restaurant, 29 Sheep Street, Cirencester. 01285 642777 (also in Cheltenham)

Siam Thai, 1 Horse Street, Chipping Sodbury 01454 850095

Tinto, 50 High Street, Stroud. 01453 756668

Farm Shops with Restaurants

Daylesford Organic Farmshop. 01608 731700 www.daylesfordorganic.com

The Organic Farm Shop, Burford Road, Cirencester. 01285 640441 www.theorganicfarmshop.co.uk

Gastro-Pubs

Bell, Alderminster. 01789 450414 www.thebellald.co.uk

Fox Inn, Lower Oddington. 01451 870555 www.foxinn.net

Gumstool Inn, Calcot Manor, Tetbury. 01666 890391 www.calcotmanor.co.uk

Bell at Sapperton. 01285 760298 www.foodatthebell.co.uk

Churchill Arms, Paxford. 01386 594000 www.thechurchillarms.com

Fox Inn, Lower Oddington. 01451 870555 www.foxinn.net

Horse & Groom, Charlton. 01666 823904 www.horseandgroominn.com

Kingham Plough. 01608 658327 www.thekinghamplough.co.uk

Kings Head Inn, Bledington. 01608 658365 www.thekingsheadinn.net

Lamb at Buckland, Lamb Lane, Buckland. 01367 870484 www.thelambbuckland.co.uk

Masons Arms, South Leigh. 01993 702485

Maytime, Asthall. 01993 822068 www.themaytime.com

Potting Shed, Crudwell. 01666 577833

Swan, Southrop. 01367 850205 www.theswanatsouthrop.co.uk

Swan Inn, Swinbrook. 01993 823339 www.theswanswinbrook.co.uk

Trouble House Inn, Nr Tetbury. 01666 502206 www.thetroublehouse.co.uk

Wheatsheaf, Northleach. 01451 860244 www.cotswoldswheatsheaf.com

Woolpack Inn, Slad. 01452 813429

Lunch In Formal Surroundings

Barnsley House (& garden visit), Nr Cirencester. 01285 740000
www.barnsleyhouse.com

Bay Tree Hotel, Sheep Street, Burford. 01993 822791
www.cotswold-inns-hotels.co.uk/baytree

Belle House Restaurant, Bar & Traiteur, Bridge Street, Pershore.
01386 555055 www.belle-house.co.uk

Bibury Court Hotel. 01285 740337 www.biburycourt.co.uk

Buckland Manor, Nr Broadway. 01386 852626
www.bucklandmanor.co.uk

Calcot Manor, Nr Tetbury. 01666 890391 www.calcotmanor.co.uk

Close Hotel, Long Street, Tetbury. 01666 502272
www.theclose-hotel.com

Corse Lawn Hotel, Nr Tewkesbury. 01452 780771
www.corselawn.com

Cotswolds88Hotel, Kemps Lane, Painswick. 01452 813688
www.cotswolds88hotel.com

Cotswold House Hotel, The Square, Chipping Campden. 01386
840330 www.cotswoldhouse.com

Grapevine Hotel, Sheep Street, Stow-On-The-Wold. 01451 830344
www.vines.co.uk

Lords of the Manor, Upper Slaughter. 01451 820243
www.lordsofthemanor.com

Restaurants With Rooms

Kingham Plough. 01608 658327 www.thekinghamplough.co.uk

St Michaels Restaurant, Victoria Street., Painswick. 01452 814555
www.stmickshouse.com

Angel, 14 Witney Street, Burford. 01993 822714
www.theangelatburford.co.uk

Old Passage, Arlingham. 01452 740547 www.theoldpassage.com

Royalist Hotel, Stow-On-The-Wold. 01451 830670
www.theroyalisthotel.com

Russell's, 20 High Street, Broadway. 01386 853555
www.russellsofbroadway.co.uk

The Rectory, Crudwell. 01666 577194 www.therectoryhotel.com

Three Ways House Hotel, Mickleton. 01386 438429
www.puddingclub.com

Wesley House, Winchcombe. 01242 602366
www.wesleyhouse.co.uk

Wild Garlic, 3 Cossack Square, Nailsworth. 01453 832615
www.wild-garlic.co.uk

Tea Rooms

Blenheim, Woodstock.

Harriets, High Street, Woodstock.

Huffkins, High Street, Burford. 01993 822126

Tisanes, 21 The Green, Broadway. 01386 853296

Town Restaurants

Allium, 1 London Street, Fairford. 01285 712200
www.allium.uk.net

Brosh, 8 Suffolk Parade, Cheltenham. 01242 227277
www.broshrestaurant.co.uk

Champignon Sauvage, 24-26 Suffolk Road, Cheltenham.
01242 573449 www.lechampignonsauvage.co.uk

Chef's Table, 49 Long Street, Tetbury. 01666 504466
www.thechefstable.co.uk

5 North Street, Winchcombe. 01242 604566

Royalist Hotel, Digbeth Street, Stow-On-The-Wold. 01451 830670
www.theroyalisthotel.com

Traditional Pubs (Some don't serve food)

Bakers Arms, Broad Campden. 01386 840515

Bathurst Arms, North Cerney. 01285 831281
www.bathurstarms.com

Bear at Bisley. 01452 770265 www.bisleybear.co.uk

Beehive, 1-3 Montpelier Villas, Cheltenham. 01242 579443

Bird in Hand Inn, Hailey. 01993 868321. www.birdinhandinn.co.uk

Butcher's Arms, Sheepscombe. 01452 812113
www.butchers-arms.co.uk

Bell, Frampton-on-Severn.

Chequers, Goddards Lane, Chipping Norton. 01608 644717
www.chequers-pub

Ebrington Arms, Ebrington. 01386 593223
www.theebringtonarms.co.uk

Falkland Arms, Great Tew. 01608 683653 www.falklandarms.org.uk

Five Mile House, Gloucester Road, Duntisbourne Abbots. 01285
821432 www.fivemilehouse.co.uk

Fleece Inn, Bretforton. 01386 831173 www.thefleeceinn.co.uk

Fox and Hounds, Great Wolford. 01608 658327
www.thekinghamplough.co.uk

Golden Heart, Birdlip. 01242 870261 www.thegoldenheart.co.uk

Hollybush Inn, Corn Street, Witney.

Kings Head Inn, Wootton. 01993 811340 www.kings-head.co.uk

Lamb Inn, Shipton-Under-Wychwood. 01993 830465
www.lambinn.co.uk

Old Spot Inn, Hill Road, Dursley. 01453 542870
www.oldspotinn.co.uk

Plough Inn, Ford. 01386 584215 www.theploughinnatford.co.uk

Ram Inn, Station Road, South Woodchester. 01453 873 329

Masons Arms, South Leigh. 01993 702485

Morris Clown, High Street, Bampton. 01993 850217

Ram Inn, South Woodchester. 01453 873 329

Royal Oak, Ramsden. 01993 868213

Seven Tuns, Chedworth. 01285 720242

Swan Inn, Swinbrook. 01993 823339 www.theswanswinbrook.co.uk

The Trout, Tadpole Bridge. 01367 870382 www.trout-inn.co.uk

Tunnel House Inn, Tarlton Road, Nr. Cirencester. 01285 770280
www.tunnelhouse.com

Three Horseshoes, Frampton-on-Severn

Three Horseshoes, Corn Street, Witney. 01993 703 086

Village Pub, Barnsley. 01285 740421 www.thevillagepub.co.uk

Volunteer, Chipping Campden. 01386 840688

Weigh Bridge Inn, Longfords, Nailsworth. 01453 832520
www.2in1Pub.co.uk

Woodstock Arms, Market Street. 01993 811251
www.woodstockarms.co.uk

Yew Tree Inn, Conderton. 01386 725364

Buckland Manor Hotel   ss

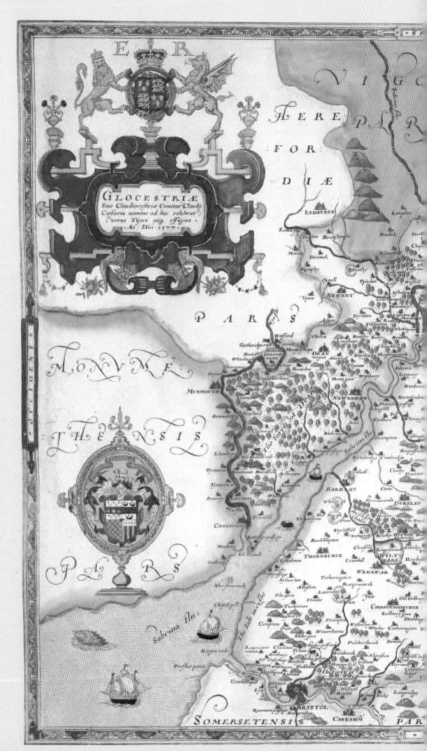

THE GOLDEN FLEECE OF THE COTSWOLD SHEEP

The Lion of the Cotswolds

Sheep have grazed on the Cotswold hills for more than 2,000 years - and the most famous breed was The Cotswold, whose lustrous, curly fleece was famous throughout Europe. Here is the story of that sheep - known as The Lion of the Cotswolds...

Today, there is not much more than a ton or two of Cotswold fleece-wool available each year. It is long-stapled (more than 6 inches), reasonably lustrous and of mid 40's quality (for comparison Merino is mid 60's plus, Lincoln about mid 30's). Until recently, Cotswold wool was for many years lumped in with other English lustre-wools - and used mainly for carpets and industrial cloths.

During the early 1980s Cotswold Woollen Weavers recognised its potential and revived its use. In particular, the natural lustre and the clarity with which it accepts dye made the wool ideal for loose-twist worsted spinning, and weaving into soft-furnishing cloths - a range of dramatic block-weave throws and rugs.

Cotswold Woollen Weavers' activities have coincided with a renewed interest in the Cotswold breed, and this is thus a good time for a re-appraisal of the breed. For too long, the historic pedigree of Cotswold wool has been ignored as irrelevant.

But it was not always so. The Cotswolds are marked with the history of the Cotswold sheep and its fleece. But, it is a puzzling, clouded history. For, although the great Wool Churches stand four-square in many a Cotswold village, as solid testimony to the power and wealth of the medieval merchants who endowed them, not much can be said with certainty about the wool which the Cotswold sheep provided. There is certainly a lot of superstition: even a bogus derivation of the very word Cotswold (sheep cot on the wold, or open hillside) has been widely used to puff the influence of wool in the area.

Certainly wool has long been an important English commodity, and the Cotswolds an important source for it. 500 years ago wise men agreed that half the wealth of England rides on the back of the sheep - wool exports paid for Richard the Lionheart's ransom to the Saracens. The Lord Chancellor sits in The House of Lords to this day on a sack stuffed with wool to show the pre-eminent position which the wool industry has played in this country's affairs. The medieval weavers of C12 Flanders happily sang:

"The best wool in Europe is Cotswold, and the best wool in England is Cotswold." But what sort of wool was it that they prized so highly?

The Medieval Cotswolds

There is evidence that the Romans brought sheep with them as they battled northwards, and perhaps they introduced them to the Cotswold hills around the important Roman settlement of Corinium, (Cirencester). They would have valued these sheep for their milk and for their fleece. Shivering Southern European mercenary soldiers needed warm winter coats. There is further evidence, based mostly on scanty skeletal remains, that these Roman imports were the ancestors of the great flocks of Medieval Cotswolds - and indeed of all the English long-wool breeds.

The temptation is to look at a Cotswold sheep today, to sink one's hand in its thick lustrous long-wool fleece, and think fondly of an unbroken pedigree stretching back 2000 years to those early Roman farmers. The problem is that for most of the intervening years virtually nothing is known for sure. Shepherds reasonably enough have rarely thought it sensible to spend their time writing down descriptions of their flocks: the first book in English entirely about sheep was not published until 1749 (Ellis- The Shepherd's Sure Guide), and the first comprehensive resumé of English wool not until 1809 (Luccock - An Essay on Wool). But by then, the early C19, the heyday of the Cotswold sheep was over. And of course, woollen cloth wears out, and is attacked by moth and mould: there is very little extant medieval woollen cloth available for analysis.

During the Early Medieval centuries England was a relatively under-populated country, with plenty of rolling hill-pasture to sustain vast land-hungry flocks of sheep kept for their fleece. Perhaps 500,000 sheep roamed the Cotswolds, and most of their wool was exported to Flanders and Lombardy - more densely populated countries which could not spare land for wool growing. Thousands upon thousands of pack-horses laden with wool-bales wound their way down from the high Cotswold hills to The Thames. They crossed the river at Radcot and proceeded southwards to Southampton, or saw their loads shipped on barges to London. The continental weavers paid royally for the wool, the Cotswold merchants grew rich and built their churches, and the English crown paid its way with the taxes levied on the trade.

But was this Golden Fleece (the Cotswold sheep was long known as The Lion of the Cotswolds) the long, heavy, lashy wool that the modern Cotswold bears, or something shorter, softer and more like the Ryeland wool from Herefordshire which was equally important to the medieval weavers?

There are memorial brasses in Northleach church which show what look like newly shorn Cotswolds just like those which crop the grass today,

and some commentators suggest the Cotswold was always a big, long-woolled breed (Youatt, for instance, quotes the sage Gervase Markham to this effect). But others suggest that the wool was once much softer: Michael Drayton, writing at the end of the C16 suggests that Cotswold wool was very fine: it comes very near that of Spain, for from it a thread may be drawn as fine as silk.

This Spanish comparison is important, because one conundrum revolves around the export - widely noted by commentators - of Cotswold sheep to Spain, particularly by Edward IV but up to 1425 when the export was banned as part of the increasingly draconian network of laws to safeguard the interests of the burgeoning English wool-weaving industry. Spain was the home of the fine-woolled Merino sheep, and it is inconceivable that English, and specifically Cotswold sheep, could have been so fine as to be worth cross-breeding with Merinos. The most likely explanation is that Cotswolds were different from Merinos: long-woolled enough to provide fleece to make alternative cloths.

Clattering Loom-shuttles

Until the late C19, and advanced mechanical innovation, it was not possible to spin worsted yarn from short fibre. The wool from which worsted yarn was spun had to be combed by hand to eliminate short hair (noils) and to align every fibre parallel to the direction of the yarn. Then tight, flat yarn could be spun and tough, sleek cloth could be woven: quite different from the spongy, less sophisticated cloths which could be woven from yarn woollen spun from shorter Merino and down-breed fleece. Perhaps medieval Cotswold sheep were shorter and softer fleeced than they are today, but their wool was still lustrous and strong enough to be ideal for worsted spinning. If nothing else, Cotswold fleece could provide Spanish soldiers with tough, resilient serge uniforms, and nobles with flowing, draping cloaks to wear over their shirts of soft, fluffy Merino.

During the C16 and C17s, the rising clatter of loom-shuttles in the valleys around Stroud presaged England's transition from raw-fleece exporter to major woollen cloth manufacturer. So complete was this change that the Crown eventually forbade the export of fleece altogether, and it remained illegal until 1824. Although, gradually, vast amounts of wool began to be imported from the wide, open spaces of Australia and South Africa (ideal for extensive sheep rearing) but it was the pre-eminence of English combing wools (including Cotswold) which helped establish England's superiority as a woollen textile manufacturer.

To some extent this issue of the nature of Cotswold wool is one of semantics: as William Marshall wrote, after he rode the Cotswold hills at the end of the C18: "The Cotswold is a breed which has been prevalent on these hills, [since] time immemorial: it has been improved, but has not changed." (During the Improving Years of the C18, the Cotswold certainly increased in size as shepherds learnt new husbandry techniques.) Or as Ezra Carman wrote disarmingly in 1892, as he strove to sum up the evidence of three hundred years of literature about Cotswold fleece:

"It is difficult to reconcile these opinions, nor indeed is it necessary; the Cotswolds beyond the memory of our day have long been a long-woolled race and valuable... for their wool."

So, superstitions and all, in this volatile world perhaps it is acceptable, even necessary, that there are these noble, mythic links with the past. If this be so, then The Golden Fleece, which might have provided uniforms for the Roman legions, paid for the Crusades, clothed C18 Europe with West of England Broadcloth and today makes splendid block-weave rugs, is certainly an ideal candidate.

Richard Martin

Cotswold Woollen Weavers, Filkins

LOCATOR MAP

For architecture, cultural festivals, luxurious hedonism, shopping sprees and walking the Cotswold Way...

Bath is arguably the most beautiful city in England. It is second to London in the number of visitors it attracts and is thus a fine place to eat, drink and be merry, and to shop and attend cultural events. The surrounding villages are accordingly affluent and well-heeled (and expensive) places to live. Bath is expensive but you can find more reasonably priced accommodation outside the town limits and many of these are listed in this book.

There are pretty and attractive villages aplenty outside Bath. The most popular being Castle Combe and Lacock. Both grew out of the wool industry, and both have been so well maintained that they amount to showcase villages. Sadly, you won't witness a herd of cattle being walked through at dawn and dusk, only perhaps the drayman delivering ale upsetting the balance of this new life.

Cross the M4 and you encounter two towns of comparative interest: Malmesbury and Tetbury. Malmesbury was the home of Athelstan, the first King of All England. And, Tetbury is the home of Prince Charles, next in line to the throne of England and its protectorates. But, if these two men and their burghs don't hold your interest, and you still have a spring in your step after tramping the streets of Bath, look to the Cotswold Way, a long distance footpath that leads north to Chipping Campden. It follows the edge of the escarpment, passes through many pretty villages and gorgeous woodland and will reward you with fine views and hours of solitary reflection. And, if trees take your fancy, you must visit Westonbirt Arboretum, an arboreal paradise, second to none.

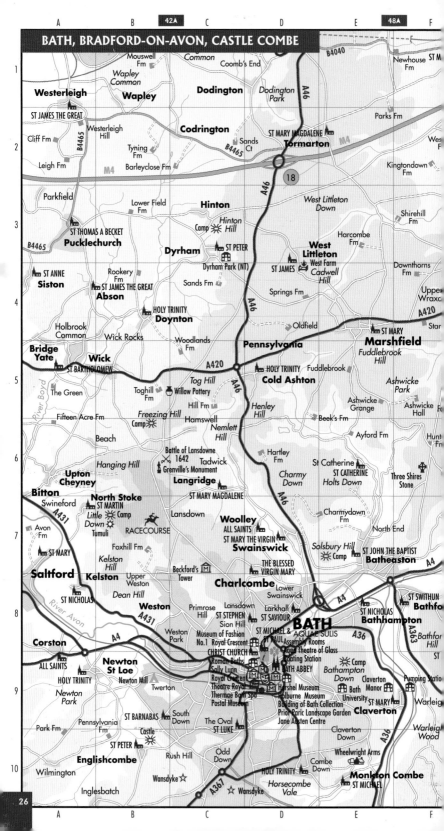

42A — 48A

A   B   C   D   E   F

1

Mouswell
Fm
Common
Coomb's End
B4040
Newhouse
Fm
ST M

Wapley
Common

Westerleigh   **Wapley**   **Dodington**   Dodington
Park   A46   Parks Fm

ST JAMES THE GREAT

2

Cliff Fm   Westerleigh
Hill   **Codrington**   ST MARY MAGDALENE   M4   Wes
F

B4465   Tyning
Fm   Sands
Ct   **Tormarton**

Leigh Fm   Barleyclose Fm   B4465   Kingtondown
Fm

M4   18

Parkfield   Lower Field
Fm   **Hinton**   West Littleton
Down   Shirehill
Fm

3

ST THOMAS A BECKET   Camp   Hinton
Hill   Harcombe
Fm

B4465   **Pucklechurch**   **Dyrham**   **West
Littleton**   Downthorns
Fm

ST ANNE   Rookery
Fm   ST PETER   West Farm
Cadwell
Hill   Uppe
Wraxc

Siston   ST JAMES THE GREAT   Dyrham Park (NT)   ST JAMES

4   **Abson**   Sands Fm   Springs Fm

HOLY TRINITY   Oldfield   ST MARY   Star

Doynton

Holbrook
Common   Wick Rocks   Woodlands
Fm   **Pennsylvania**   **Marshfield**

**Bridge
Yate**   **Wick**   A420   HOLY TRINITY   Fuddlebrook   Fuddlebrook
Hill

5   ST BARTHOLOMEW   **Cold Ashton**   Ashwicke
Park

The Green   Tog Hill   Henley
Hill   Ashwicke
Grange   Ashwicke
Hall

Toghill
Fm   Willow Pottery   Hill Fm

Fifteen Acre Fm   Freezing Hill   Hamswell   Beek's Fm   Ayford Fm

Camp   Nemlett
Hill   Hunt
Fr

Beach

6   Hanging Hill   Battle of Lansdowne
1642
Grenville's Monument   Tadwick   Hartley
Fm   St Catherine   Three Shires
Stone

**Upton
Cheyney**   **Langridge**   Charmy
Down   ST CATHERINE
Holts Down

Bitton   ST MARY MAGDALENE   Charmydown
Fm

Swineford   **North Stoke**   Lansdown   North End

A431   ST MARTIN   **Woolley**

7   Avon
Fm   Little
Down   Camp   ALL SAINTS   Solsbury Hill   ST JOHN THE BAPTIST

Tumuli   RACECOURSE   ST MARY THE VIRGIN   Camp   **Batheaston**

ST MARY   Foxhill Fm   **Swainswick**   A4

Kelston
Hill   Beckford's
Tower   THE BLESSED
VIRGIN MARY

Saltford   **Kelston**   Upper
Weston   **Charlcombe**   ST SWITHUN

ST NICHOLAS   Dean Hill   Lower
Swainswick   ST NICHOLAS   **Bathfo**

8   **Weston**   Primrose
Hill   Lansdown   Larkhall   **Bathhampton**

A431   Weston
Park   ST STEPHEN   ST SAVIOUR   **BATH**   Bathfor
Hill

Sion Hill   ST MICHAEL &   A36   A363

Museum of Fashion   ST PAUL   AQUAE SULIS   Aqua Theatre of Glass

Corston   No.1 Royal Crescent   Assembly Rooms   Boating Station   Camp

CHRIST CHURCH   BATH ABBEY   Bathampton
Down   Pumping Statio

ALL SAINTS   **Newton
St Loe**   Roman Baths   Bath   Claverton
Manor   ST MARY

HOLY TRINITY   Newton Mill   Sally Lunn   University

9   Newton
Park   Twerton   Royal Crescent   Herschel Museum   Building of Bath Collection   Warleig

Theatre Royal   Holburne Museum

Thermae Bath Spa   Prior Park Landscape Garden   **Claverton**

Postal Museum   Jane Austen Centre

ST BARNABAS   South
Down   The Oval
ST LUKE   Claverton
Down   Warleigh
Wood

Park Fm   Pennsylvania
Fm   Castle

10   ST PETER   Odd
Down   Wheelwright Arms

Englishcombe   Rush Hill   Combe
Down

Wilmington   Wansdyke   Wansdyke   HOLY TRINITY   **Monkton Combe**

Inglesbatch   A367   Horsecombe
Vale   ST MICHAEL

A   B   C   D   E   F

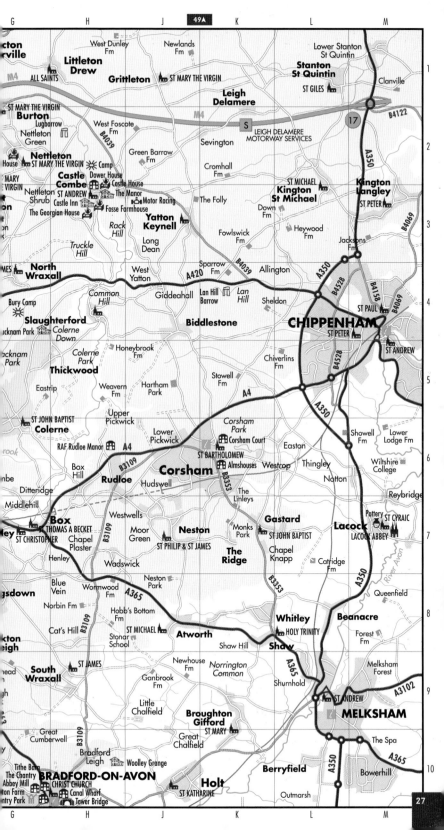

1

West Dunley Fm
Newlands Fm
Littleton Drew
ALL SAINTS
Grittleton
ST MARY THE VIRGIN
Lower Stanton St Quintin
Stanton St Quintin
ST GILES
Clanville

Leigh Delamere

M4

2

ST MARY THE VIRGIN
Burton
Lugbarrow
Nettleton Green
West Foscote Fm
B4039
Green Barrow Fm
Sevington
S LEIGH DELAMERE MOTORWAY SERVICES
17
A350
B4122

MARY VIRGIN
House
Nettleton
ST MARY THE VIRGIN
Camp
Cromhall Fm
ST MICHAEL
Kington St Michael
Kington Langley
ST PETER

3

Castle Combe
Dower House
Castle House
The Folly
Down Fm
B4069

Nettleton Shrub
ST ANDREW
The Manor
Motor Racing
Heywood Fm
Jacksons Fm

Castle Inn
The Georgian House
Fosse Farmhouse
Yatton Keynell
Fowlswick Fm

Rack Hill
Long Dean

Truckle Hill

4

North Wraxall
West Yatton
Giddeahall
A420
Sparrow Fm
B4039
Allington
A350
B4528
B4158
B4069
ST PAUL

Bury Camp
Common Hill
Lan Hill Barrow
Lan Hill
Sheldon
CHIPPENHAM

Slaughterford
ST PETER
ST ANDREW

cknam Park
Colerne Down
Biddlestone

5

acknam Park
Thickwood
Honeybrook Fm
Chiverlins Fm
B4528

Eastrip
Colerne Park
Weavern Fm
Hartham Park
Stowell Fm
A4
A350

ST JOHN BAPTIST
Colerne
Upper Pickwick
Lower Pickwick
Corsham Park
Easton
Thingley
Showell Fm
Lower Lodge Fm

6

rook
RAF Rudloe Manor
A4
Corsham Court
ST BARTHOLOMEW
Westcrop
Notton
Wiltshire College

Box Hill
B3109
Corsham
Almshouses
B4528
Reybridge

mbe
Ditteridge
Rudloe
Hudswell
The Linleys

ey
Middlehill

7

Box
THOMAS A BECKET
Westwells
Moor Green
Neston
Monks Park
Gastard
ST JOHN BAPTIST
Lacock
LACOCK ABBEY
Pottery
ST CYRIAC

ST CHRISTOPHER
Chapel Plaster
ST PHILIP & ST JAMES
The Ridge
Chapel Knapp
B3353

Henley
Wadswick
Catridge Fm

8

sdown
Blue Vein
Wormwood Fm
A365
Neston Park
B3353
Whitley
HOLY TRINITY
Beanacre
Queenfield

Norbin Fm
Hobb's Bottom
Forest Fm
River Avon

kton eigh
Cat's Hill
B3109
ST MICHAEL
Stonar School
Atworth
Shaw Hill
Shaw
A365
Melksham Forest
A3102

9

head
South Wraxall
ST JAMES
Newhouse Fm
Norrington Common
Shurnhold
ST ANDREW
MELKSHAM
A350

Ganbrook Fm
Little Chalfield

10

Great Cumberwell
B3109
Broughton Gifford
ST MARY
Great Chalfield
Berryfield
A350
The Spa
A365
Bowerhill

Tithe Barn
The Chantry
Abbey Mill
Bradford Leigh
Woolley Grange
BRADFORD-ON-AVON
Holt
ST KATHARINE
Outmarsh

ton Farm
ntry Park
CHRIST CHURCH
Canal Wharf
Tower Bridge

Bath Abbey

BATH

Is Bath the most beautiful city in England? Many believe so, for it is second only to London in the number of visitors it attracts. It will captivate you today as it has done so down the centuries, from the Romans to Jane Austen, to Robert Southey and the Romantic Poets, to the Rugby aficionados jostling to get into the Recreation Ground. There is surely only one way to see Bath (apart from the top of an open double-decker bus, or from a hot-air balloon) and that is to walk. So, prepare yourself, first with a good night's sleep, and second with a comfortable pair of shoes and a clear map. The day will be long and exhausting. Your eyes will be worn out with an overload of images, and your feet in need of a soothing bath. However, the next day you will be raring to go and see more of this visual feast and to revisit your favourite crescent. You have become a Bathophile. The Bath springs or hot waters were discovered by the mythical King Bladud (or Blaiddyd) in 863 BC, King of the Britons, and father of King Lear. The Celts venerated the site but it was the Romans in about 60-70 AD who developed the hot springs and built a wall around the 23 acre site naming it Aquae Sulis. The site held warm to hot to very cold baths, sweating

rooms, massage areas and fitness rooms. It prospered for 400 years until the Romans withdrew from Britain in 410 AD. In 973 the Abbey was chosen as the setting for the coronation of King Edgar, and in 1157 it received the seat of a Bishopric. The city saw much prosperity in the Middle Ages due to the sale of Cotswold wool. The building of today's Abbey started in the C15. But the heyday of Bath began over a 40-year period when three men of immense vision transformed the city with a populace of 3,000 into the Georgian city of 30,000 citizens. The three men were Beau Nash (Master of Ceremonies, manners and fashion), John Wood, (architect), and Ralph Allen, (benefactor, financier and quarry owner who supplied the building materials). Today, Bath is an educational centre and host to many festivals: Literature, Music, Cricket, to name but a few. It is a bustling shopping centre with more than your average number of independent retailers. For those seeking refreshment there appears to be a café or bar on every corner and it boasts some of the West Country's finest restaurants. Listed and described below are the most notable attractions to visit. (E8)
www.visitbath.co.uk

Special Places of Interest...

Assembly Rooms (NT), Bennett Street. Designed in 1769 by John Wood the Younger, these public rooms epitomise the elegance of fashion - conscious life in Georgian society. These magnificent rooms were let out for parties and functions in the C18 as they are today. Café.
Open daily 10.30-5.
(D9) 01225 4771734
www.nationaltrust.org.uk

Bath Abbey. The Church of St Peter and St Paul has seen three churches occupy this site: an Anglo-Saxon church in 757 and a Norman Cathedral in 1090 but later in 1137 much of this was destroyed by fire. Today's building was founded in 1499 to replace the ruin damaged in the fire. But it had again to be rebuilt in 1611 following Henry VIII's Dissolution of the Monasteries. In simple architectural terms it can be described as Perpendicular Gothic and cruciform in plan. The fan vaulting of the Nave is very fine and was designed by Robert and William Vertue designers of Henry VII's chapel in Westminster Abbey. It was never finished until Gilbert Scott completed the original designs in the 1860s. Note the Stairway to Heaven on the West Front. Tower Tours.
Open daily. (D9) 01225 422462
www.bathabbey.org

| 3500 BC | Neolithic farmers and herdsmen clear the forests | 43 | Romans invade Britain |
| 3000 BC | Hetty Pegler's Tump and Belas Knapp long barrow, along with thousands of others are established across Britain | 44 | Celts build a shrine to the goddess Sulis |

Bath Aqua Theatre of Glass, 105-107 Walcot Street.
Demonstrations of glass blowing (from 10.30am) with a history of glass, stained glass, and museum. Gift shop. Open daily 9.30-5. (D9) 01225 311183
www.bathaquaglass.com

Bath Boating Station, Forrester Road. Try your hand at Wind in the Willows on the River Avon. You can hire skiffs (rowing boats), punts and canoes (Canadian and kayaks) and navigate between Bathampton Weir and Pulteney Bridge. Boatman Restaurant. Self-catering units. Open daily 10-6. (D9) 01225 312900
www.bathboating.co.uk

Bath Rugby Club, Recreation Ground. Loyalty to this club hath no bounds. The West Country's premier rugby club has won glory in all competitions, from the Heineken Cup to the Premier Division. Who can forget the sight of Jeremy Guscott, Stuart Barnes and Ben Clarke in full flow? (D9) 01225 325200 www.bathrugby.com

Beckford's Tower, Lansdown Road. Designed by Henry Goodridge in 1825 for the eccentric collector William Beckford (1760-1844) to house his library of rare books, prints and paintings. For panoramic views over Bath you must climb the spiral staircase of the 120ft neo-classical Tower. Open East to 31 Oct W/Es &

BH Ms 10.30-5. (C7) 01225 338727
www.bath-preservation-trust.org.uk

Building of Bath Collection, The Paragon. A fascinating study of how Bath was transformed from a provincial town into the world-renowned Georgian city thought of (at the time) as the finest city in Western Europe, and how classical design influenced the architects, builders and visionaries. Open mid-Apr to 30 Oct, W/Es & BHs 10.30-5. (D9) 01225 338727
www.bath-preservation-trust.org.uk

Fashion Museum, Assembly Rooms. A major collection started by Doris Langley Moore, collector, costume designer and author. From the C18 to the present day: with accessories, corsets, 'Dress of the Year', archives and research facilities. Open daily from 10.30-4. (D9) 01225 477173
www.museumofcostume.co.uk

Georgian Garden, Royal Victoria Park. A place to sit and meditate after pounding the streets amidst a simple, formal garden of variegated leaves and double-flowers. Open daily. (D9)

Herschel Museum of Astronomy, 19 New King Street.
A celebration of the many achievements of William and Caroline Herschel, distinguished astronomers and talented musicians

whose research broached new knowledge of the solar system. In 1781 William discovered Uranus. Open daily except W Feb to mid-Dec, M-F 1-5, Sa, Su & BHs 11-5. (D9) 01225 446865
www.bath-preservation-trust.org.uk

Holburne Museum of Art, Great Pulteney Street.
A collection of fine, decorative art founded by Sir William Holburne in the C19. The paintings include landscapes by Guardi and Turner, portraits by Stubs, Zoffany and Gainsborough. Closed for renovation. (D9) 01225 466669
www.bath.ac.uk/holburne

Jane Austen Centre, 40 Gay Street. Jane lived in Bath from 1801-1806 and the experience had a profound effect on her writing. There are costume displays from TV's Persuasion and guided tours of Jane's Bath. Bookshop. Tearoom. Open daily. (D9) 01225 443000
www.janeausten.co.uk

The Little Theatre Cinema, St Michael's Place. Part of the Picturehouse chain of cinemas showing a mix of mainstream and art house films. Built in 1935, the cinema has retained the charm of the 30s whilst being refurbished with up-to-date technology and comfort. (D9) 0871 704 2061
www.picturehouses.co.uk

Pulteney Street

The Circus

Museum of Bath at Work, Julian Road. Set in a C18 Real Tennis Court the museum traces the development of Bath from the C17 to the present day by illustrating engineering, printing, tourism and car making. Open daily Jan to Nov 10.30-5. (D9) 01225 318348 www.bath-at-work.org.uk

Museum of East Asian Art, 12 Bennett Street. Founded by Brian McElney whose collection of fine ceramics, jades and bronzes from China, Japan, Korea and South East Asia date from 5,000 BC to the present day. Open Tu-Sa 10-5, Su 12-5. (D9) 01225 464640 www.meaa.org.uk

No 1 Royal Crescent. Built between 1767 and 1774 by John Wood the Younger to be the finest house in Bath. It was considered the very embodiment of C18 urban architecture and was used to accommodate wealthy visitors and royalty. It reflects a vivid picture of Georgian Bath and you, too, can

The Drawing Room, No 1 Royal Crescent ss

577 Native Britains beaten by Saxons (from Germania) at Battle of Dyrham (three British Kings killed in combat)

600
675

Christianity takes an increasing hold on spiritual life
King Osric establishes a monastic house in Bath

Pulteney Bridge

bathe in the brilliance of C18 life by experiencing the Entrance Hall, Dining Room, Study, Drawing Room, Bedroom and Kitchen. Open Tu-Su 10.30-5. (D9) 01225 428126 www.bath-preservation-trust.org.uk

Postal Museum, 27 Northgate Street. History of the postal system from ancient Egypt to today and the men who developed Bath's system: Ralph Allen, John Palmer and Thomas Moore Musgrave. Wonderful display of the British postbox. Open M-Sa 11-5 (4.30 in winter). (D9) 01225 460333 www.bathpostalmuseum.org

Prior Park Landscape Garden (NT). The brainchild of C18 entrepreneur Ralph Allen. Within an enchanting and wild wood lies a Palladian bridge. The views of Bath from here are spectacular. Parking only for the disabled. Access is via a steep path from the railway station passing by Widcombe's shops. Open daily except Tu, mid-Feb to 30 Oct and winter W/Es, 11-5.30 (dusk in winter). (D9) 01225 833422 www.nationaltrust.org.uk

Pulteney Bridge. Built by Robert Adam in 1773 for the entrepreneur Francis Pulteney who planned to connect Bath with his new town, Bathwick. The plans were shelved

and this was sadly Adam's only building in Bath. It was based on the Ponte Vecchio (Florence) and the Ponte di Rialto (Venice). (D9)

Roman Baths, Abbey Church Yard. The centre of this great city, and the centrifugal force of nature that created Bath. This is where the story began in 863 BC when King Bladud discovered the hot springs whose rich mineral waters were to have magical healing powers. The Romans built a great temple around the spring and dedicated it to the goddess, Sulis Minerva. What is extraordinary to fathom is that the hot water erupts at 46 degrees centigrade at a rate of 240,000 gallons (1,170,000 litres) per day. Where does it all go after this, you

Sally Lunn's Refreshment House & Museum

may well ask? The main features are: the Sacred Spring, the Roman Temple, the Roman Bath House and the Georgian Pump Room, a neo-classical salon where the hot spa water is available for consumption, along with morning coffee, lunch and afternoon teas. Open daily from 9.30 to dusk. (D9) 01225 477785 www.romanbaths.co.uk

Sally Lunn's Refreshment House & Museum, 4 North Parade Passage. The oldest house in Bath, and home of the original Bath bun. It houses a museum as well as providing coffee, lunch and cream teas. Open daily. (D9) 01225 461634 www.sallylunns.co.uk

The Circus. Originally named King's Circus, the vision and brilliance of John Wood the Elder was built between 1754 and 1768. Sadly, he died and never saw his plans reach fruition. It was left to his son to complete the project. It was John Wood's intention to create a classical Palladian architectural landscape inspired by Rome's Colosseum. The Circus is made up of 33 terraced houses. Thomas Gainsborough lived in No.17 from 1765-1774. In 1942 several were destroyed during the blitz. (D9)

The Royal Crescent

The Royal Crescent. Built by John Wood the Younger between 1767 and 1774, and all houses were occupied by 1778. Today the 30 original homes are split into flats, houses and a hotel and many are privately owned. A Society was founded in 1973 to protect the Crescent for future generations. Interestingly, it took the Society 18 years to persuade the council to ban tourist buses and coaches from entering the crescent. (D9) www.royalcrescentbath.com

Theatre Royal. A lively theatre with a busy Young People's Theatre, and locally sponsored events. It is one of the country's oldest theatres, first built by George Trim in 1705 with many guises thereafter. The present building was renovated in 1982 and opened with A Midsummer Night's Dream starring Paul Scofield, Marsha Hunt and Jack Shepherd. Vaults Restaurant. (D9) 01225 448844 www.theatreroyal.org.uk

Thermae Bath Spa. Combine the rich mineral waters of Bath with contemporary design and the full range of spa treatments, and you have this haven of relaxation and hedonism. You can enjoy two-hour, four-hour or full day sessions intermingled with the aromatic steam rooms and various massages on offer. Children under 16 are not permitted. Open daily from 9am. (D9) 01225 331234 www.thermaebathspa.com

Victoria Art Gallery, Bridge Street. The gallery provides a full programme of contemporary art, decorative art and British paintings by Sickert, Whistler, Zoffany and Gainsborough. Don't miss the hilarious caricatures depicting C18 Bath life. Open Tu-Sa 10-5, Su 1.30-5. (D9) 01225 477233 www.victoriagal.org.uk

Where to Eat & Drink...

Browns, Orange Grove. Browns does not offer an intimate dining experience (100 seats) but the menu and ambiance will be familiar to many with a Browns in their locale and sometimes there is comfort in familiarity, especially when it tastes so good! Menu based on classic recognisable dishes. The building was once a police station and a Magistrates Court and retains the entrance doors suitable for horse drawn Police vehicles! Open from 10am. (D9) 01225 461199 www.browns-restaurants.co.uk

Casanis, 4 Saville Row. A relatively new but already popular French bistro restaurant which has carved out a little corner of France in the south-west of England and oozes Gallic charm. The unfussy interior complements the authentic French menu (which includes regional specialities). 'A place where locals feel at home and visitors feel special'. (D9) 01225 780055 www.casanis.co.uk

Demuths Vegetarian Restaurant, 2 North Parade Passage. Long-established restaurant catering for vegetarians and vegans as well as all who love a tasty feast. Unpretentious and uncomplicated vegetarian food. Open for breakfast, lunch and dinner.

Demuths Vegetarian Restaurant ss

Hole in the Wall   ss

Special childrens' menu. Organic wine list. Demuths also runs a cookery school. (D9) 01225 446059 www.demuths.co.uk

Firehouse Rotisserie, 2 John Street. The owners of the Firehouse have transferred a little bit of the American Southwest to a listed Georgian building that was formerly a wool shop; from the rustic interior and furnishings, to the menu influenced by Californian, Mexican, Pacific Rim and Creole cuisine. Remains very popular and fresh after 12 years. Open for lunch and dinner. (D9) 01225 482070 www.firehouserotisserie.co.uk

FishWorks, 6 Green Street. The original FishWorks, 6 Green Street has a relaxed atmosphere with comfortable seating, plenty of tables plus covered and heated decking area. Also a fishmonger's counter with an extensive range of fish and shellfish brought in everyday. They say: "We're all about eating, buying and enjoying fabulous seafood." I can't put it any better! (D9) 01225 448 707 www.fishworks.co.uk

Hole in the Wall, 16 George Street. This central restaurant offers a cosy ambience and the best seasonal produce turned into modern British cuisine. The co-owner is MD of the local independent wine merchant so the wine menu is varied in terms of choice and price and you can even sample wine from a Gloucestershire vineyard. Pre-theatre, and seasonally changing menus. Open M-Sa lunch, dinner, Su dinner. (D9) 01225 425242 www.theholeinthewall.co.uk

Hop Pole, 7 Albion Buildings. One of the Bath Ales Brewery's pubs situated right opposite Royal Victoria Park. Ignore the uninspiring exterior; once you pass through the door, the Hop Pole is a comfortable and spacious pub with excellent beers (of course) and food and a delightful city centre garden oasis for summer afternoon tipples. Described as 'a country pub in the heart of the city'. (D9) 01225 446327 www.bathales.com/pubs/hop.html

Hudson Steakhouse Bar & Grill, 14 London Street. A mix of steakhouse upstairs and lively cocktail bar downstairs all set in an old Edwardian pub. This apparent clash of genres results in a relaxed and surprisingly glamorous restaurant. Steaks are slow-matured for 28 days and come from grass-fed herds of Angus and Limousin Staffordshire cattle. Also fusion, seafood and classic dishes. (D9) 01225 332323 www.hudsonbars.com

King William, 36 Thomas Street. This tastefully designed pub serves award winning food along with a drinks menu that includes four tasty real ales from local microbreweries - all kept cool in their very own Georgian wine cellar! Repeated appearances in the Which? Good Food Guide is testament to the quality of the menu. (D9) 01225 428096 www.kingwilliampub.com

Loch Fyne Bath, 24 Milsom Street. Renowned fish restaurant chain. Open for breakfast, lunch and dinner and now serving a selection of meat dishes as well as excellent dishes made from fresh seafood and shellfish obtained from sustainable sources. Bedrooms upstairs at Milsoms, boutique hotel. (D9) 01225 750120 www.lochfyne.com

Olive Tree, Queensberry Hotel, Russel Street. A sophisticated restaurant with modern art lining the walls set in the basement of a luxury contemporary boutique hotel. Classy, very high quality and delicious modern British cuisine served with understated skill in a relaxed environment. Rarely does the quality of a hotel restaurant match the quality of the hotel itself. In this case, both get high marks. (D9) 01225 447928 www.thequeensberry.co.uk

Restaurant de l'Arche, 2-3 Queen Street. French restaurant and champagne lounge set in a charming city centre location. The wooden floors, rich red walls and white tablecloths with the sparkle of wine glasses lends a satisfying ambience of quality to this restaurant. The chef has a long history of working at successful top notch venues and the food he delivers here can only increase his reputation for excellence. (D9) 01225 444403 www.thearchbath.co.uk

Woods, 9-13 Alfred Street. Woods is owned and run by an anglo-French couple and their children and the Gallic in this paring shines through in the design of the place from the wicker chairs outside the front of the restaurant to the paraphernalia on the walls inside. Menus offer a range of gourmet European dishes. (D9) 01225 314812 www.woodsrestaurant.com

Bath Boating Station

1085	William I declares the intent of the Domesday Book whilst holding court at Gloucester	1087 1089	Burford granted a charter The nave of Gloucester Cathedral undergoes construction

33

Dorian House ss

Where to Stay...

4 Brock Street. You can't get much better in terms of location, and the B&B accommodation is pretty special too. Set between the Royal Crescent, The Circus and Victoria Park this Georgian house has been decorated with great care and period style. The rooms are full of books, antique furniture and paintings. (D9) 01225 460536 www.no4brockstreet.co.uk

14 Raby Place, Bathwick Hill. Small B&B set in a Regency house filled with modern art and stunning pictures and objects scattered throughout. (D9) 01225 465120

77 Great Pulteney Street. Situated, as it is, right in the centre of trendy Bath, this B&B seems reasonably priced. One comfortable and airy room that makes you feel like you are staying with friends. (D9) 01225 466659 www.77pulteneyst.co.uk

Bath Paradise, 86-88 Holloway. Small, privately owned hotel located in a pretty Georgian house and garden. Raised above the town, the views are excellent. Accommodation is a mix of traditional elegance and modern comfort. (D9) 01225 317723 www.paradise-house.co.uk

Bath Priory Hotel, Weston Road. The Priory epitomises luxury and efficiency. Comfortable rooms with delightful garden views from the windows. 2009 heralds the arrival of Michael Caines as Executive Head Chef at the Michelin-starred Priory restaurant. Fresh from his success at the Bath Priory's sister hotel in

Devon, Caines will bring his uniquely classic yet innovative style to dining here. (D9) 01225 331922. www.thebathpriory.co.uk

Bathwick Gardens, 95 Sydney Place. Bathwick Gardens is a Regency townhouse B&B, the façade adorned with wrought iron balustrades. The interior is tastefully decorated with period touches. A self-catering four-bed coach house situated at the bottom of the garden is also available. (D9) 01225 469435 www.bathwickgardens.co.uk

Dorian House, 1 Upper Oldfield Park. Think of the Dorian (Grey) that walks and not the image trapped on canvas when you think of Dorian House. For every inch of this B&B is gorgeous and full of period charm. From the bedrooms upstairs to the drawing room and gardens downstairs. (D9) 01225 426336 www.dorianhouse.co.uk

Dukes Hotel, Great Pulteney Street. In the heart of Bath sits this Grade I Palladian townhouse. Faithfully restored to high

Georgian standards with a layer of contemporary comforts, Dukes has a pleasing ambience. Bedrooms and suites are tastefully dressed in period furnishings and fabrics. Cavendish Restaurant & Bar. (D9) 01225 787960 www.dukesbath.co.uk

Grey Lodge, Summer Lane, Combe Down. Simple, well equipped B&B which enjoys the benefits of being in a rural outskirt of Bath. Walks and nature are on the doorstep and Bath is only a 10 minute drive away. (D10) 01225 832069 www.greylodge.co.uk

The Grove, Lyncombe Vale Road. The Grove is a classic Georgian house set in a 200 year old, flower filled garden. Accommodation is spacious and the interior is filled with books, paintings and figurative bronzes. Robert Hornyold-Strickland is a sculptor and will show you round his studio. The house has an interesting past - its gardens were once part of the pleasure gardens connected to a local spa. More recently, an underground room was discovered that is thought to be the original Georgian icehouse. (D9) 01225 484282 www.bathbandb.com

Milsoms Hotel, 24 Milsom Street. Milsoms Hotels are part of the Loch Fyne Restaurant group and represent 'restaurants with rooms' in the truest sense. Built around a Loch Fyne restaurant, this small stylish hotel has dispensed with a concierge and room service and in their stead is a modern pared back elegance in concord with a Grade II listed building in the centre of an historic city. Relaxing and elegant simplicity. (D9) 01225 750128 www.milsomshotel.co.uk

Bath Priory Hotel ss

The Royal Crescent Hotel   ss

Newton Mill Holiday Park and Campsite, Newton Road. Caravanning and camping site open all year. Idyllic setting in a sheltered valley bordered by trees and a meandering stream. Convenience store and licensed bar/restaurant. (B9) 01225 333909 www.newtonmillpark.co.uk

The Royal Crescent Hotel, 16 Royal Crescent. The Royal Crescent occupies two listed buildings which were built by John Wood the Younger and have remained fairly unchanged since the C18. This makes a perfect setting for what is an extravagantly luxurious hotel full of period details. Step into the Royal and you enter a more sumptuous world - one of overstated luxury. Rooms are filled with period details and paintings from C18 masters.

Behind the hotel lies a surprise - the beautiful and secluded gardens, perfect for afternoon tea, and overlooked by the Dower House restaurant and bar. The former coach houses are now the Bath House Spa. (D9) 01225 823333 www.royalcrescent.co.uk

Tasburgh House, Warminster Road. The hotel is set on the outskirts of Bath in seven acres of gardens and meadow park running down to the Kennet and Avon canal making you feel like you're in the countryside whilst remaining close to the city centre. Rooms are tastefully decorated and the service is friendly and efficient. Try breakfast in the conservatory, drinks on the garden terrace or a quick game on the croquet lawn. (E8) 01225 425096 www.bathtasburgh.co.uk

Special Places To Visit Outside Bath...

Claverton Church of St Mary. Norman church renovated in 1858. Ralph Allen, who financed the building of Georgian Bath, is buried here. Peel of bells. (E9)

The American Museum in Britain, Claverton Manor. An important Museum of Americana that displays fine American furniture and decorative arts and fosters anglo-american friendship. Fascinating collection of American furniture, decorative arts, silver, and textiles taking you on a journey through American history. Good resource for students. Café. Gift shop. Open mid-Mar to 1 Nov Tu-Su 12-5 late Nov-mid-Dec (E9) 01225 460503 www.americanmuseum.org

| 1176 | Death of 'Fair Rosamund Clifford' mistress to Henry 11 | 1232 | Lacock Abbey founded by Ela, Countess of Salisbury |
| 1227 | Northleach is founded as a new market town by the Abbot of Gloucester | 1246 | Hailes Abbey founded by the Earl of Cornwall, son of King John |

35

Dyrham Park

Claverton Pumping Station.

This attractive Grade II listed building is built of Bath stone and is a feature on the Kennet and Avon canal. From 1813-1952 it pumped water from the river Avon into the canal 47 feet above. (F9) www.claverton.org

Dyrham Park. (NT) C17 William and Mary mansion house set in a deer park with elegant formal gardens. The house belonged to the family of Sir William Blathwayt's wife, Mary Wynter. Blathwayt was secretary of war to William III (1671-1720). Sir William started to remodel the dilapidated Tudor mansion on site in 1692-1699. Victorian domestic quarters, Splendid collection of Dutch paintings. Film location for 'Remains of the Day' (1993). Open mid-March -1 Nov daily except W & Th 11-5. Park open all year. (C3) 0117 9372501 www.nationaltrust.org.uk

Willow Pottery, Toghill House Farm. Ceramics by Kim Donaldson. (C5) 01225 891919

Grenville Monument (EH). This was built in honour of Sir Bevil Grenville who led his Cornish Pikemen in the Battle of Lansdowne in 1643 during the English Civil War. Erected on the spot where he lay mortally wounded. He was taken to nearby Cold Ashton manor where he died. (B6)

Where to Stay outside Bath...

Lucknam Park, Colerne.

Drive six miles from Bath and enter another era. This Palladian manor house built in 1720 was a family home until 1987 when it was transformed into a Country House Hotel lovingly restored to the elegance and style of the Georgian period. Set in 500 acres of listed parkland and gardens the hotel offers luxurious comfort in its 41 bedrooms including 13 suites. Fine dining in the Park Restaurant. More humble dining in the Brasserie. Spa, Equestrian Centre. (G5) 01225 742777 www.lucknampark.co.uk

Whatley Manor, Easton Grey. Set in a 12-acre traditional English country garden, Whatley Manor is a beautifully restored Cotswold manor house made to feel more like a private home than a hotel. Bedrooms and suites are filled with contemporary and antique furnishings feeding the senses. For those mixing business with pleasure, there is a boardroom and business centre including 40-seat cinema. Spa. (G6) 01666 822888 www.whatleymanor.com

Wheelwrights Arms Hotel, Monkton Combe.

A C18 carpenter's home and workshop converted into a public house in 1871 with the workshop transformed into charming, light and airy B&B accommodation in 1981. (E10) 01225 722287 www.wheelwrightsarms.co.uk

Grenville Monument

1253   Lady Berkeley obtains a grant for Wotton's market and fair

1265   Simon de Montfort, along with 18 barons, 160 knights and 4000 men-at-arms are slain at the Battle of Evesham

Tithe Barn, Barton Farm Country Park

BRADFORD-ON-AVON

Situated in the Vale of Pewsey and on an adjoining hillside, Bradford-On-Avon is the last Cotswold town in west Wiltshire close to the borders of Somerset. The town centre is full of narrow streets lined with shops as well as impressive Roman and Norman architecture. It is dissected by the River Avon and the Kennet and Avon canal which provide a glimpse into the mill-related past of the town. The surrounding hillside is scattered with weavers' cottages of all shapes and sizes built in Cotswold stone. A climb through the narrow passageways between the houses and up to St Mary's Tor provides an excellent vantage point to view the town in its entirety, and beyond it the Marlborough Downs, the Mendip Hills and Westbury White Horse. (H10)

Special Places of Interest...

Abbey Mill. Built in the mid-1800s Abbey Mill has been used as a cloth mill, a rubber factory, offices and is finally being transformed into luxury flats. Best seen from across the river. (H10)

Barton Farm Country Park. A 36-acre park bounded by the River Avon on one side and the Kennet and Avon Canal on the other. The park offers something for everyone from walking, rowing, and fishing to relaxing with a picnic by the river. Sections of the park are managed specifically to encourage a wide range of wildlife. At the entrance to the park are the C14 farmhouse, granary and tithe barn of the original Barton Grange farm. Open all year, free of charge. (H10)

Canal Wharf & Lock. There are two wharfs on the Kennet and Avon Canal both of which were busy commercial wharfs from 1810 to 1930. Lock Inn Cottage café at the lower wharf. Larger wharf is the upper wharf by the lock. (H10)

Holy Trinity Church. The church is originally Norman and was extensively modified in the early 1300s and throughout the following century. (H10) 01225 864444

Pack Horse Bridge. The Pack Horse bridge, spanning the River Avon, was built in C14 to allow produce to be carried across the river by packhorses for storage in the tithe barn at Barton Grange farm. (H10)

Saxon Church. Near to Trinity Church is the Saxon church of St Laurence. This C7 building is all that remains of a monastery which once existed in the area. Throughout the C17 and C18 the Saxon church had various secular uses as, among other things, an ossuary, cottages and a free school for boys. Now protected by a trust. (H10)

The Chantry. Visible from the churchyard this striking building was once the home of a successful local clothier. (H10)

The Shambles. A crooked lane running between Silver Street & Market Street with a variety of shops. The name derives from the Anglo-Saxon word 'scamel', meaning a bench on which goods were laid out for sale. (H10)

Tithe Barn. Formerly part of the estate of Shaftesbury Abbey, the C14 barn was used to collect 'tithes' or income in the form of produce and livestock for the Abbey. The barn is 51 metres (168ft) long and has a spectacular timber-cruck roof which is one of the largest stone roofs in Europe. Open all year 10.30am-4pm. Free. (H10)

Canal Wharf & Lock

Terrace of Georgian houses, Bradford-On-Avon

1270   A phial of Christ's blood is presented to Hailes Abbey which becomes a major destination for pilgrims   1300   Gloucester Abbey owns a herd of 10,000 sheep

1327   Edward II murdered at Berkeley Castle and buried in Gloucester Cathedral   **37**

Town Bridge

Bradford Old Windmill

Town Bridge. It crosses the 'broad ford' on the Avon which is likely to be the origin of the name Bradford-On-Avon. Built by the Normans, the bridge was too narrow and so a second bridge was built alongside to widen it - you can see the join under the bridge. You can also still see two ribbed and pointed arches of the original bridge on the eastern side. The tiny C17 building on the bridge was originally a chapel. Later it became a small prison or 'Blind House' where local drunks were left overnight to cool off. (H10)

Where to Eat & Drink...

Bridge Tea Rooms, 24a Bridge Street. Housed in a charmingly wonky former blacksmith's cottage dating from 1675, the tea room specialises in traditional afternoon tea and cakes served by waitresses in Victorian costume. Also open for evening meals. (H10) 01225 865537 www.thebridgeatbradford.co.uk

Fat Fowl Restaurant, Silver Street. The Fat Fowl, right in the centre of town, is a bustling licensed café with an outdoor terrace during the day and a busy restaurant in the evening. Open for breakfast, lunch and dinner everyday, and tapas in the Roost Tapas bar. (H10) 01225 863111 www.fatfowl.com

Where to Stay...

Bradford Old Windmill, 4 Mason's Lane. This quirky and historic windmill, set high above Bradford, is stuffed with character, with romantically themed bedrooms especially those set up in the circular rafters. (H10) 01225 866842 www.bradfordoldwindmill.co.uk

Castle Inn, Mount Pleasant. Revived from dilapidation and a failing reputation, this listed Georgian building is now a thriving freehouse pub with boutique bedrooms, stunning views and a large and sunny garden and terrace. (G10) 01225 865 657 www.flatcappers.co.uk

Clifton House, Bath Road. Originally a coaching inn dating from the C17 with a Victorian façade, Clifton House has a charming and comfortable interior. Guests are encouraged to spend lazy Sundays lounging in their four-poster bed, the drawing room or garden with the Sunday papers. (G10) 01225 309 399 www.cliftonhouse-boa.co.uk

Woolley Grange, Woolley Green. This luxury Family Hotel is set in a beautiful Jacobean Manor House. All the comforts parents might crave and all the adventure a child could want. (H10) 01225 864705 www.woolleygrangehotel.co.uk

Saxon Church of St Laurence

CASTLE COMBE

One of the prettiest and most visited villages in the Cotswolds lies sheltered in a hidden valley surrounded by steep, wooded hills. In former times, an important medieval, wool centre evidenced by the weavers and clothiers' cottages that descend from the Market Cross to By Brook, and the three-arch bridge. There is parking at the top and bottom end of the village. Given its popularity with coach parties of Americans and Japanese, no wonder the number of gift shops and inns. Its great claim to fame followed its appearance in the 1966 film of Doctor Doolittle starring Rex Harrison. The village remains a popular location for TV commercials and period dramas because of its rows of quaint cottages undisturbed by time. (H3) www.castle-combe.com

Special Places of Interest...

Colham Farm Trail. The circular trail starts opposite the Dower House in Castle Combe and takes you through ancient woodland in Parsonage Wood and down into the By Brook valley where the meadow is a Site of Special Scientific Interest. Resident species include the green winged meadow orchid. (H3)

Dower House. The finest house in the village built in the C17. Note the beautiful shell-hooded doorway. (H3)

Motor Racing Circuit. Regular car and motorcycle race days take place through the summer at one of the longest established circuits in the UK. (J3) 01249 782417
www.castlecombecircuit.co.uk

St Andrew's Church. Originally C13, the nave was added in the C14 and the tower completed in the C16. In the 1850s much of the church had to be rebuilt. Note the beautiful fan vaulting reminiscent of Bath Abbey. Also the medieval faceless clock, one of the most ancient working clocks in the country. (H3)

Village Museum. Run by villagers, this tiny museum gives a fascinating insight into the history of the village and its surrounding countryside. Many artefacts including archaeological finds and old photographs and maps. Open East to

By Brook & Cottages, Castle Combe

Oct Su and BHs 2-5 or by prior arrangement. (H3) 01249 782250
www.museum.castle-combe.com

Where to Eat & Drink...

White Hart, Market Place. C14 pub at the heart of the village with a sunny conservatory and patio gardens to the rear. (H3) 01249 782295

Where to Stay in Castle Combe...

Castle House B&B. In the centre of Castle Combe is Castle House - built in 1672 and originally the George Inn. If you would like to stay in the room used by Sienna Miller in the movie Stardust, book the beautiful, simply furnished attic bedroom with crooked low wooden beams and nooks and crannies. Guests have their own breakfast/sitting area. (H3) 01249 782227

Castle Inn Hotel. This is a pretty honey-coloured building set in the market place. Many features of the original C12 construction remain

thanks to considerate restoration. The eleven bedrooms are individual in character. You can choose fine dining in the restaurant or more simple bar food in the bar itself. (H3) 01249 783030
www.castle-inn.info

Georgian House B&B. Ideally situated in the village centre next to the White Hart Pub and opposite the Castle Inn. The house was used as Hercule Poirot's home in 'The Murder of Roger Ackroyd'. Simple and comfortable design in the ensuite bedroom. (H3) 01249 783009

Manor House Hotel. This charming C14 hotel combines a historical setting with modern comforts. Stylish bedrooms are located in the main building or in the quaint neighbouring Mews Cottages. Plenty of places to hide away in peace and quiet around the building or the 365 acres of gardens and woodland. The restaurant has been awarded a Michelin Star. (H3) 01249 782206
www.manorhouse.co.uk

The High Street, Castle Combe

Corsham Court

Outside Castle Combe...

White House B&B, Nettleton.
Set in open countryside two miles outside Castle Combe. Accommodation is in an annexe to a thatched cottage containing bedroom and shower room. There are plenty of places to sit and relax in the orchard and garden. (G2) 01249 782359 www.thewhitehousebandb.com

West Farm B&B, West Littleton.
The family-run working farm has a substantial climber-covered red-roofed farmhouse. Ensuite bedrooms are bright and airy. (D3) 01225 891249 www.westfarmbandb.co.uk

CORSHAM

Attractive town of Cotswold stone and lime-washed houses dominated by the Methuen-Campbell's home, Corsham Court. Make sure you have time to admire the exterior of the noted Almshouses. (J6)

Special Places of Interest...

Corsham Court. Home of the Methuen-Campbells since the C15. The current inhabitants are 8th generation. The building dates back to 978 when it was a Summer Palace for the Kings of Wessex. Major alterations were undertaken in the C16 and C18s with the house being converted to an E-plan in 1582. In C19, however, major dry rot problems were found which set back the family's finances. The gardens were laid out by Capability Brown. The current mansion has a superb collection of paintings by Joshua Reynolds, Van Dyke and Phillipo Lippi among others, as well as Chippendale furniture. Part of the building is currently used by Bath Spa University's Art Department. Open summer, late Mar to 30 Sept daily except M & F 2-5.30, winter 1 Oct to late Mar W/Es 2-4.30 (closed Dec). (K6) 01249 712214 www.corsham-court.co.uk

RAF Rudloe Manor (now known as JSU Corsham). This was a Royal Air Force station above an MOD underground tunnel complex which, during WWII, was the Central Ammunitions Depot for the UK and the world's largest underground factory. A Beaverbrook aircraft engine factory was also created here as a fallback should the factories in Bristol be damaged by bombing - but it was never used. The labyrinth of caverns supplied 2,250,000 square feet (209,000 m2) of space, divided into many smaller chambers and including 14 miles of conveyor belts. There was cause for much rumour and conspiracy theories during its time and until very recently most of Corsham's inhabitants were unaware of the tunnel complex, some parts of

Almshouses, Corsham

1400   Burford now established as one of the Cotswolds most important wool-markets

1401   Death of William Grevel, Chipping Campden's great beneficiary

Lacock Abbey

which are still classified. Nowadays, a wine merchant rents out some areas for wine storage and amateur cavers often explore (and graffiti) the tunnels. (H6)

LACOCK

This is a show village owned and protected by the National Trust. You could be forgiven for thinking you were on a film set. Not surprisingly, it is a favourite for location scouts. Pride and Prejudice, Cranford and Wolfman are just some of the TV/film projects carried out here. The houses are lime-washed and half-timbered, and many date from the C13. There are some old inns and tearooms, and gift shops awaiting your custom. (M7)

Special Places of Interest...

Lacock Abbey (NT). Founded in 1232 by Lady Ela, the Countess of Salisbury, as a nunnery for the Augustinian order. The abbey

George Inn, Lacock

prospered from the wool trade in the Middle Ages but its religious foundation came to a sad end following the Dissolution of the Monasteries. It was converted into a country house around 1540 and eventually passed into the Talbot family. In the C19 William Fox-Talbot lived here and began experimenting with photography. In 1835 he invented the negative-positive process. His achievements can be seen in the museum. The gardens are a great attraction especially the Victorian woodland and Fox-Talbot's Botanic Garden. Abbey & Museum open daily mid-Mar to 1 Nov from 11 am (Abbey closed Tu & W, Museum open winter W/Es). (M7) 01249 730459
www.nationaltrust.org.uk

Lacock Pottery, 1 The Tanyard. Coloured glazes cover the stoneware pieces. The B&B is set in the old workhouse. A most impressive building overlooking the church. (M7) 01249 730266
www.lacockbedandbreakfast.com

Where to Eat & Drink...

George Inn, 4 West Street. The George Inn dates back to 1361. Its interior is so evocative of ye olde worlde that you would be forgiven for imagining that the man at the bar is Cromwell and that the dogwheel by the huge open fireplace is still being turned by a specially bred dog known as a Turnspit. 01249 730263
www.wadworth.co.uk/lacock/george_inn

Where to Stay...

Old Rectory, Cantax Hill. Built in 1866, this Victorian Gothic house has an impressive entrance hall with original Victorian tiles and stained glass windows. The bedrooms are elegant with large windows, and guests have use of the drawing room, dining room and garden including orchard and croquet lawn. 01249 730335
www.oldrectorylacock.co.uk

Sign of the Angel, Church Street. C15 inn that is full of character. Upstairs is a cosy wood panelled lounge. Crooked corridors and low doorways lead into the snug bedrooms which are furnished with dark, carved, period furniture. One has an enormous carved bed that once belonged to Isambard Kingdom Brunel. Bedrooms also in the Garden Cottage. 01249 730230
www.lacock.co.uk

Thatch Cottage, Folly Lane. Why not stay in your own cute C16 thatch cottage? Enjoy the privacy of your own living room and front door without the inconvenience of having to fix breakfast– the main house kitchen is adjacent. 01249 730398
www.thatchcottagelacock.com

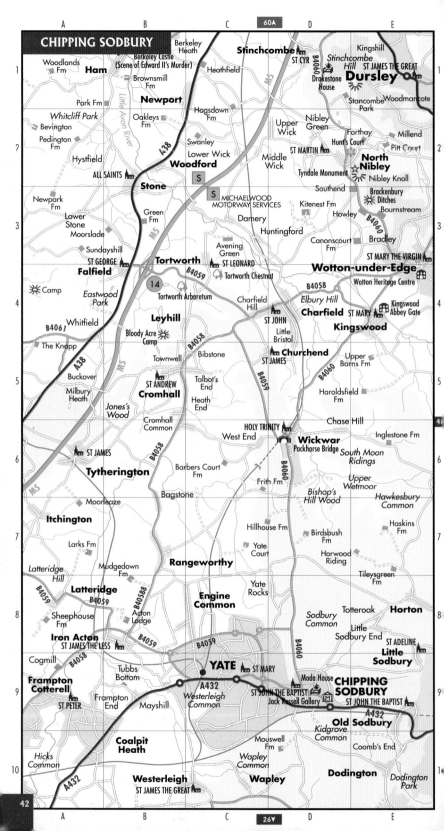

Tortworth Chestnut

CHIPPING SODBURY

An ancient medieval town that has escaped the hectic intrusions of tourism, and with its close neighbour Yate (which provides the commerce) has become a quality place to live and work. The wide main street formerly held sheep fairs and market fairs. There are a number of places to eat and drink: for coffees and cakes, the smart Hamptons Deli, for a taste of the Mediterranean, La Passione is popular on 01454 326444, but the most highly recommended eatery is Siam Thai at the bottom of the High Street on 01454 850095. (D9)

Where to Stay...

The Moda House, 1 High Street. Enjoy B&B with an international flavour. If you can pull yourself away from the photo-covered walls, you will settle easily into the comforts of this idiosyncratic C18 home. 10 comfy bedrooms. Relaxed sitting room and snugs, ideal for families. Wifi. (D9) 01454 312135 www.modahouse.co.uk

Special Places of Interest in Chipping Sodbury...

Jack Russell Gallery, 41 High Street. Jack was Gloucestershire's and England's wicketkeeper and (saviour) batsman for many years in the late 1980s and 90s. He started painting cricket scenes in the West Indies in 1990 and has since built an international reputation. His paintings cover diverse subjects such as cricket, landscape, the legal profession, portraits and wildlife. Originals and prints for sale. Open M-Sa 9.30-1. (D9) 01454 329583 www.jackrussell.co.uk

Outside Chipping Sodbury...

Brackenbury Ditches. An unexcavated Iron Age earthwork in an impregnable position on the Cotswold Way. The ramparts and entrance are vaguely visible from the south side. Good viewpoint. (E3)

Kingswood Abbey Gatehouse. Almost sole remnant of Abbey built in the C16 for the Cistercian Order.

Of interest, the richly decorated mullioned window. Open daily to view. (E4)

Tortworth Chestnut. An enormous sweet chestnut tree. Age is unknown but reckoned to be about 1,000 years old. She sits in St Leonard's churchyard and continues to gather legends. Follow the signs to the Farm shop and continue down lane for a further 200 yards. (C4)

Tyndale Monument. Built by the people of Berkeley in 1866 to honour the memory of their famous son and martyr William Tyndale, 1490-1536. Tyndale translated the Old and New Testaments which was considered an heretical offence and he was duly executed. His work became the foundation of the King James Version of the Bible. The monument rises to 111 feet and has an inner spiral staircase which ascends to a stupendous viewpoint. Open as locally advertised. (E2)

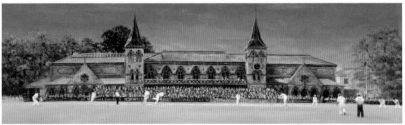
Cheltenham College by Jack Russell, Jack Russell Gallery ss

Field of Poppies, Withington

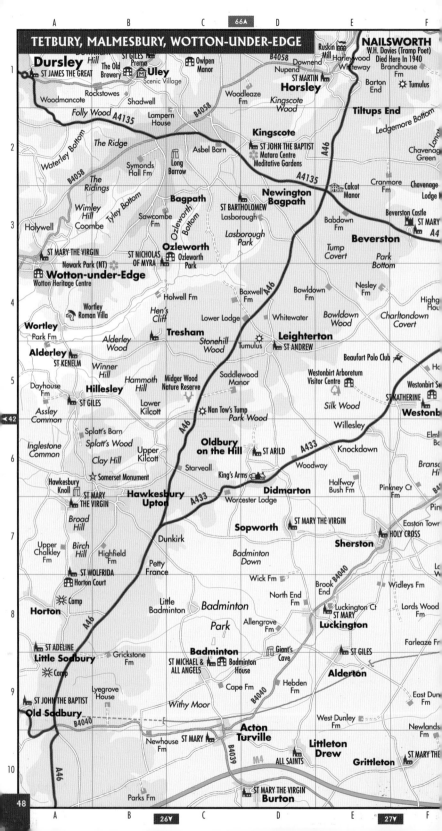

TETBURY, MALMESBURY, WOTTON-UNDER-EDGE

NAILSWORTH
W.H. Davies (Tramp Poet)
Died Here In 1940

Ruskin Mill
Harleywood
Whiteway
Brandhouse
Fm
Tumulus

Dursley
ST JAMES THE GREAT

Downham Hill
The Old Brewery
ST GILES
Prema
Uley
Scenic Village

Owlpen Manor

Downend
Nupend
B4058
ST MARTIN
Horsley

Woodmancote
Rockstowes
Shadwell

Folly Wood A4135
Lampern House
B4058
Woodleaze Fm

Kingscote Wood

Barton End

Tiltups End

Ledgemore Bottom

Chavenage Green

1

Waterley Bottom
The Ridge
The Ridings
B4058

Symonds Hall Fm
Long Barrow

Asbel Barn

Kingscote
ST JOHN THE BAPTIST
Matara Centre
Meditative Gardens

A46
A4135

Calcot Manor

Cranmore Fm

Chavenage Lodge

2

Holywell
ST MARY THE VIRGIN

Wimley Hill Coombe
Tyley Bottom

Sawcombe Fm

Bagpath
Ozleworth Bottom

ST BARTHOLOMEW
Lasborough

Lasborough Park

Newington Bagpath

Babdown Fm

Tump Covert

Park Bottom

Beverston Castle
ST MARY
A4

Beverston

3

Newark Park (NT)
ST NICHOLAS OF MYRA
Ozleworth
Ozleworth Park

Wotton-under-Edge
Wotton Heritage Centre

Holwell Fm

Boxwell Fm
A46

Bowldown Fm

Nesley Fm

Highg Hou

4

Wortley
Park Fm
Wortley Roman Villa

Hen's Cliff

Lower Lodge

Whitewater

Bowldown Wood

Charltondown Covert

Alderley
ST KENELM

Alderley Wood
Tresham

Stonehill Wood
Tumulus
ST ANDREW
Leighterton

Beaufort Polo Club

5

Dayhouse Fm
Hillesley
ST GILES

Winner Hill
Hammoth Hill

Midger Wood Nature Reserve

Saddlewood Manor

Westonbirt Arboretum Visitor Centre

Silk Wood

Westonbirt Se
ST KATHERINE

Westonb

Assley Common

Lower Kilcott

Nan Tow's Tump
Park Wood

Willesley

Inglestone Common
Splatt's Barn
Splatt's Wood
Clay Hill

Upper Kilcott

Oldbury on the Hill
ST ARILD

A433

Knockdown

Woodway

Elml
B

Bransc Hi

6

Hawkesbury Knoll
Somerset Monument
ST MARY THE VIRGIN
Hawkesbury Upton

Starveall

King's Arms

Halfway Bush Fm

Pinkney Ct Fm

Pin

A433

Worcester Lodge
Didmarton

7

Broad Hill

Dunkirk

ST MARY THE VIRGIN

Sopworth

HOLY CROSS
Easton Town

Upper Chalkley Fm
Birch Hill
Highfield Fm

Petty France

Badminton Down

Sherston

8

ST WOLFRIDA
Horton Court
Camp

Little Badminton

Badminton Park

Wick Fm

North End Fm

Brook End
B4040

Luckington Ct
ST MARY
Luckington

Widleys Fm

Lords Wood
B40

Farleaze Fm

Horton

Allengrove Fm

ST ADELINE
Little Sodbury
Camp

Grickstone Fm

Badminton
ST MICHAEL & ALL ANGELS
Badminton House

Giant's Cave

ST GILES

Alderton

9

ST JOHN THE BAPTIST
Old Sodbury
B4040

Lyegrove House

Withy Moor

Cape Fm

Hebden Fm

East Dun

West Dunley Fm

Newlands Fm

ST MARY THE

A46
M4

Newhouse Fm
ST MARY
Acton Turville

ALL SAINTS
Littleton Drew

Grittleton

10

B4039

Parks Fm

ST MARY THE VIRGIN
Burton

◀42

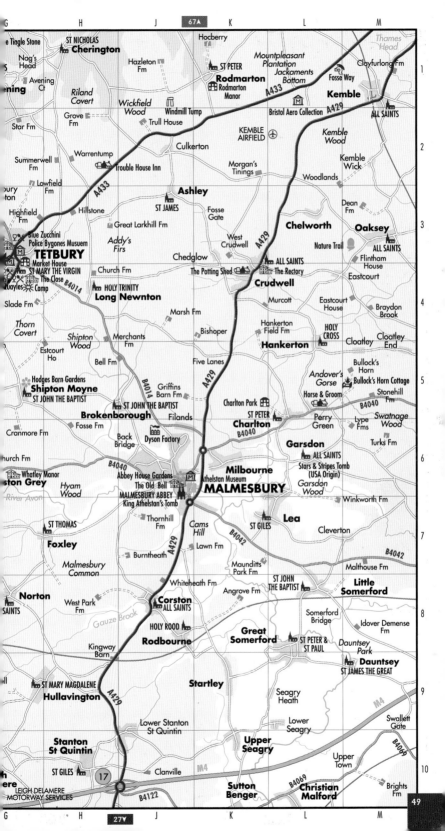

Chavenage

TETBURY

A market town with a fine church, St. Mary's. The town's recent claim to fame has been due to its proximity to Highgrove, Prince Charles' home at Doughton. The opening of his Highgrove shop on the High Street has brought more visitors to the town with coach outings bringing the traffic to a standstill. How this helps the rest of the town's merchants, one can only surmise. Today it is the Cotswold's major centre for antiques. It has also had much welcome investment in the shape of new shops, galleries and places to eat and drink. Nearby is Gatcombe Park, the home of Anne, The Princess Royal. The Woolsack Races on May Bank Holiday are fun to watch and cause great merriment if you are not forced to carry the heavy woolsack. Those with weak backs (or strong common sense) are best left to be onlookers. (G3)

Market House, Tetbury

Special Places of Interest...

Beverston Church of St Mary. Saxon sculptures. Norman additions. Three pointed arches on south arcade are of interest. Screen with some C15 work. (F3)

Beverston Castle. A substantial ruin incorporated into a C17 house. King Harold stayed here in 1051. It was besieged by King Stephen in 1145. The Berkeleys lorded over it and added a gatehouse. The gardens have an impressive collection of orchids and are open for the National Garden Scheme. (F3)

Chavenage. A haunted Elizabethan manor house that has remained virtually unchanged for 400 years. A replica of a bygone age. It contains two complete tapestry rooms, furniture and relics of the Civil War. Guided tours by the family. Specialises in weddings and corporate events. Open East Su & M, also May to Sept Th & Su 2-5. (F3) 01666 502329 www.chavenage.com

Market House. A substantial building of c.1655 supported by thick Tuscan pillars. It dominates the Market Place of this affluent little town and is often the venue for Saturday markets. (G3)

Matara Centre Meditative Gardens, Kingscote Park. Labyrinths, ponds, sculptures, Shinto woodlands, meadows and a Meditative Walled Garden. A place of calm and healing. Specialises in weddings with accommodation on hand. Open May to Sept Tu & Th 1-5. (D2) 01453 861050 www.matara.co.uk

Nan Tow's Tump. A long barrow. 9ft high and 100ft in diameter crowned with trees. Believed to contain skeleton of Nan Tow, a local Witch buried upright. (C5)

Parish Church of St Mary the Virgin. The Early Gothic revivalism gives the interior a sparse ambience. There are some box pews of interest. The whole is surrounded by an enclosed cloister housing some ancient tombs of knights and local dignitaries. It is best viewed from afar, across from the fields on the south side of town. (G3)

WESTONBIRT ARBORETUM

If you believe trees to be the most beautiful things in creation then a visit to this wonderland must be at the top of your agenda. Here, in this arboreal paradise garden, you will find 600 acres of magnificent trees and shrubs from around the world. With no less than 15,500 individual specimens of 3,000 different tree types, and a good 17 miles of footpaths ahead, you will need comfy footwear. Needless to say, it is quite a sight in spring and autumn, and popular too. Oak Hall Visitor Centre, giftshop and courtyard cafe. Plant centre. Open daily 9-dusk, from 8 at W/Es. (E5) 01666 880220 www.forestry.gov.uk/westonbirt

Westonbirt School.
Girls independent school. Grade 1 listed house. Former home of Robert Stayner Holford (1808-1892), the founder of Westonbirt Arboretum. Formal Italian gardens noted for exotic trees, shrubs and rustic walks. Gardens open, as locally advertised. (F5) 01666 880333 www.westonbirt.gloucs.sch.uk

Where to Eat & Drink...

Blue Zucchini Brasserie, 7-9 Church Street. Perfect for a coffee break, lunch and meeting up with friends. (G3) 01666 505 852

Chef's Table, 49 Long Street. You can dine upstairs in the Deli or downstairs in the Bistro, or take the cooked food home with you. Perhaps, brush up on your culinary skills with award-winning chef, Michael Bedford, at his Cookery School. (G3) 01666 504466 www.thechefstable.co.uk

Close Hotel, Long Street. This traditional Cotswold hotel built a fine reputation but has since been overtaken by the more contemporary and luxurious. However, lunch is exceptional value and a comfortable chair awaits you whilst you digest and look forward to your afternoon cuppa. (G3) 01666 502272 www.theclose-hotel.com

Quayles, 1 Long Street. Delicatessen and coffee shop ideal for resting and watching the passers-by. (G3) 01666 505151 www.quayles.co.uk

Trouble House ss

Trouble House, Cirencester Road. Considered to be aptly named as it has been the site of agricultural riots and civil war conflicts among other travails. Today, locals claim a ghostly blue lady floats through the bar after closing time. The surroundings are pleasant and unpretentious with ancient beams and fireplaces. The menu is praised for being a clever mix of fancy dining and more simple fare. (H2) 01666 502206 www.thetroublehouse.co.uk

Where to Stay...

Calcot Manor. This is a leisure complex combining a top English country hotel furnished in contemporary, up-to-the-minute designs that flow with ease into the C14 Cistercian barns, and all ideally suited for a family, business or leisurely stay. Adjacent you have Calcot Spa for health, beauty and relaxation - put simply, pampering the Self. And if, after all this hedonism, you need some simple refreshment, a glass of ale, or some nourishment, then pop in to the Gumstool Inn next door. Location is ideal for exploring the southern Cotswolds and Bath. (E3) 01666 890391 www.calcotmanor.co.uk

Lodge Farm B&B, Tetbury. The owners stock pure bred Hebridean black sheep, as well as thoroughbreds they are breeding to produce Event horses. Opposite the Elizabethan Mansion Chavenage House. 01666 505339 www.lodgefarm.co.uk

Talboys House, Church Street. Formerly owned by Richard Talboys, a wealthy wool merchant who traded with the Far East and Orient. The décor is sumptuous and evokes travels in India and the sub-continent. Double and single rooms available. (G3) 01666 503597 www.talboyshouse.com

The Ormond, 23 Long Street. This former coaching inn has been completely revamped into a modern small hotel furnished with colour and panache. Restaurant, bar, lounge and courtyard for al fresco refreshments. (G3) 01666 505690 www.theormond.co.uk

The Kings Arm's, Didmarton. C17 coaching inn on the edge of the Badminton Estate. Specialises in dishes of seasonal game and English lamb. B&B. (D6) 01454 238245 www.kingsarmsdidmarton.co.uk

Calcot Spa ss

1490   St Mary's Church, Fairford is almost completely rebuilt by
       John Tame, wool-merchant
1499   Bishop Oliver King begins construction of Bath Abbey
1500   Stroud now the centre of the Cotswold cloth industry

53

Special Country Places of Interest...

Badminton House. The home of the Dukes of Beaufort and venue for the annual Badminton Horse Trials. The estate was bought by the Worcesters in 1682. It was the 3rd Duke who was responsible for the house as we see it today. First, he invited James Gibbs to set about remodelling the East and West wings, then William Kent finished the North Front in the Palladian style. Fox hunting has been a great passion of the Beauforts. Their early forebears hunted all the way to London and back. Publishing was another passion. From 1885 to 1902 they devised The Badminton Library of Sports & Pastimes - an aristocratic leather bound series of books that was like a combination of Punch and your High Street cricket or football magazine, albeit a little more high brow. And, of course, the game of Badminton was reintroduced here in 1873 following its Indian origins. The house is closed to the public. The closest you'll get is to visit during the Three Day Horse Trials. (C9)

MALMESBURY

Claims to be the oldest borough in England (although Barnstaple in North Devon may dispute this) - established in 880 AD. Military strategists have described its hilltop location as the best naturally defended inland position of all

The Entrance to the Abbey Church of St Peter & St Paul, Malmesbury

ancient settlements. No wonder then that King Athelstan, the first King of all England, chose it as his home. Set on the edge of the Cotswold escarpment, it is a cheaper place to stay than the more central towns. Its

spirit though lies with the Wiltshire landscape. Dysons, the innovative design company of vacuum cleaners, is the major employer and has brought some much needed zest, style and money to this isolated town. However James Dyson was not the first inventor to work in the town. You must go back to the free-spirited monk, Eilmer, in the C11, who designed and built his own hang glider (see Malmesbury Abbey for details). (J6)

Special Places of Interest...

Abbey House Gardens. The home of the Naked Gardeners so be prepared for a surprise! View their website for Clothes Optional Days. There are bulbs galore, especially the 70,000 tulips in Spring and a massive range of 2,200 different roses, herbaceous borders, specimen trees and shrubs. Open daily 21 Mar to end Oct 11-5.30. (J6) 01666 822212 www.abbeyhousegardens.co.uk

Abbey House Gardens ss

Athelstan Museum, Cross Hayes.
Wonderful collection of Roman and
Saxon coin as well as bicycles, fire
engines, Tom Girtin drawings and
local bygones. Open daily 10.30-4.30.
(J6) 01666 829258
www.athelstanmuseum.org.uk

Charlton Park. Palatial mansion
built in 1607. Home to the Earls of
Suffolk since the C16. There are 4,500
acres of arable and woodland with
trout fishing and game shooting on
hand. It is also the venue for WOMAD,
the World of Music, Arts & Dance
festival, with its own park and camp
facility. (L5) 01666 822146
www.charltonpark.co.uk

Dyson Factory, Tetbury Hill.
The headquarters of the firm
established by James Dyson: a
temple of innovation and
engineering design, and world leader
in the manufacture of vacuum
cleaners and hand dryers. It is quite a
success story. Dyson is the market
leader in the USA. The first vacuum
cleaner took 5 years and 5,127
prototypes to develop. (J6)
01666 827200 www.dyson.co.uk

**Malmesbury Abbey Church of
St Peter & St Paul.** Founded as a
Benedictine Monastery in 676 AD by
the saintly and scholarly Brother
Aldhelm. King Athelstan was buried
here in 941 AD. By the C11 the
monastery held the second largest
library in Europe and was a place of
learning and pilgrimage. The Abbey
was built and completed by 1180. The
tall spire rose to 431 feet (131m) and
was to be seen for miles around.
However, in 1500 it collapsed
destroying the Nave and the Transept.

Dyson Factory   ss

A few years later, in 1550, the West
Tower also collapsed. What you see
today is less than half of the original
structure. Yet it still remains a
formidable church, and a sight to
behold. It was also a place of great
inspiration, for in 1010 the monk
Eilmer of Malmesbury became the
first man to fly by jumping off the
roof of the Tower and flying his hang
glider 200 yards before crashing and
breaking both his legs - Leonardo da
Vinci was to design a similar
machine 350 years later. Open daily
East-Oct 10-5, Nov-East 10-4. (J6)
www.malmesburyabbey.com

Market Cross. Built in 1490 to
shelter the poor and despondent
from the rain. (J6)

Where to Stay, Eat & Drink...

**Bullocks Horn Cottage,
Charlton.** Log fires in winter and
in summer dine outside in the cool
shade of the arbour or by candlelight
in the conservatory. 01666 577600
www.bullockshorn.co.uk

**The Horse and Groom Inn,
The Street, Charlton.** All the
charm of a true country inn in a
beautiful setting. Great food and
stylish bedrooms and even an
outside bar for those warm summer
nights! 01666 823904 www.
horseandgroominn.com

The Old Bell Hotel, Abbey Row.
England's oldest purpose built hotel
dating back to 1220. A fine place to
stay if you seek comfort coupled
with historic charm. Dine in the
formal Edwardian Restaurant, or
the less formal Hanks Room. (J6)
01666 822344 www.oldbellhotel.co.uk

Potting Shed Pub, Crudwell. A
more traditional gastro-pub, if that is
not a contradiction in terms. The
interior is trendy and modern without
being overbearingly so. Good choice
of beers on tap and tasty food without
the fiddly garnishes. Two acres of
garden including a vegetable plot
which supplies the pub kitchen. (K4)
01666 577833
www.thepottingshedpub.com

The Rectory, Crudwell.
This is a really lovely C16 house that
has been transformed into a small,
comfortable country house hotel
with 12 bedrooms. Three acres with
Victorian walled garden, croquet
lawn and heated outdoor swimming
pool. Beauty and Health therapies on
hand. Noted, however, for its superb
cuisine. (L3) 01666 577194
www.therectoryhotel.com

The Rectory, Crudwell ss

1535   The Dissolution of the Monasteries sees the destruction
of the monastic estates at Cirencester, Hailes, Gloucester
and Winchcombe

1536   William Tyndale, the first translator of the Bible is burnt
at the stake for heresy

Ozleworth Park

WOTTON-UNDER-EDGE

As the name suggests, Wotton hangs on the southern edge of the Cotswold escarpment. In its long history, the Berkeley family has dominated the town with varying success. King John's mercenaries devastated the Berkeley's property in the C11. Later, the simmering dispute between the de Lisles and the Berkeleys was sorted out in the latter's favour at the Battle at Nibley Green in 1470. The Berkeleys were generous patrons; Katherine Lady Berkeley established one of the country's first grammar schools here in 1384. Weaving and cloth-making grew from cottage industries in the C13. Wotton is a quiet market town with some splendid C17 and C18 buildings. Isaac Pitman, 1813-97, who invented shorthand lived on Orchard Street. The Ram Inn is probably the town's oldest building, but it is to St Mary the Virgin that all historians will be drawn. (A4)

Special Places of Interest...

Newark Park, Ozleworth (NT). Former Tudor hunting lodge with an eclectic art collection. Countryside walks. Plant sales. Open Mar to May W & Th, (& W/Es June to 1 Nov) 11-4. (B4) 01793 817666 www.nationaltrust.org.uk

Ozleworth Park. C18 house with rose garden and spacious lawns. Next door, Church of St Nicholas with its C12 hexagonal tower, rare weathercock and C13 font. (B3)

St Mary the Virgin, Wotton-Under-Edge.
The first church on this site was probably destroyed by King John's mercenaries in the C11. The present structure was consecrated in 1283. Its Perpendicular tower, one of the county's finest, has corner buttresses crowned with crocketed pinnacles. The marble tomb and the C15 brasses of Thomas, Lord Berkeley and his wife are outstanding. Note the C16

stained glass. Edward Barnsley in the Gimson tradition (Arts & Crafts Movement) designed the new altar and reredos on the north wall. The organ originally came from St. Martin in the Fields and had been a gift from George 1. George Handel played on it. Yet the church lacks the beauty of Burford or Chipping Campden and cannot be described as a notable "Wool" church. (A3)

The Bottoms, Waterley Bottom, Tyley Bottom and Ozleworth Bottom. Deep combes (valleys) of rare and solitary beauty rich in wild flowers and bird life. And all can be viewed from countless footpaths. Strange to believe, but in the C17 and C18 Waterley operated 15 fulling mills (to cleanse and thicken cloth) within a radius of 5 miles. (B3)

Wortley Roman Villa. Believed to be in existence from the C1 to C4. It was accidentally discovered in 1981 when an archaeological dig by the University of Keele unveiled Roman and Saxon coins, painted wall plaster, pottery and a damaged hypocaust. Much is now on display in Stroud Museum. (A4)

Wotton Heritage Centre, The Chipping. Run by the local Historical Society. Museum and research room. Open Tu-F 10-1 & 2-5 (2-4 in winter), Sa 10-1. (A4) 01453 521541 www.wottonheritage.com

Waterley Bottom

1540 Newark Park is designed by Sir Nicholas Poyntz
1540 Winchcombe becomes a tobacco growing area
1542 The Crown sells Hailes Abbey to an agent who demolishes it
57

For art and bohemia, 'Wool' churches, river valleys, Roman remains, gastro-pubs, hunting, industrial archaeology, gardens, idyllic villages, rolling hills and woodland.

You are now in the heart of the Cotswold experience. From the deep-sided valleys surrounding Stroud to the gentler slopes of the southern Wolds drained by the rivers Churn, Coln and Windrush. Out of these valleys have sprung hamlets with matching stone…made up of the manor house beside the church surrounded by cottages covered in roses and clematis.

The property developer has been busy in this Cotswold landscape. Rarely do you spy an old barn or hayloft that has not been converted into a domestic dwelling. Never has the picture-postcard village looked so perfect.

The Roman influence is easily seen in the fast-flowing A-roads that pass by Cirencester: Fosse Way, Ermin Way and Akeman Street where you can imagine the auxiliary cavalry units charging up and down these thoroughfares . A visit to the Corinium Museum will connect you to Hadrian and Caesar and you will learn that the conquering Romans built Corinium Dobunnorum (Cirencester) into the second largest Roman settlement in Britain with a populace of 12,000 inhabitants.

A few miles east of Cirencester lies the medieval town of Fairford, home to perhaps the finest stained glass in the Cotswolds, an example of which is displayed on the opposite page.

In the Stroud area there is much to interest the industrial archaeologist. Tours are organised to the woollen mills where you can see for yourself the looms in action.

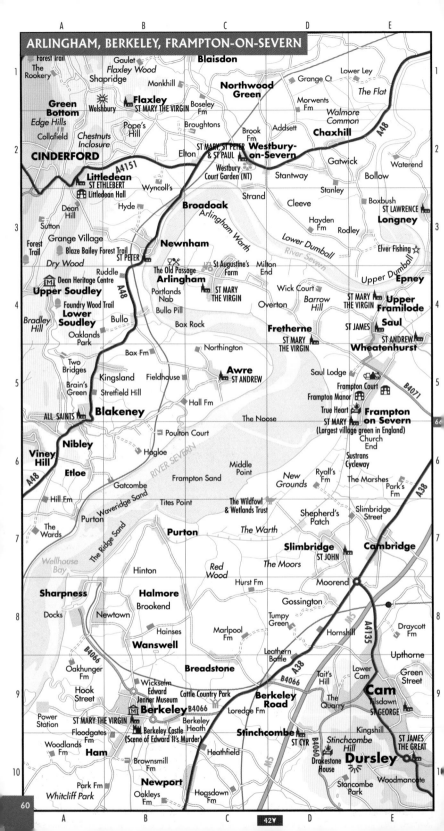

A   B   C   D   E

1

Forest Trail
The Rookery
Gaulet
Flaxley Wood
Shapridge
Monkhill
Blaisdon
Lower Ley
The Flat
Grange Ct

Green Bottom
Welshbury
Edge Hills
Collafield
Chestnuts Inclosure
Flaxley
ST MARY THE VIRGIN
Pope's Hill
Boseley Fm
Broughtons
Northwood Green
Morwents Fm
Walmore Common
Addsett
Chaxhill
A48

2

CINDERFORD
A4151
Elton
Brook Fm
Westbury-on-Severn
ST MARY, ST PETER & ST PAUL
Westbury Court Garden (NT)
Stantway
Gatwick
Stanley
Waterend
Bollow

Littledean
ST ETHLEBERT
Littledean Hall
Wyncoll's
Hyde
Broadoak
Arlingham Warth
Strand
Cleeve
Hayden Fm
Rodley
Boxbush
ST LAWRENCE
Longney

3

Dean Hill
Sutton
Grange Village
Blaze Bailey Forest Trail
ST PETER
Dry Wood
Ruddle
Newnham
The Old Passage
Arlingham
St Augustine's Farm
Milton End
Lower Dumball
River Severn
Upper Dumball
Elver Fishing
Epney

Forest Trail
Dean Heritage Centre
Upper Soudley
Foundry Wood Trail
Lower Soudley
Bradley Hill
Bullo
Portlands Nab
Bullo Pill
St Mary the Virgin
ST MARY THE VIRGIN
Wick Court
Overton
Barrow Hill
ST MARY THE VIRGIN
Upper Framilode
ST JAMES
Saul
ST ANDREW
Wheatenhurst

4

Oaklands Park
Box Rock
Box Fm
Northington
Fretherne
ST MARY THE VIRGIN

Two Bridges
Brain's Green
Kingsland
Stretfield Hill
Fieldhouse
Hall Fm
Awre
ST ANDREW
The Noose
Saul Lodge
Frampton Court
Frampton Manor
True Heart
ST MARY
Frampton on Severn
(Largest village green in England)
B4071

5

ALL SAINTS
Blakeney
Poulton Court
Church End

Nibley
Hagloe
Middle Point
Sustrans Cycleway
6

Viney Hill
Etloe
A48
Hill Fm
Gatcombe
Waveridge Sand
RIVER SEVERN
Frampton Sand
Tites Point
New Grounds
Ryall's Fm
The Marshes
Park's Fm

Purton
The Ridge Sand
Purton
The Warth
The Wildfowl & Wetlands Trust
Shepherd's Patch
Slimbridge Street
7

Wellhouse Bay
Hinton
Red Wood
The Moors
Slimbridge
ST JOHN
Cambridge
A38

8

Sharpness
Docks
Newtown
Halmore
Brookend
Hainses
Wanswell
Hurst Fm
Gossington
Tumpy Green
Moorend
Hornshill
A4135
Draycott Fm
Upthorne

9

B4066
Oakhunger Fm
Hook Street
Wickselm
Edward Jenner Museum
Berkeley
Cattle Country Park
B4066
Loredge Fm
Breadstone
Berkeley Road
B4066
Tait's Hill
The Quarry
Lower Cam
Green Street
Cam
Tilsdown
ST GEORGE

Power Station
ST MARY THE VIRGIN
Floodgates Fm
Berkeley Heath
Berkeley Castle
(Scene of Edward II's Murder)
Stinchcombe
ST CYR
Stinchcombe Hill
Drakestone House
Kingshill
ST JAMES THE GREAT

10

Woodlands Fm
Ham
Brownsmill Fm
Heathfield
Dursley
Woodmancote

Park Fm
Whitcliff Park
Newport
Oakleys Fm
Hogsdown Fm
Stancombe Park

A   B   C   D   E
42▼

ARLINGHAM PENINSULA

One of Gloucestershire's hidden gems tucked away between a sweeping bend in the River Severn's southern course. Centuries of floods and silt have turned this peninsula into rich agricultural land. You can enjoy all of this by following one or all of the four circular walks that start from a map board beside the Red Lion Inn on Arlingham's High Street. All walks have kissing gates and bridges, and can be muddy. So take your pick of either the Hare Walk, Gloucester Cattle Walk, Salmon Walk or the Skylark Walk, before or after luncheon. All walks take about 2.5 hours and are between 4.5 to 5 miles in length. (C3)

Special Places to Visit, Eat, Drink & Sleep...

The Old Passage. This restaurant with rooms has a magical and spellbinding quality and the new owners have redecorated the restaurant itself into a light and airy space with fine views across the Severn, only bettered by the view from the luxurious bedrooms above. This continues to be a sea-foodies delight: prawns, devilled whitebait, freshly shucked oyster, Pembrokeshire lobster, roast halibut, the list goes on. Meat, too. Accommodation. Special Severn Bore breakfasts. Closed Ms. (B3) 01452 740547 www.theoldpassage.com

St Augustine's Farm.
Working farm where you can stroke and feed the animals, and buy free range eggs. Open Mar to Oct Tu-Su 11-5. (C3) 01452 740277 www.staugustinesfarm.co.uk

BERKELEY

An attractive small town with wide streets that stands at the centre of the Vale of Berkeley. It has been at the heart of English history for over 1,000 years, all vividly displayed in its three outstanding attractions: Berkeley Castle, the Edward Jenner Museum and St Mary's Church. For some refreshment there is the Berkeley Arms Hotel with coffee lounge, bars and a restaurant. (B9) 01453 811177 www.theberkeleyarms.com

The Old Passage ss

Special Places of Interest...

Berkeley Castle. Home of the Berkeley family for the last 850 years. It remains a splendidly preserved Norman fortress with an enclosing curtain wall. Scene of Edward II's murder in 1327. Lovely terraced gardens. Superb Butterfly House. Open East to Oct Su & BH Ms, Su-Th June to Aug, 11-5.30. (B9) 01453 810332 www.berkeley-castle.com

Cattle Country Park. American bison, and other unusual breeds of cattle, with wild boar in special enclosures. Play area. Pets corner. Open W/Es and BHs 10-5. (C9) www.cattlecountry.co.uk

Berkeley Castle ss

The Berkeley Family tomb, Church of St Mary's

Edward Jenner Museum.

A Queen Anne House with traditional and modern displays that celebrate the life of Edward Jenner, the surgeon who discovered a vaccine for smallpox. Open Apr to end Sept, Tu-Sa & BH Ms 12.30-5.30, Su 1-5.30, & daily June to Aug, Oct Su 1-5.30. (B9) 01453 810631
www.jennermuseum.com

Parish Church of St Mary's.

One of Gloucestershire's most historic and interesting churches with a mass of features: Ring of ten bells, Norman doorway, C12 font, C13 chancel, C13-15 murals, C15 rood screen, C16 brass, Berkeley family tombs from the C15; and life-size effigies in alabaster, Jenner family vault and separate Gothic tower built in 1753. (B9)
www.stmarys-berkeley.co.uk

DURSLEY

This ancient market town nestling in a wooded valley on the very edge of the Cotswold escarpment modestly hides its innovative and industrial past. The Market House is a magnificent building that was funded by the Estcourt family of Shipton Moyne in 1738. It has a hipped tile roof and white-washed stone columns. There are some splendid Georgian town houses on the northern fringes of the town. Industry and enterprise are synonymous with Dursley's heritage: from the manufacture of C15 woollen cloth to the mighty C19 diesel, paraffin and petrol engines built by the engineering firm of R A Lister who also employed the failed inventor and genius, Mikael Pedersen. Pedersen invented the centrifugal cream separator (cream and whey from milk) and the Dursley Pedersen Bicycle, a machine of classic design and rare beauty. Architectural innovation carries on with the new library in May Lane and the splendid new school on the Berkeley Road. Let's hope Dursley is another Cotswold town (like its neighbours, Nailsworth and Tetbury) that is on the up. For some much-needed refreshment try "the pub of a thousand locals'" - The Old Spot Inn on Hill Road. The pub of the late, much missed, Old Ric (Sainty). One of CAMRA's favourites and if you are drawn to fine watering holes then rest your heels here awhile. (E10) 01453 542870 www.oldspotinn.co.uk

Stinchcombe Common.

Superb viewpoint over the Vale of Berkeley and River Severn. Walks. Golf courses. (D10)

Drakestone House, Stinchcombe. A small estate

boasting a fine Arts & Crafts building in a magnificent setting on the edge of beech woods. 01453 542140

FRAMPTON-ON-SEVERN

An enchanting, straggling village with one of the largest village greens in England. Cricket is played here in summer on Saturday afternoons - so beware of flying projectiles and men dressed in shimmering white garb running before your windscreen. It is a haven of wild flowers, bird life and insects due to the absence of ploughing, spraying or cultivation for the past 250 years. Two inns side The Green: The Bell and The Three Horseshoes. (E5)
www.framptononsevern.com

Elver Fishing. The elver is a baby eel which arrives here in Spring after a two-year journey from the Sargasso Sea. They are fished with nets at Epney on the Severn and considered to be a culinary delicacy (if par-boiled and fried in bacon fat), and are reputed to be aphrodisiac in effect. The elvers mature in isolated ponds then return across the Atlantic to spawn. On Easter Monday, Frampton-On-Severn holds an elver eating contest. The winners are then allowed to rest in a quiet bedchamber with their beloveds, sic. (E5)

The Dursley Pedersen Bicycle

Special Places of Interest...

Frampton Court. A Grade I Vanbrugh House, garden and family home. Fine panelling, original furniture and porcelain,1732. Superb Gothic C18 garden building, The Orangery for self-catering accommodation (sleeps 8). Fine landscaping with park, lake and ornamental canal. Home of the 'The Frampton Flora' a famous wild flower painting. C16 Wool Barn for hire. Country fair in September. (E5) 01452 740698 www.framptoncourtestate.co.uk

Frampton Manor. Grade I timber-framed medieval Manor House with walled garden and barn. C12 Birthplace of 'Fair Rosamund'

Westbury Court Garden

Flamingos, Wildfowl & Wetlands Trust

Clifford, mistress to Henry II. House and garden open by written appointment for groups of 10 or more. (E5) Tours: 01452 740268.

Where to Stay...

The True Heart, The Street. This is a truly sweet little cottage with all the right credentials. It's eco-friendly, fair trade, organic, stylish and comfortable. Within walking distance of the two inns, and a maze of footpaths. (E5) 01452 740504 www.thetrueheart.co.uk

Special Places to Visit...

Wildfowl & Wetlands Trust, Slimbridge. Founded by the late Sir Peter Scott in 1946, and home to the world's largest collection of flamingos, swans, geese and ducks - with over 35,000 wildfowl in winter. In historic terms it is most probably the birthplace of modern conservation. Restaurant. Shop. Picnic areas. Free wheelchairs for the disabled. Open daily; Apr to Oct daily 9.30-5.30, Nov-Mar daily 9.30-5. (C7) 01453 891900 www.wwt.org.uk

And, across the river...

Littledean Hall. One of the oldest houses in Britain dating from C11. Archaeological site. Lovely ancient trees. No longer open to the public. (A3)

Westbury Court Garden (NT). C17 Dutch water garden laid out between 1696 and 1705. Designed with canals, yew hedge and vegetable plots. Open East to Oct W-Su & BH Ms 10-5. Open daily July & Aug 10-5. (C2) 01452 760461 www.nationaltrust.org.uk

1570 The "Great Rebuilding" of England begins
1576 Chavenage developed into a substantial manor
1582 Wiliam Shakespeare licensed to marry the pregnant Anne Hathaway
63

FREE HOUSE
FOSTONS ASH

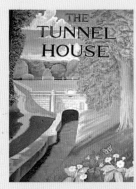

THE TUNNEL HOUSE

The Brandy Cask

FREE HOUSE
BUTCHERS ARMS
Omnia subiecisti sub pedibus, oves et boves

SWAN

The George Hotel
HOOK NORTON
EST. ALES 1849

RAM INN

FREE HOUSE
PUBLIC WEIGHBRIDGE
THE WEIGHBRIDGE

FREE HOUSE
Hunt on CAT & CUSTARD

MILLERS ARMS

VILLAGE PUB
FREEHOUSE

The Maytime Inn
FREE HOUSE

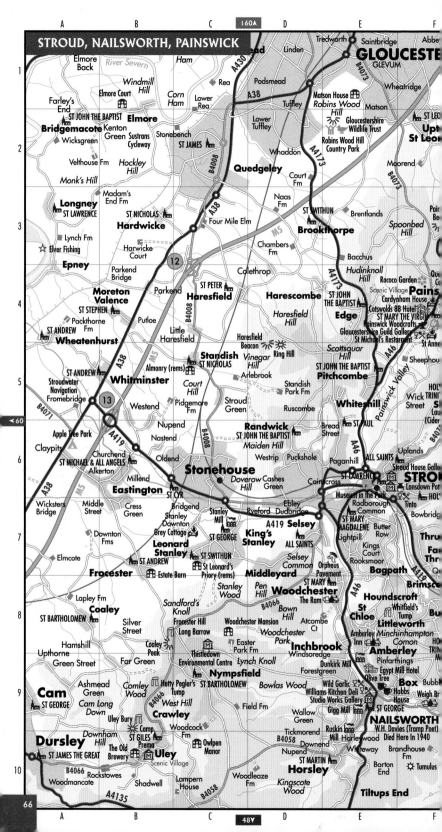

STROUD, NAILSWORTH, PAINSWICK

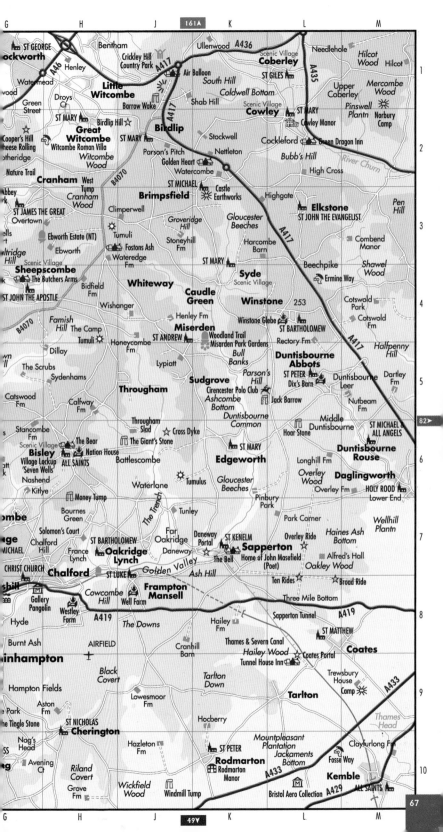

Saltridge Wood, Sheepscombe

STROUD

This is not a pretty, pretty almost too perfect Cotswold town. No. Stroud was as close to the dirt of the industrial revolution as any other town in the Gloucestershire Cotswolds. It has few architectural gems. However, its attraction lies in its energy and artistic ambitions (or pretensions). There has been a liberal, bohemian attitude at play here since the group of Tolstoyan Anarchists settled at Whiteways in 1898. There is a lively community of writers and artists living in the surrounding valleys. Many will have read Laurie Lee's Cider With Rosie about his early life in the Slad Valley but artists Michael Cardew, Lyn Chadwick and Norman Jewson settled here too. And Damien Hirst has a business making up his prints and artworks in nearby Chalford. So perhaps the claim that it is the Arts and Crafts centre of the Cotswolds is justified. A busy café culture pervades too. The weaving industry all began in a couple of cottages up the hill in Bisley, This moved into the town where 150 mills were soon in action using the water from the valleys. But, as the C19 progressed, much of this cloth making moved north to the West Riding of Yorkshire. The surrounding valleys provide wonderful walks through combes and woodland that are so very different from the Central Wolds. Look out for the Subscription Rooms built around 1833. Fringe Festival in 2nd week of September. Arts Festival in October. (F6) www.stroudfringe.co.uk

Special Places to Visit...

Stroud Valley Cycle Trail. A flattish route ideal for family cycling takes you along the Nailsworth valley, a former railway track. Start from the Kings Stanley car park, cross the A46, to Dudbridge Roundabout and follow the trail to Egypt Mill. (D7)

Gallery Pangolin, Chalford. Specialises in contemporary bronze sculptures that have been caste in their foundry, and also sculptures and drawings. Open M-F 10-6, Sa 10-1. (H8) 01453 886527 www.gallery-pangolin.com

Lansdown Pottery. A small group of potters work here developing their own different styles. It is also a centre for learning and art shows with the Studio, Glaze room, Kiln Room and extensive Library. Open M-F 10-5. (E6) 01453 753051 www.lansdownpottery.co.uk

Museum In The Park, Stratford Park. Innovative and colourful displays and changing exhibitions ranging from Dinosaurs to the Uley Roman Temple to the world's first lawnmower and contemporary sculpture. Open Apr to Sept Tu-F 10-5, W/Es & BHs 11-5. Oct to Mar Tu-F 10-4, W/Es 11-4. (E6) 01453 763394 www.museuminthepark.org.uk

Stroud House Gallery, Station Road. A presentation of contemporary art in 5 spacious rooms. Around 10 annual exhibitions. Open W-Sa 10.30-5. (E6) 01453 750575 www.stroudhousegallery.co.uk

Gallery Pangolin ss

1585   William Shakespeare's twins Judith and Hamnet born   1587   Endymion Porter born at The Manor, Aston-sub-Edge patron of the poets Robert Herrick and Ben Jonson

Woodchester Roman Villa.
This huge villa was excavated by
Lysons in 1993 and revealed 64
rooms including the Orpheus
Pavement. Today there is little to see.
The pavement lies buried and plans
to uncover it lie dormant. You can see
a replica at Prinknash Abbey. (E7)

Where to Eat & Drink...

Tinto, 50 High Street.
Intimate, friendly, delicious.
(E6) 01453 756668

MINCHINHAMPTON

A large village noted for the Market
House, Holy Trinity and rows of
weavers' cottages. The Parish Church
of the Holy Trinity has an unusual
coronet Tower and some richly ornate
monuments. A living and working
village, off the tourist route, and
better for it. The wide, open spaces
have room for three golf courses. So
pack your clubs and tees. (F9)

Market House. Impressive building
built in 1698 with stone columns and
row of wooden pillars. (F8)

Minchinhampton Common
(NT). A wide, open space popular
with dog walkers, horse riding. The
Saxons final resting place, the Long
Barrows and Earthworks. (F8)

NAILSWORTH

In the last few years this little town
has come alive! Transformed into a
thriving, bustling shopping centre
with bakery, restaurants, tearooms,
arts and craft shops. An eclectic mix
of Cotswold domestic and industrial
architecture is on the hillside
overlooking a wooded valley. A
convenient centre for visiting Bath
and the southern Cotswolds. (E9)

Special Places to Visit...

Dunkirk Mill Centre.
A mill with machinery driven by
the largest working water wheel in
Gloucestershire. Displays on the
finishing processes of fulling, teasel
raising and cross cutting. Access
is via the Cycle Track by Egypt Mill.
Open Apr to Sept on odd W/Es 2-4.
(E9) 01453 766273
www.stroud-textile.org.uk

Wild Garlic   ss

Gigg Mill, Old Bristol Road.
Historic mill with weaving shed
containing ancient and modern
looms. Open as Dunkirk Mill,
above. (E9)

Ruskin Mill. A thriving arts,
craft and education centre set in a
restored 1820s woollen mill. (E9)
01453 837521 www.rmet.co.uk

**Studio Works Gallery,
26 Fountain Street.** Work by
Paul Bradley; Early Studio Pottery,
Clive Bowen and others. Open daily.
(E9) 01453 833733

Where to Eat & Drink...

Hobbs House, 4 George Street.
Busy bakery and deli serving coffee,
cakes, paninis and sandwiches.
(E9) 01453 839396
www.hobbshousebakery.co.uk

Olive Tree, 28 George Street.
Just the place to sit and wile away
lazy days in the sunshine, or perhaps
to write the next Harry Potter.
Breakfasts, coffee, lunch and suppers.

Daily Specials can be Fish Pie,
Ratatouille Crumble or Rump Steak.
Open M-Sa from 8.30am.
(E9) 01453 834802
www.theolivetree-nailsworth.com

Weigh Bridge Inn, Longfords.
Home of the famous 2 in 1 pie.
Half of the bowl contains the filling
of your choice: steak and mushroom,
chicken, ham and leek, pork, bacon
and celery...the other half is
brimming with home made
cauliflower cheese. Freehouse with
log fires and cosy corners to sample
fine ales. (E9) 01453 832520
www.2in1Pub.co.uk

Wild Garlic, 3 Cossack Square.
Warm ambience, fresh organic
produce, making friends, modern
British food cooked by the former
head chef of nearby Calcot Manor.
There is also a bright and colourful
bedroom to rest in, and digest
your food. (E9) 01453 832615
www.wild-garlic.co.uk

Rococo Garden, Painswick

Williams Kitchen, 3 Fountain Street. In need of a lunch time sandwich, or fresh bass to take home and bake. This deli has been spoiling the locals for so long they have probably forgotten how lucky they are to have it. Open daily. (E9) 01453 835507 www.fishandseafood.co.uk

Egypt Mill Hotel. Former C16 cloth mill and dye house with its machinery on view. 28 bedrooms decorated in a comfortable contemporary style with a mix of beams and rusticity. Restaurant. Child friendly. (E9) 01453 833449 www.egyptmill.com

PAINSWICK

Its local description as 'The Queen of the Cotswolds' is fully justified. The houses and cottages are built from a grey, almost white limestone, in marked contrast to Broadway and Chipping Campden, and some of the buildings have an almost Palladian, yet statuesque quality about them. Look out for the Court House and the Cotswolds88hotel. Wander down the pretty side streets and visit the churchyard famous for the legendary 99 yew trees. The 100th yew tree has been planted time and again but has never survived. Painswick is one of the gems of the southern Cotswolds and is a worthy base from which to explore this region. It is also connected to a network of footpaths including the Cotswold Way so you can arrive by car or taxi and then just

walk for the rest of your stay. (F4)

Special Places to Visit...

Gloucestershire Guild Gallery, Painswick Centre. The best of contemporary craftsmanship direct from the makers in their own gallery. Commissions undertaken. Open Tu-Sa 10-5. (F4) 01452 814745 www.guildcrafts.org.uk

Little Fleece Bookshop, Bisley Street. A traditional C17 Cotswold house that portrays the Arts & Crafts style. It is a private dwelling open as

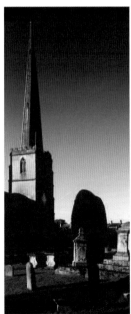

Painswick

an antiquarian and second-hand bookshop. (F4) 01452 812264

Rococo Garden. A beautiful C18 Rococo garden in 6 acres dating from a period of flamboyant and romantic garden design nestles in a hidden Cotswold valley. Be sure you visit in February for the display of magical snowdrops. Open daily mid-Jan to end Oct, 11-5. Restaurant and Gift Shop. (F4) 01452 813204 www.rococogarden.co.uk

Painswick Beacon. Fine viewpoint. Footpaths. Parking. (F3)

Painswick Woodcrafts, 3 New Street. Dennis French specialises in British woodware, hand-turned on the lathe - table lamps, bowls, vases. Open W-Sa & BH Ms from 9.30. (F4) 01452 814195 www.painswickwoodcrafts.co.uk

Prinknash Abbey Park. Benedictine Monastery with C14 and C15 origins set amidst an idyllic, rolling landscape. Abbey church opens 8-5. Monastery garden with possible Tudor origins. Café opens W-Su and displays a replica of the Great Orpheus Pavement originally found in Woodchester but now buried and more than likely never to be exposed again for fear of contamination. Grounds open daily. (G2) 01452 812455 www.prinknashabbey.org.uk

Prinknash Bird Park. Collection of over 50 wildfowl, waterfowl and tame deer. Open daily from 10. (F2) 01452 812727 www.prinknash-bird-and-deerpark.com

1611   The King James Version of the Bible incorporates much of Tyndale's work   1612   Robert Dover holds the first Cotswold Olympicks at Chipping Campden

It is the soaring spire that will first captivate you then, as you enter, it will be the line of yew trees and then, as you wander around the churchyard, the tombs or monuments carved with their intricate figures. But do look up and admire the gold clock. The spire has been struck by lightning on many occasions including 1763 and 1883. The 100th yew tree always withers away. (F4)

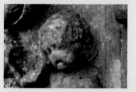

Edgeworth

Where to Eat & Drink...

St Michaels Restaurant, Victoria Street. A family run restaurant with weekly-changing menu. Everything is sourced locally, even berries and wild mushrooms in season from the nearby fields and hedgerows. Three stylish bedrooms for B&B. (F4) 01452 814555 www.stmickshouse.com

Where to Stay...

Cardynham House, Tibbiwell Street. A luxurious B&B set within an enchanting C15-16 former wool merchant's home. Each room is individually decorated from 'Old Tuscany' to 'Cottage Rose' but if you seek a real treat try the 'Pool Room'. Bistro. (F4) 01452 814006 www.cardynham.co.uk

Cotswolds88Hotel, Kemps Lane. This Palladian-style Cotswold rectory has been transformed by interior designer Marchella De Angelis into a lifestyle-boutique hotel in homage to the avant-garde artist, Leigh Bowery. It's wacky, bright, eclectic, interesting...it invites opinion. The transformation has been a cause of some controversy, not least from its former owner. One of those places you will either love or hate. Best give it a go. (F4) 01452 813688 www.cotswolds88hotel.com

St Anne's B&B, Gloucester Street. A listed C18 former wool merchant's house with a relaxed family atmosphere. Within easy walking distance of pubs and restaurants. (F4) 01452 812879 www.st-annes-painswick.co.uk

Villages of Interest...

Bisley. Home of the writer Jilly Cooper and the sculptor, the late Lynn Chadwick. Noted for the Well Dressing on Ascension Day and its rows of beautiful stone cottages. (H6)

Sapperton. In a splendid position overlooking woodland and the Golden Valley. Home of the William Morris protégés, Ernest Gimson and Sydney and Ernest Barnsley of the Cotswold Arts and Crafts Movement, creators of beautiful furniture who also built their own cottages in the village. Their fame rose after completing restorative work at nearby Pinsbury Park which became, during World War II, home to the Poet Laureate, John Masefield. Ernest Gimson died young at 59 and is buried in the churchyard. The area is rich in industrial heritage, woodland and circular walks. Two inns, the Daneway and the gastro-pub, The Bell, are on hand to refresh you. (K7)

Sheepscombe. A straggling village surrounded by beautiful woodland, rolling pastures and green hills. The view down the valley looking towards Painswick church is a beauty. It is the ancestral home of Laurie Lee whose parents moved to Slad. He maintained a connection with the village by purchasing the field for the cricket club, so named Laurie Field and which remains part of his Estate. A network of footpaths leads through woodland to Painswick, Cranham and Slad. (G4)

Bisley

1612   Chipping Campden's Almshouses built by Sir Balptist Hicks   1613   Sir Baptist Hicks' Chipping Campden mansion burnt down by Royalist troops to prevent capture by Parliamentary forces

A group of isolated hamlets dotted along a beautiful wooded valley. Duntisbourne Abbot stands at the head of the valley. The Dunt Brook flows through each hamlet. The road to Duntisbourne Leer runs adjacent to the stream. Middle Duntisbourne and Duntisbourne Rouse are two farming hamlets, the latter famous for its idyllic Saxon Church. (L5)

Frocester Court's Medieval Estate Barn

Cotswold Canals. The Stroudwater Navigation was opened in 1779 linking Stroud to the River Severn in order to serve the cloth industry of the Stroud Valleys. The Thames and Severn Canal was built to link the Stroudwater to the River Thames via the Sapperton Tunnel. The towpath is open and the best places to see the restored canal are at Eastington, near Stonehouse, and at both portals of the Sapperton Tunnel, and west of the Spine Road in the Cotswold Water Park. The restoration work is on-going and is actively creating freshwater habitats where wildflowers

Slad. One of the Stroud villages where cloth was spun in the little cottages before it all moved to South Riding, Yorkshire. Hundreds flock here to walk in the shadow of Laurie Lee's Cider With Rosie and to sample the brew still available in the Woolpack. If you have recently read the book which captures an England long forgotten, you will recognise the woods and valleys described. You may wish to make your way to Bulls Cross, the hanging place, and now the start point for many walks. Laurie Lee lies buried in the churchyard, opposite the Woolpack. (F5)

Uley. A long, attractive village with some fine Georgian houses, and famous as a centre of the cloth industry in the C17 and C18s. In 1608 three Uley clothiers acted for 29 local broadcloth weavers, and the 13 weavers from Owlpen. Uley is also the site of a Roman settlement. (B10)

Uley Bury

Special Places of Interest...

Bristol Aero Collection, Kemble Airfield, Hangar A1. Designs and produce from two factories; Bristol Aeroplane Company-British Aerospace at Filton, and Rolls-Royce at Patchway. Aircraft, Missile and space systems. Open East to Oct M & Su from 10, Nov to East M only. (L10) 01285 771204 www.bristolaero.com

abound, notably 'Lilies of the Valley'. (L8) 01285 643440 www.cotswoldcanals.com

Elmore Court. Home of the de Guise family, Baronets of Gloucestershire. This grade II listed mansion has recently been the subject of a Channel 4 TV series to save it from falling into further disrepair. We await the success of their hopeful intentions with interest. (B1)

Frocester Court's Medieval Estate Barn. This is an enormous barn built between 1284 and 1306. It remains the second largest in England and is one of the best preserved with massive oak roof. It is used every day by the farmer who owns it. For conducted tours (of 5 or more) phone 01453 823250. (B7)

Jet Age Museum, Brockworth Enterprise School. Collection of Gloucester built aircraft with artefacts representing the county's contribution to aviation. See website for opening times. (H1) www.jetagemuseum.org

Laurie Lee's Resting Place, Slad

1616   Death of William Shakespeare   1620   Lygon Arms developed from small manor house into larger building

Misarden Park Gardens

Owlpen Manor

Misarden Park Gardens.
The home of the Wills family, of tobacco fame, has shrubs, a traditional rose garden, perennial borders, extensive yew topiary, magnolia Goulangeana and spring bulbs amidst a picturesque woodland setting. Rill and Summerhouse. The Elizabethan mansion has mullion windows and was extended by Waterhouses in the C19 and by Lutyens who added a new wing between 1920-21. The gardens are open Apr to Sept Tu, W & Th, 10-4.30. Nursery open daily except M, Apr to mid-Oct. (K5) 01285 821303 www.misardenpark.co.uk

Owlpen Manor. An iconic group of picturesque Cotswold buildings: Manor House, Tithe Barn, Church, Mill and Court House. Water Garden and terrace. The Tudor manor dates

from 1450 to 1616 but the whole estate has 900 years of history to tell. Open May to Sept Tu, Th & Su 2-5. Grounds and restaurant open 12.00. Holiday cottages for hire. (C10) 01453 860261 www.owlpen.com

Prema, Uley. Independent rural arts centre shows new work by emerging artists in their converted chapel. Open M-F. (B10) 01453 860703 www.prema.demon.co.uk

Rodmarton Manor, Cirencester.
This is a unique building built by Ernest Barnsley and his Cotswold group of craftsmen for the Biddulph family from 1909 to 1929. It displays Cotswold "Arts and Crafts" furniture, metalwork and wall hangings. The 8-acre garden is a series of outdoor rooms and is a marvel throughout

the year. Refreshments. Open Feb, then May to Sept W, Sa & BHs 2-5. (K10) 01285 841253 www.rodmarton-manor.co.uk

Stanley Mill, Stonehouse.
Built in 1812, the mill has an exceptional interior where you can watch demonstrations of wool carding and mule spinning. To visit book on 01453 766273 (C7)

St Mary's Mill, Chalford.
An 1820 mill housing a large water wheel and a powerful Tangye steam engine. Open for Open Days on 01453 766273 (H8)

The Old Brewery, Uley.
The mill owner, Samuel Price, built this brewery in 1833 to assuage his workers' thirst. It was restored in 1984 and has since won many awards for their Old Spot, Pigs Ear and Uley Bitter. It is not open to prying visitors, only the trade. You can sample their wares in the Old Crown Inn at the top of the village, or in various hostelries around the Cotswolds. (B10)

Thistledown Environment Centre, Nymspfield.
Promotes the awareness of agricultural and environmental practices by tackling ecological issues head-on in a fun way. Follow the adventure, sculpture and wildlife trails. Organic campsite. Open daily 10-5.30. (C8) 01453 860420 www.thistledown.org.uk

Woodcarving from the demolished Sapperton House in Sapperton Church

Cam Long Down from Coaley Peak

Whiteway Colony. Founded in 1898 by a group of Tolstoyan Anarchists made up of liberal minded teachers and clerks from Croydon who found land they could buy for £7 an acre and who built small, wooden houses. They grew their own vegetables, buried their own dead and invited musicians and intellectuals to visit them. The men wore shorts and beards, the women smocks. They housed a number of Republican refugees from the Spanish Civil War who influenced Laurie Lee's education and travels. Today many of their descendants still live here. You can buy fresh honey and vegetables from them. (J4)

Woodchester Mansion. Be prepared for a good 1-mile walk from the car park down to this unfinished masterpiece of Victorian stone masonry set in a secret Cotswold valley. The restoration project is on-going and ambitious. Bat Exhibition. Open late Mar to end Oct most W/Es 12-5. (C8) 01453 861541 www.woodchestermansion.org.uk

Woodchester Mansion

Churches to visit...

Coates. Norman. Perpendicular tower. Brasses. Best viewed from across the fields. (L8)

Coberley. C15 Gargoyles. Enter through farm gates. (L1)

Daglingworth. Saxon carvings. (M6)

Duntisbourne Rouse. Small Saxon. Saddleback Tower. Norman additions. Lovely situation. (M6)

Edgeworth. Early Saxon with some Norman additions: nave, chancel and south door. A restored C13 porch and C14 stained glass. Look for the cross in the churchyard with medieval base and mutilated head. (K6)

Elkstone. Famous Norman Cotswold church known for its Tympanum and claimed to be the highest in the Cotswolds. (L3)

Miserden. Late Saxon in origin, with a Norman font and windows. Some C16 tombs in churchyard. Sadly much was destroyed by the amateur architect, the Reverend W H Lowder, in 1886. Note the War Memorial by Lutyens and the beech and yew trees. (J4)

Sapperton. Noted for its monuments, oak panelling supplied from the Manor House and woodcarvings, its hundreds of crocuses in Spring, and not forgetting its superb position overlooking the Golden Valley. (K7)

Selsey. Spectacular position set high on the Cotswold escarpment. Stained glass by pre-Raphaelites, Edward Burne-Jones and William Morris. (D7)

Uley. In a spectacular position overlooking the valley. Noted for the Norman font, fine roof and stained glass. (B10)

Special Places of Natural Interest...

Cam Long Down. A humpbacked ridge of oolitic limestone that once seen is never forgotten. From the top it's a good viewpoint touched by the Cotswold Way surrounded by beech woods and bracken. (A9)

Chalford Valley Nature Trail. Passes beside the River Frome and the Thames & Severn Canal. Parking near Round House by the Industrial Estate. (H8)

Coaley Peak. On the edge of the Cotswold escarpment affording fine views. Picnic area. Ice Cream van. (B8)

Cooper's Hill. 137 acres of common land in which to roam wild. Criss-crossed by nature trails. Start from the car park at Fiddler's Elbow. The scene of the Cheese-Rolling ceremony on Whit Monday at 6pm - a large cheese (originally representing the Sun in a Pagan ceremony) is chased down the hill. Only for the fittest, and craziest at heart, for limbs have known to be fractured here on many occasions. Scene of an Iron Age fort. (G2)

Cranham Woods. Bluebells and white garlic bloom in Spring and a web of footpaths spread throughout this tangled woodland. Best approached from Birdlip in early summer when the foliage is green and new. (H3)

THE COTSWOLD HORSE

The horse, Equus ferus caballus, has evolved over 45 to 55 million years and began to be domesticated about 4000 BC and by 2000 BC their use had spread across much of Europe, Central Asia and the Middle East. The only wild horse still in existence is the Przewalski, of Mongolian origin and now a protected species.

To many who live in the Cotswolds the horse is synonymous with their lifestyle. Whether it be hunting with hounds, training hunters for racing, point-to-pointing, playing polo, running a livery stable or just owning a horse for the simple pleasure of exercise, and because you adore these beautiful creatures. You can't travel very far in the Cotswolds without coming across a horse being ridden down a country lane or seeing ponies chasing each other around a field. The Cotswold countryside is criss-crossed with hundreds of miles of bridleways. For starters, you could try the Sabrina Way, a 44-mile (70km) route from Forthampton to Great Barrington. For details of more routes log on to www.ride-uk.org.uk. For those wishing to join this merry band there are many riding stables just itching to teach you.

The Cotswold calendar is full of events from Cheltenham's National Hunt festival in March, to the Badminton Horse Trials in May, to the Gatcombe Park festival in August. In between are point-to-points, pony club meets and hunts.

Cam Long Dow

Ebworth Estate (NT). Woodland walks through beech woods rich in wildlife managed by English Nature. No parking facilities. (H3) 01452 814213

Frocester Hill. A viewpoint rising to 778 feet provides superb views over the Severn Estuary, Welsh Hills and Forest of Dean. (C8)

Gloucestershire Wildlife Trust, Robinswood Hill Country Park. Visitor Centre, exhibition and giftshop. Open daily 9-5, W/Es 11-4.30. (E2) 01452 383333
www.gloucestershirewildlifetrust.co.uk

Golden Valley. Runs from Sapperton to Chalford, and is especially fine with the arrival of the autumnal colours of beech, ash and oak. (G8)

Haresfield Beacon & Standish Wood (NT). High open grassland at 700 feet that was a natural fort held by Iron Age and Roman settlements. Delightful when the bluebells and primroses bloom in the Spring. (D4)

Rodborough Common (NT). 800 acres of open space provides great walks and views across the Stroud Valleys. (E7)

Ancient Monuments to visit...

Barrow Wake. Deep scarp edge. Favourite viewpoint. Roman pottery found at the bottom of scarp. Car park. (J1)

Ermin Way. Roman road linking Cirencester with Gloucester and Kingsholm - two encampments on

the edge of Roman civilisation. Built and manned by troops. This undulating road still leaves a marked pattern across the landscape. (L4)

Hetty Pegler's Tump Uley Tumulus. Neolithic Long Barrow 120ft x 22ft, 4 chambers, 38 skeletons found in C19. Torch and wellington boots needed. (B9)

Uley Bury Iron Age Hill Fort. This is the Cotswolds' most famous Iron Age site. The deep ramparts provide superb views across the Severn Vale, Welsh Hills, Dursley and Owlpen Woods. It's an enclosed area of about 32 acres and is used for arable crops. Of more interest, it has an easy circular walk possible for large-wheeled pushchairs. (B9)

Haresfield Beacon

1642 Lord Chandos turns Sudeley Castle into a Royalist fortress   1643 Gloucester and Painswick are under siege during Civil War

Hostelries Worthy of a Special Visit...

Bear at Bisley. Bisley's oldest pub is traditional and friendly. Bar is well stocked with a range of traditional ales. (H6) 01452 770265 www.bisleybear.co.uk

Bell at Sapperton. Popular dining pub given to natural stonewalls and polished flagstone floors. Winter log fires provide a comfortable ambience. Local beers. Al fresco in summer. (K7) 01285 760298 www.foodatthebell.co.uk

Butcher's Arms, Sheepscombe. The Butcher's Arms has an unlikely national claim to fame - the much photographed carved sign of a butcher sipping a pint of beer with a pig tethered to his leg. 'Pie and a Pint' meal deal. (G4) 01452 812113 www.butchers-arms.co.uk

Five Mile House, Gloucester Road, Duntisbourne Abbots. Billed as 'a traditional pub serving food, not a restaurant'. Children and dogs welcome. (M4) 01285 821432 www.fivemilehouse.co.uk

Golden Heart, Birdlip. Centuries-old pub serving a range of local ales and food from sandwiches to four course meals. Focus on locally sourced produce. (K2) 01242 870261 www.thegoldenheart.co.uk

Ram Inn, Station Road, South Woodchester. Large outside sitting area. (E8) 01453 873 329

Tunnel House Inn, Tarlton Road, nr. Cirencester. Rural pub in idyllic location beside the Thames and Severn Canal. Children's play area. Dogs welcome. (L9) 01285 770280 www.tunnelhouse.com

Woolpack Inn, Slad. Traditional Cotswold pub with exceptional food simply cooked, and home to a cup of Rosie's cider and the spirit of Laurie Lee. Newspaper, views, cricketers...bliss. 01452 813429 (F5)

Where to Stay...

Amberley Inn. This old favourite overlooks the five Stroud valleys. The kitchen provides meals using local Cotswold ingredients. Pretty rooms. B&B. (E8) 01453 872565 www.theamberley.co.uk

Apple Tree Park, Eastington. New camping and caravan site with 100 pitches in 6 acres a mile from the A38. (B6) 07708 221457

Cowley Manor. A chic and stylish country hotel set in 55 acres with four lakes and a Victorian cascade. Techno-gadgets galore. Child-friendly (including Play Stations). Spa with all the pampering you need. (L2) 01242 870900 www.cowleymanor.com

Dix's Barn, Duntisbourne Abbots. This converted barn overlooks the Area of Outstanding Natural Beauty. Fishing and riding nearby. 01285 821249

Grey Cottage, Bath Road, Leonard Stanley. Comfortable C19 cottage with lots of personal details. Dinners by arrangement. No dogs. No children U-10. (C7) 01453 822515 www.greycottage.ik.com

Nation House B&B, 3 George Street, Bisley. Three cottages knocked into one makes for a splendid home and warm-hearted welcome. Family, double and single

Cowley Manor ss

Bell at Sapperton

rooms available. Ideal base. (H6) 01452 770197

Well Farm, Frampton Mansell. Charming building set in 20 acres of fields and garden in a peaceful location with stunning views. (J8) 01285 760651 www.well-farm.co.uk

Westley Farm, Chalford. 80 acre hill farm of ancient woodlands, flower-rich hay meadows, and steep banks of limestone grassland with traditional stone (self-catering) cottages spread over the hillside. For the more adventurous try one of the two Turkoman style yurt tents situated in 'the diddlydumps'. 01285 760262 www.westleyfarm.co.uk

Winstone Glebe B&B, Winstone. This small Georgian rectory provides traditional hospitality and English country house comforts. Dinner cooked by a former Cordon Bleu chef is a welcome option. (L4) 01285 821451 www.winstoneglebe.com

1644 King Charles 1 seeks refuge in Moreton-in-Marsh
1644 Sudeley Castle is partially demolished during siege
1646 Battle of Stow the final (and bloodiest) battle of the Civil War
81

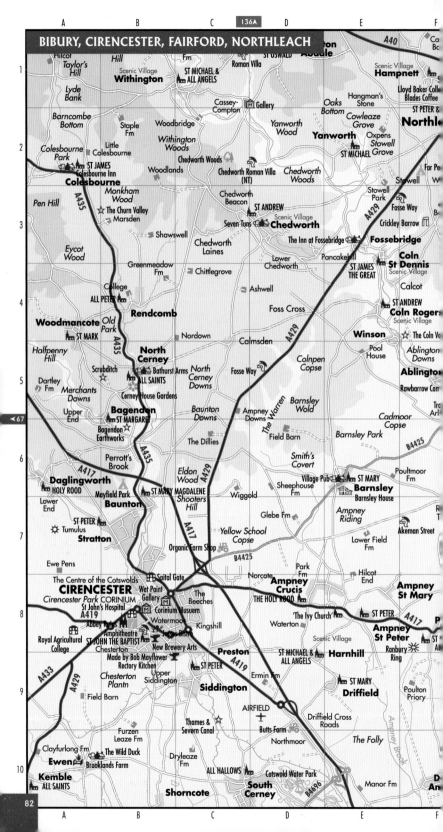

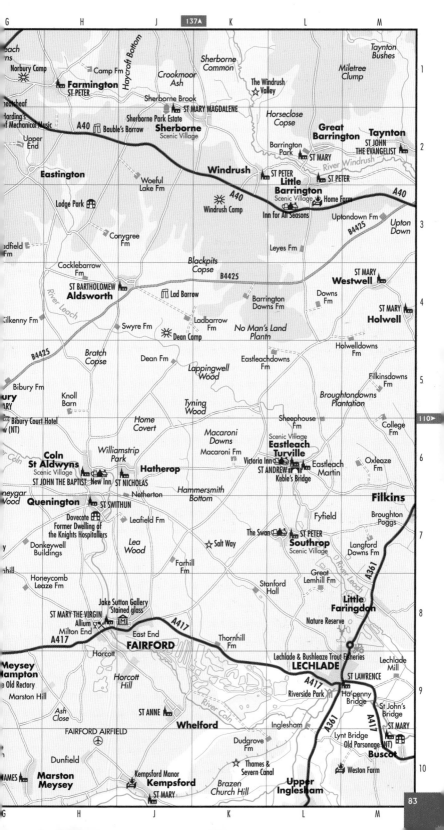

G   H   J   K   L   M

Taynton
Bushes

Norbury Camp
Camp Fm
Miletree
Clump

Farmington
ST PETER

Haycroft Bottom

Crookmoor
Ash

Sherborne
Common

The Windrush
Valley

1

Sherborne Brook

Harding's
f Mechanical Music

Upper
End

A40

Sherborne Park Estate
Bauble's Barrow

ST MARY MAGDALENE

Sherborne
Scenic Village

Horseclose
Copse

Great
Barrington

Taynton
ST JOHN
THE EVANGELIST

2

Eastington

Woeful
Lake Fm

Windrush

A40

Barrington
Park

ST MARY

River Windrush

ST PETER

Little
Barrington
Scenic Village
Inn for All Seasons

ST PETER

Home Farm

A40

Lodge Park

Windrush Camp

Uptondown Fm

B4425

Upton
Down

3

adfield
Fm

Conygree
Fm

Leyes Fm

Cocklebarrow
Fm

Blackpits
Copse

B4425

ST MARY

Westwell

ilkenny Fm

ST BARTHOLOMEW
Aldsworth

Lad Barrow

Barrington
Downs Fm

Downs
Fm

ST MARY

Holwell

4

Swyre Fm

Ladbarrow
Fm

Dean Camp

No Man's Land
Plantn

B4425

Bratch
Copse

Dean Fm

Lappingwell
Wood

Eastleachdowns
Fm

Holwelldowns
Fm

Filkinsdowns
Fm

5

Bibury Fm

ury
ARY

Knoll
Barn

Tyning
Wood

Broughtondowns
Plantation

Bibury Court Hotel
w (NT)

Home
Covert

Macaroni
Downs

Sheephouse
Fm

Scenic Village

College
Fm

110►

Williamstrip
Park

Macaroni Fm

Eastleach
Turville

Oxleaze
Fm

6

Coln
St Aldwyns
Scenic Village
ST JOHN THE BAPTIST   New Inn

Hatherop
ST NICHOLAS

Hammersmith
Bottom

Victoria Inn
ST ANDREW
Keble's Bridge

Eastleach
Martin

neygar
ood

Quenington
ST SWITHUN

Netherton

Fyfield

Filkins

Broughton
Poggs

7

Dovecote
Former Dwelling of
the Knights Hospitallers

Leafield Fm

Lea
Wood

Salt Way

The Swan
Southrop
Scenic Village

ST PETER

Langford
Downs Fm

A361

Donkeywell
Buildings

hill

Farhill
Fm

Great
Lemhill Fm

River Leach

Honeycomb
Leaze Fm

Jake Sutton Gallery
'Stained glass'

Stanford
Hall

Little
Faringdon

8

ST MARY THE VIRGIN
Allium
Milton End

East End

A417

Thornhill
Fm

Nature Reserve

A417

FAIRFORD

Horcott

Lechlade & Bushleaze Trout Fisheries

Lechlade
Mill

Meysey
ampton
e Old Rectory

Marston Hill

Horcott
Hill

LECHLADE
A417

Riverside Park

Ha'penny
Bridge

ST LAWRENCE

St John's
Bridge

9

Ash
Close

ST ANNE

Whelford

River Coln

Inglesham

A361

A417

ST MARY

FAIRFORD AIRFIELD

Lynt Bridge
Old Parsonage (NT)

Buscot

Dunfield

Dudgrove
Fm

Thames &
Severn Canal

Weston Farm

10

HAMES

Marston
Meysey

Kempsford Manor

Kempsford
ST MARY

Brazen
Church Hill

Upper
Inglesham

G   H   J   K   L   M

William Morris described Bibury as one of the prettiest villages in England, and few would argue with him. It attracts the crowds and is thus the stop-off point for many coach tours. It is a honey-pot village made up of rose-covered cottages set behind idyllic kitchen gardens, and all overlook the sleepy River Coln inhabited by swans, trout and duckling. During the C17 Bibury was notorious as a buccaneering centre for gambling and horse racing. (G5)

Bibury Cottage Garden

Bibury Trout Farm

Special Places to Visit...

Arlington Row (NT). These iconic cottages were originally monastic wool barns. However, in the C17 they were converted into weavers' homes. Now domestic dwellings, they overlook Rack Isle, a four-acre water meadow where cloth was once hung out to dry. (G5)

Arlington Mill. A beautiful, historic C17 watermill beside the River Coln. Formerly a countryside museum, but sadly all the artefacts were sold off and it is now a domestic property, closed to the public and currently up for sale. (F5)

Bibury Trout Farm. This working trout farm lies in a beautiful setting beside the River Coln. You can feed the fish, or try your hand at fly fishing in the Beginner's Fishery (hours vary). There are fresh and prepared trout on sale, as well as plants and shrubs. Gift shop. Light refreshments. Open summer M-Sa 9-6, Su 10-6, winter daily 9-4. (F5) 01285 740215 www.biburytroutfarm.co.uk

Church of St Mary. If you seek a refuge from the hurly burly of Bibury's tourists then walk along the banks of the River Coln and you'll soon find the entrance to this pretty church. With evidence of Saxon remains, Norman font and superb sculptured table tombs. (G5)

Where to Stay, Eat & Drink...

Bibury Court Hotel. An impressive Cotswold mansion lying in an idyllic spot beside the River Coln. You are provided with old-style, traditional comfort at an engaging price. The locals are very fond of their lunches in The Conservatory. Open all year. (G5) 01285 740337 www.biburycourt.co.uk

New Inn, Coln St Aldwyn. Charming C16 ivy-clad inn delivers a combination of hotel-pub-restaurant. Efficient service, affordable cuisine and

contemporary-style bedrooms. (H6) 01285 750651 www.new-inn.co.uk

The Swan Hotel. Few hotels have such a fabulous location as this. Overlooking the trout stream that is the River Coln. Photographed by every Bibury visitor. It is an iconic site. Café Swan (brasserie). Fishing rights. 18 luxurious bedrooms. (G5) 01285 740695 www.cotswold-inns-hotels.co.uk

New Inn, Coln St Aldwyn

The Swan Hotel, Bibury

1647   Thomas Cromwell and Ireton visit Chavenage to persuade Colonel Nathaniel Stephens to vote for Charles I's impeachment

1649   The Burford Levellers, a cornet and two corporals, are court-martialled and shot against the church wall

87

CIRENCESTER

One of the finest and most affluent town in the Cotswolds lies surrounded by a plethora of attractive villages whose populace (often second home owners) tend to shop and hobnob in Ciren (as the locals call it). The smart shops and bars reflect the riches of its patrons. As the Roman town Corinium, it became the second largest Roman town (after London) in Britain. Its strategic position at the confluence of the major routes (the Fosse Way, Ermin Way and Akeman Street) combined with the vast rolling sheep pastures brought great wealth in the Middle Ages. The history of Cirencester and the Cotswolds is well documented at the impressive Corinium Museum. On the outskirts of the town stands the Royal Agricultural College, famous for producing generations of estate managers and farmers from all classes of society. All the best eating places appear to be on Black Jack Street. Monday and Friday are market days. July Carnival. (B8)

Palm Sunday Procession, Parish Church of St John the Baptist

New Brewery Arts ss

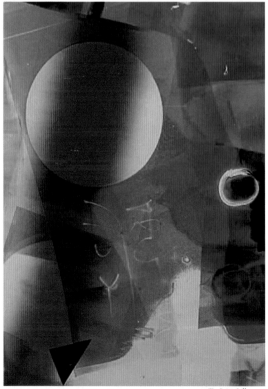

Wet Paint Gallery ss

Special Places to Visit...

Cirencester Abbey.
Only the Abbey grounds remain.
A peaceful enclave behind the
Parish Church of St John the
Baptist. Open daily. (B8)

Cirencester Park.
Belongs to the Bathurst family
who have generously opened their
grounds for many years giving you
the opportunity to walk in 3,000
acres of landscaped parkland, and
along a five-mile avenue of horse
chestnuts and hardwoods that
were planted in the early C18.
The C18 mansion is home to
Lord and Lady Apsley and is not
open to the general public. If you
like hobnobbing with celebrities you
have the opportunity to do so by
watching polo on most Sundays at
3pm, from May to September, see
www.cirencesterpolo.co.uk or
01285 653225. The park opens
daily all year from 8am to 5pm.
Separate entrance to the Cricket
and Tennis clubs on the Stroud road.
(A8) www.cirencesterpark.co.uk

Corinium Museum.
Impressive collection of Roman
remains clearly displayed to relate
the development of the Cotswolds
from the earliest times with special
reference to the Roman period.
Open daily all year M-Sa 10-5,
Su 2-5. Attached to Jack's Coffee
Shop. (B8) 01285 655611
www.coriniummuseum.co.uk

**New Brewery Arts, Brewery
Court.** A centre for excellence in
contemporary arts and crafts with
Exhibition Gallery, coffee house,
shop, theatre and resident craft
workers. Open M-Sa 9-5, Sun
10-4 (B8) 01285 657181
www.newbreweryarts.org.uk

**Parish Church of St John
the Baptist.** A fine mix of the C14
and C15, the largest of the 'Wool'
churches, and the easiest to recognize
with its three-storied, fan-vaulted
porch. The porch, formerly the Town
Hall, overshadows the Market Place.
C15 'wine glass' pulpit, Ann Boleyn
Cup, and many fine brasses. Open
M-Sa 9.30-5 Su in winter 2.15-5.30,
in summer 12.30-6. (B8)

| 1689 | Nailsworth's Quaker Meeting House built | 1694 | Hetty Pegler (owner of field surrounding the |
| 1692 | Rebuilding of Dyrham Park | | burial mound) dies |

Just look around and you know these gardens have been created by persons of immense enthusiasm, passion and experimentation. And you have a garden of maturity, too. Old roses and herbaceous borders sit well beside the walled kitchen/flower garden. You may purchase plants from their important plant collections. Open end of Jan (snowdrops) to end July, Tu W F & Su, 10-5, and by appointment. (B5) 01285 831300
www.cerneygardens.com

No. 12 Park Street, Cirencester ss

St John's Hospital.
Founded by Henry II, later absorbed by the Abbey. Next door, Almshouses dated 1826. (B8)

The Organic Farm Shop, Burford Road.
They claim 'Eating organic is eating from the Earth, Back to nature avoid of pesticides. All growing freely without insecticides.' Café. Open Tu-Sa 9-5, Sun 11-4. (C7) 01285 640441
www.theorganicfarmshop.co.uk

Wet Paint Gallery, 14 London Rd.
Colourful, abstract and modern landscapes, ceramics and glass. Open M-F 10-5. (C8) 01285 644990
www.contemporary-art-holdings.co.uk

Just Outside Cirencester...

Akeman Street. Roman road built to provide communications between military units and their forts. Best seen near Coln St Aldwyn and Quenington. (E7)

Bagendon Earthworks (Dykes). Remains of the Dobunni tribes' headquarters which was the capital of the Cotswolds in the C1 AD. The settlement was abandoned ten years after the Roman Conquest. Iron Age silver coins excavated here. (B6)

Butts Farm (& Farm Shop). Rare breeds, sheep, fowl, pigs and cattle in 30 acres of meadowland. Tractor safari. Picnics. Pets' corner. Open East to Oct half term Tu-Su & BHs 10.30-5. (D9) 01285 862224
www.thebuttsfarmshop.com

Where to Eat & Drink in Cirencester...

Jesse's Bistro, Black Jack Street. Butchers in the Cotswolds for many generations so if they can't get their meat right, what hope for the rest of us? The fresh fish trawls in from Newlyn. Open for lunch, M-Sa and dinner, W-Sa. (B8) 01285 641497
www.jessesbistro.co.uk

'Made By Bob'. Set in the Corn Hall, a new food emporium open from 7.30 for breakfast, lunch and afternoon teas. It's got Ciren's Ladies of Means in a frenzy of excitement, all rushing in for their champagne cocktails and made-up TV dinners.
www.foodmadebybob.com

Mayflower Chinese Restaurant, 29 Sheep Street.
If you like Chinese food then book into this sophisticated, mouth-watering restaurant where you can revel in a full panoply of oriental flavours. (B8) 01285 642777

Rectory Kitchen, Off Black Jack Street.
For home-made soups, cakes and deli, none comes better, and all at a reasonable price. 01285 644700
www.therectorykitchen.com

If you enjoy a friendly pint and pub-grub
Try The Crown just up from the corner of Black Jack Street, or the Twelve Bells on Lewis Lane. Bon appetit. (B8)

Where to Stay...

Mayfield Park. Set on the north side of Cirencester this popular site welcomes tents and caravans. (B6) 01285 831301
www.mayfieldpark.co.uk

No.107 Gloucester Street, Cirencester. Tucked away in a narrow courtyard is this delightful B&B with all the comforts of home. Within walking distance of Ciren's pubs and eating-out emporia. (B8) 01285 657861

No.12 Park Street, Cirencester. If style and gracious comfort is to your liking then this Grade II Georgian townhouse offering luxurious B&B may be just what you are looking for. (B8) 01285 640232
www.no12cirencester.co.uk

Rectory Kitchen, Cirencester ss

1703 A gale blows in the West Window of Fairford's stained glass
1704 John Wood (architect) the Elder born
1705 Richard "Beau" Nash becomes Bath's Master of Ceremonies

The former home of the garden expert, the late Rosemary Verey. A chic hotel and spa offering discreet and impeccable service, great food and state-of-the-art technology. A visit to this extraordinary garden may cost you lunch but it will be a worthwhile and memorable experience. Make sure you visit the vegetable garden. Cinema Club. (E6) 01285 740000 www.barnsleyhouse.com

E · LABORE · STABILITAS

TENEURDE

Yanworth Village Sign

Keble's Bridge, Eastleach

EASTLEACH

The twin hamlets of Eastleach Turville and Eastleach Martin face each other across the River Leach. The ancient clapper bridge (Keble's Bridge) connects the two. In spring, hundreds of daffodils grow on both banks, and hidden behind the trees is the Norman Church of St Michael and St Martin. Across the river the tiny church of St Andrews. Good village hostelry, the Victoria Inn. (L6)

Keble's Bridge. This was most likely built by the Keble family whose descendant, John Keble, was curate here in 1815. He founded the Oxford Movement, and is know for his volume of religious verse The Christian Year. (L6)

Church of St Michael & St Martin.
Founded by Richard Fitzpons, one of William the Conqueror's knights. It has a C14 north transept, decorated windows and a memorable exterior beside the river, fronted by daffodils in spring. It closed for services in 1982. (L6)

Church of St Andrews. Hidden beneath the trees this tiny church has a more interesting interior than its neighbour. Note the splendid C14 saddleback-tower of a Transitional and Early English period style. A Norman doorway c.1130 with a carved Tympanum of Christ. (L6)

Macaroni Downs.
Quite a sight. These rolling sheep pastures were once the location for Regency derring-do, gambling and horse racing. Now just munched by sheep. (K6)

FAIRFORD

An attractive market town on the tranquil River Coln, noted for the fine 'Wool' Church with its C15 stained glass windows. Mill. C6 Saxon cemetery. (J8)

Special Places of Interest...

**Jake Sutton Gallery,
10 High Street.**
An exhibition of Dance and Ballerinas - bright watercolour scenes, charcoal drawings and prints. Open Sa 10-5, or by appointment. (J8) 01285 712500
www.jakesutton.co.uk

Clara, Jake Sutton Gallery, Fairford

Where to Eat, Drink & Be Merry...

Allium, 1 London Street.
A relaxed contemporary restaurant with friendly service, daily changing lunch menus and a seasonal evening menu. Also monthly cookery demonstrations and wine tastings. 01285 712200 www.allium.uk.net

This perfect, late C15 Perpendicular church is world-famous for the outstanding 28 stained glass windows depicting scenes from Genesis to the Last Judgement. Of further interest are the carved misericords and recumbent brasses. Open 9.30-5.30 for visits and guided tours.
(J8) 01285 712611

Keith Harding's World of Mechanical Music

The Wheatsheaf, Northleach ss

Chedworth Roman Villa

Hostelries Worthy of a Visit...

Bathurst Arms, North Cerney.
Always a favourite with students from the RAC, and families on long summer evenings.
(B5) 01285 831281
www.bathurstarms.com

Colesbourne Inn.
Delicious Sunday lunches. The décor needs lifting to be more inviting. (A2) 01242 870376
www.thecolesbourneinn.co.uk

Inn For All Seasons, Little Barrington. A welcome hostelry on the London to Cheltenham road. B&B. (L3) 01451 844324
www.innforallseasons.co.uk

Seven Tuns, Chedworth.
Basic pub given to long evenings of vivid conversation, dominoes and bountiful pints of golden ale.
(D3) 01285 720242

Where to Stay...

Brooklands Farm, Ewen.
Two miles from the source of the Thames and close to the National Thames Path. Two comfortable rooms. Home cooked food. Quiet garden to the rear. 01285 770487

Kempsford Manor, High Street.
Beautiful gardens surround this charming C17-18 manor house that is often a venue for artistic workshops and village cricket. A place to retreat

to and be at peace with yourself and the world. (H8) 01285 810131

The Inn at Fossebridge.
With Liz Jenkins' enthusiasm and hospitality you can be assured of a good time. Here it's all about old-fashioned manners, comfort food, flagstone floors and log fires.
(E3) 01285 720721
www.fossebridgeinn.co.uk

The Old Rectory, Meysey Hampton. Lovely family home. Bask in convivial hospitality surrounded by antiques and creaking floorboards. Comfy beds. (G9) 01285 851200
www.meyseyoldrectory.co.uk

NORTHLEACH

An attractive Cotswold village noted for its church and Market Place. Often overlooked because the A40 now bypasses the village which at

1715 Mineral springs are discovered in Cheltenham
1721 Construction of Witney's Blanket Hall
1730 Sapperton House is demolished by Lord Bathurst and much of the woodwork is transferred to make up the church pews, next door

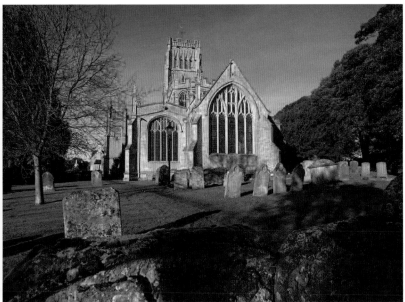

Parish Church of St Peter & St Paul, Northleach

first left it out on a limb. The village elders have done much to restore the lifeblood of this little community. It is worth a journey for the church, buildings and museums. (F2)

Special Places of Interest...

Keith Harding's World of Mechanical Music, High Street.
One of the finest attractions in the Cotswolds where you will always be met with a cheery welcome. An enchanting wonderland of mechanical musical instruments, clocks and restored musical boxes. 'Magical Musicals'. Gift shop. Open daily 10-6. (G2) 01451 860181 www.mechanicalmusic.co.uk

Lloyd Baker Countryside Collection & Blades Coffee Shop, The Old Prison.
Fascinating medley of agricultural implements: carts and bygone machinery. Free entry via Blades, who serve snacks and light lunches. Monthly food events and special Blues/Jazz evenings. Open Apr to Oct M-F 9-4.30, Sa 10-4.30. (F1)

Parish Church of St Peter & St Paul. C15. The South Porch has been described as the most lovely in all England: Tall pinnacles and statue filled niches. From afar, the

church appears to hover above the town. Brasses of wealthy wool barons. Guided tours: 01451 861172. (F2)

Where to Eat, Drink & Stay...

Far Peak Camping. A simple campsite centred right in the middle of the Cotswolds, within walking distance of Northleach. (F2) 01285 720858 www.farpeakcamping.co.uk

Home Farm, Little Barrington.
Robin and Sylvia will welcome you warmly to their golden stoned Cotswold home. Robin's family have lived here for 200 years and he will regale you with tales of derring-do. Sylvia's talents lie with interior design and the culinary arts. Good value B&B. (L2) 01451 844300

The Wheatsheaf, West End, Northleach. A friendly C17 coaching inn that invites long hours beside log fires, and lazy mornings lounging in their comfy beds. Lunch and suppers to be recommended. B&B. Book club. Music nights. (G2) 01451 860244 www.cotswoldswheatsheaf.com

Just Outside Northleach...

Chedworth Roman Villa (NT). Discovered in 1864 by a local

gamekeeper and later excavated between 1864 and 1866 revealing remains of a Romano-British villa containing mosaics, baths and hypocausts. Family trails. Museum. Open daily except Mondays Mar to mid-Nov, from 10am. (D2) 01242 890256 www.nationaltrust.org.uk

Chedworth Woods. A network of footpaths that criss-cross through tangled woodland close to the Roman Villa. (C2)

Churn Valley. A memorable route from Seven Springs to Cirencester follows one of England's most scenic drives. The variety of the trees and the sunken river valley are a sight to behold. Beware, this is a fast road and accidents are frequent. (A2)

Coln Valley. Charming valley with typically quaint Cotswold villages: Calcot, Coln Rogers, Coln St Dennis, Winson and Ablington. (E4)

Compton Cassey Gallery.
An eclectic mix of art and wildlife sculpture with a Summer exhibition of paintings in July & August. Jonathan Poole also represents the Art Estates of John Lennon, Ronnie Wood and Miles Davis. (C1) 01242 890224 www.jonathanpoole.co.uk

Bagendon

Churches of Interest...

Ampney Crucis. C14 wall paintings (being restored). Saxon, Early Norman and Perpendicular features. Life-size effigies. Jacobean pews. (D8)

Ampney St Mary. Wall paintings from the C12 to the C15. Norman font with chevron moulding. Isolated in field. Rarely open. (E8)

Baunton. C14 wall painting of St Christopher. Remains of rood screen. Tudor doorway. (B7)

Bagendon. In fabulous, central position in small hamlet. Stained glass. Norman arcade. (B5)

Chedworth. Norman origins. C15 'wine glass' pulpit. Gargoyles. 'Wool' church. (D3)

Coln St Dennis. Picturesque. Massive Norman tower. (E3)

Eastleach Martin. Norman. Hipped roof. Beautiful place. Daffodils in spring. (L6)

North Cerney. Saddle-back tower. Rood loft. C15 stained glass. (B5)

Rendcomb. Perpendicular. Norman font. (B4)

Southrop. Norman nave. C12 font. (K7)

Stowell. Doom painting. Norman. (E2)

Fairford Church Cat

Chedworth

Eastleach Martin

| 1754 | John Wood the Elder begins work on The Circus | 1770 | Construction of Bibury's bridge opposite the Swan Hotel |
| 1767 | Construction of Royal Crescent, Bath begins | 1774 | Royal Crescent construction completed |

101

Tombstone, Northleach

The Coln Valley is an example of the quintessential Cotswold river valley. There are five other rivers or streams that drain the Cotswold escarpment. All of them (the Churn, Evenlode, Glyme, Stour and Windrush) flow in a parallel, south-easterly direction eventually to enter the River Thames. These rivers meander through green pastures, home to cattle and sheep, the moorhen and heron, brown and rainbow trout. It can be an idyllic Cotswold scene, as seen in Bibury or the Chedworth Woods.

Rainbow Trout by Jane Bury

LECHLADE

A pleasant market town bejewelled with many fine C18 and C19 buildings. C15 'Wool' Church with fine Priest's Door. A busy boating and fishing centre given that it is the highest navigable point of the River Thames. Marina. (L9)

Lechlade & Bushleaze Trout Fisheries. Stocked with brown and rainbow trout (and the odd Pike) for day and half-day, and evening fishing exploits. Tackle shop, loos, tuition and boat hire on hand. 01367 253266 www.lechladetrout.co.uk

Where to Stay...

Weston Farm, Buscot Wick. 500 acre organic farm with farmhouse built in the C17. Tastefully decorated and furnished, inviting comfort and relaxation, both in the house and garden. 01367 252222

Sculpture, Keynes Country Park

Country Inns (Pubs)...

Village Pub, Barnsley. A warren of little rooms serving ambitious pub food and local beers. Child/dog friendly. B&B. Part of the Barnsley House empire, opposite. They have also just taken over the Wagon Wheel in Bibury - a welcome move. (E6) 01285 740421 www.thevillagepub.co.uk

The Swan, Southrop. This is more chic restaurant than country pub and is marketed toward the affluent London weekenders who play at country bumpkin for the weekend. Perfect if you like to spy on celebs in mufty (usually a disappointment) but you may get a crooked neck for all your troubles, and a hefty bill. (K7) 01367 850205 www.theswanatsouthrop.co.uk

Wild Duck at Ewen. A pub popular with students from the RAC, and Londoners down for the weekend in their Chelsea tractors. If you can put up with the drawling voices and the posh totty you may enjoy the comfortable décor and family portraits, the lazy ambience given to long drinking binges and boisterous conversation. But first book a taxi home or take a chauffeur. (A10) 01285 770310 www.thewildduckinn.co.uk

Special Places To Visit...

Cotswold Water Park. This covers an area of 40 square miles of countryside and is split into three sections: the Western section, the Keynes Country Park and the Eastern Section (near Fairford). www.waterpark.org There are 140 lakes, 74 fishing lakes, 10 lakes with SSSI status, 40 different lake owners

Village Pub sign, Barnsley

and 150km of pathways, bridleways and cycleways. 20,000 people live in the park's 14 main settlements. The extraction of the gravel and sand deposits from the 'catchment area' of the Upper Thames left large holes that were in 1967 designated to become a water park. From its humble beginnings at the South Cerney Sailing Club the park now attracts more than half-a-million visitors a year. Children love the sandy beach and sculptures at Keynes whilst the more active are beckoned to the wakeboarding and slalom skis at WM Ski on Spine Road www.wmski.com A visit to the Gateway Centre on Spine Road is recommended before you explore the park where you can eat and drink at the Coot's Café daily from 9-5. Just opposite is the retailer Cotswold Outdoor for all your walking and camping supplies. Further down the road overlooking Spring Lake, the Lakeside Brasserie for coffees, beers, pizzas, burgers and children's meals. www.watermarkclub.co.uk (D10)

Wakeboarding, WM Ski

Little Barrington

Lodge Park (NT). A 'little' property with a big (boozy) history. A grandstand (folly) built by John 'Crump' Dutton in 1634 so he could watch deer coursing in comfort and share his passion for gambling, drinking and entertaining with his friends. Open mid Mar to 1 Nov, F & W/Es 11-4. (H3) 01451 844130 www.nationaltrust.org.uk

Sherborne Park Estate (NT). Waymarked walks through woods and parkland with fine views. (J2) www.nationaltrust.org.uk

Windrush Valley. A slow, trickling stream in summer with a tendency to flood in winter. The river snakes its way through quiet golden villages, creating the idyllic Cotswold scene. (K2)

Brewing, scenic villages, blanket making, Blenheim, birthplace of Sir Winston Churchill.

The West Cotswolds extends from the flat Thames basin in the south up into the more typically hilly undulating countryside around Chipping Norton and the beautiful Windrush Valley dissects the region.

This area has traditionally been a coaching route on the A40 London to Gloucester road. It is awash with hostelries and now has a broad selection of pubs with an excellent reputation for eating and drinking. One of the areas best independent breweries, Hook Norton, is based here too.

Burford was home to one of the area's most famous historic incidents involving the Burford Levellers who are famed with having started civil rights in this country. During the English Civil War, three Parliamentarian soldiers who felt Cromwell was getting too big for his boots stood up against him and were put to death in Burford churchyard for their troubles. This event is celebrated annually with much gusto and beer.

Many of the villages in the West Cotswolds are feeder villages for Oxford. Great Tew is arguably one of the most beautiful villages in the Cotswolds. Witney is a former blanket making town and was, along with the hilltop village, Chipping Norton, a wool trading market town. And, of course, there is Blenheim, famously the birthplace of Winston Churchill.

Basket of Cotswold Wool, Cotswold Woollen Weavers

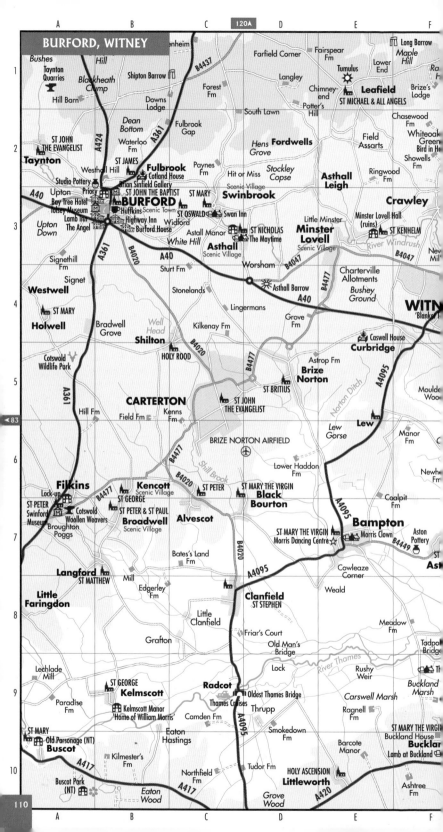

BURFORD, WITNEY

A **B** **C** **D** **E** **F**

Bushes
Blenheim
Long Barrow
Taynton Quarries
Blackheath Clump
Hill
Shipton Barrow
Farfield Corner
Fairspear Fm
Maple Hill
Ra
H
Hill Barn
Downs Lodge
Forest Fm
Langley
Chimney-end
Lower End
Tumulus
Brize's Lodge
Leafield
Chasewood Fm

1

Dean Bottom
Fulbrook Gap
South Lawn
Potter's Hill
ST MICHAEL & ALL ANGELS
Whiteoak Green
Bird in He
ST JOHN THE EVANGELIST
Waterloo Fm
Hens Grove
Fordwells
Field Assarts
Showells Fm

Taynton
A424
ST JAMES
Paynes Fm
Stockley Copse
Asthall Leigh
Ringwood Fm

2

Westhall Hill
Fulbrook
Cotland House
Hit or Miss
A361
Studio Pottery
Brian Sinfield Gallery
Scenic Village
Crawley

Upton
Priory
ST JOHN THE BAPTIST
ST MARY
Swinbrook
Little Minster
Minster Lovell Hall (ruins)

A40
Bay Tree Hotel
BURFORD
Scenic Town
ST OSWALD
Swan Inn
ST KENHELM
Tolsey Museum
Huffkins
Widford
ST NICHOLAS
Minster Lovell
New Mil

3

Upton Down
Lamb Inn
Highway Inn
The Angel
Burford House
Astall Manor
The Maytime
Scenic Village
River Windrush
B4047

Signethill Fm
White Hill
Asthall
Scenic Village
Charterville Allotments

Signet
A4020
A40
Sturt Fm
Worsham
B4047
B4477
Bushey Ground

Westwell
Stonelands
Asthall Barrow
A40
Grove Fm

4

Holwell
ST MARY
Bradwell Grove
Well Head
Lingermans
WITN
'Blanket I

Cotswold Wildlife Park
Shilton
HOLY ROOD
Kilkenay Fm
Caswell House
Curbridge

CARTERTON
Kenns Fm
B4020
Astrop Fm
Brize Norton
A4095

5

A361
Hill Fm
Field Fm
B4477
ST BRITIUS
ST JOHN THE EVANGELIST
Norton Ditch
Lew
Manor Fm

◄83
BRIZE NORTON AIRFIELD
Lew Gorse
Newhe
Fm

6

Filkins
Kencott
Scenic Village
B4477
Shill Brook
ST PETER
ST MARY THE VIRGIN
Lower Haddon Fm
Coalpit Fm

Lock-up
ST GEORGE
B4020
Black Bourton
A4095

ST PETER
Swinford Museum
Cotswold Woollen Weavers
ST PETER & ST PAUL
Broadwell
Scenic Village
Alvescot
ST MARY THE VIRGIN
Morris Dancing Centre
Bampton
Morris Clown
Aston Pottery

7

Broughton Poggs
Bates's Land Fm
B4020
Cowleaze Corner
B4449
Ast

Langford
ST MATTHEW
Mill
Edgerley Fm
A4095
Weald

Little Faringdon
Little Clanfield
Clanfield
ST STEPHEN
Meadow Fm

8

Grafton
Friar's Court
Old Man's Bridge
Tadpo
Bridge

Lechlade Mill
ST GEORGE
Lock
River Thames
Rushy Weir
Buckland Marsh

9

Paradise Fm
Kelmscott
Radcot
Oldest Thames Bridge
Carswell Marsh
Ragnell Fm

Kelmscott Manor
'Home of William Morris'
Thames Cruises
Thrupp
Camden Fm
ST MARY THE VIRGIN
Buckland House

ST MARY
Old Parsonage (NT)
Eaton Hastings
Smokedown Fm
Barcote Manor
Bucklan
Lamb at Buckland

Buscot
Kilmester's Fm
Northfield Fm
Tudor Fm
HOLY ASCENSION

10

Buscot Park (NT)
A417
Eaton Wood
A417
Littleworth
Grove Wood
A420
Ashtree Fm

A **B** **C** **D** **E** **F**

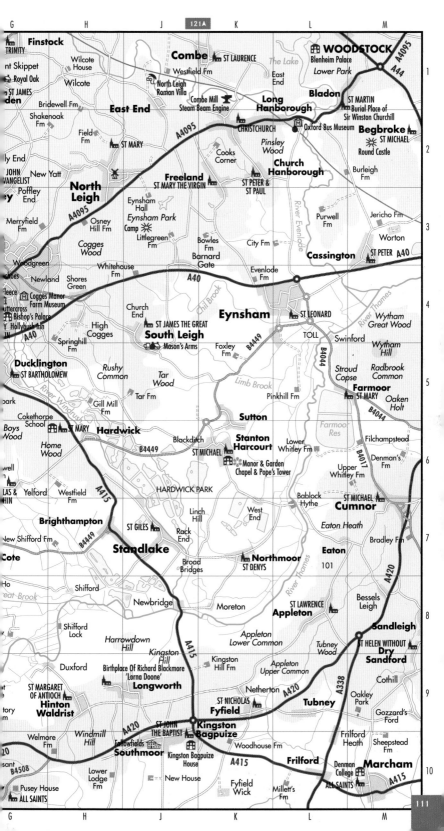

BURFORD

The first major Cotswold town you come to if travelling from the east, and what an introduction. The wide High Street, with its classical gables atop some gracious houses, slopes down to the River Windrush. It was once an important coach and wool centre bursting with activity, hostelries and dens of rumbustious entertainment. A history of civil rights and religious tolerance prevailed here with the Burford Levellers. On 17 May 1649, three soldiers were executed in Burford Churchyard on the orders of Oliver Cromwell. These three had sought to undermine the authority of Cromwell whom they considered to be a dictator rather than a liberator. This event is celebrated every year with song, dance and speeches.

Today there are the splendid inns and pretty cottages hidden down the side streets. The churchyard is a quiet spot with some beautifully decorated table tombs. The town has a wide selection of hotels, inns and tearooms and a couple of delis to make up lunchtime sandwiches. Feast of the Dragon and Street Fair in June. (B3)

Reflections of Burford's High Street

Special Places of Interest...

Brian Sinfield Gallery, 57 High Street. Highly respected gallery featuring changing exhibitions of modern and contemporary paintings, sculpture and ceramics. Open Tu-Sa, 10-5. (B3) 01993 824464 www.briansinfield.com

Burford Priory. This was the former home of Benedictine nuns who have since moved to Broad Marston. It is hidden behind high walls and is Jacobean in style and has a history dating from the C13 when it was a Hospital of St John in 1226. Recently sold as a private residence. (B3)

Cotswold Wildlife Park. A full score of animals, birds and reptiles from all corners of the globe beautifully laid out in 120 acres of gardens and parkland. Adventure playground. Tropical House. Children's farmyard. Facilities for the disabled. Picnic area. Café. Open daily 10-7 (winter 10-4.30). (A5) 01993 823006 www.cotswoldwildlifepark.co.uk

Burford High Street

Studio Pottery, 4 Bear Court. The work of some of Britain's most respected potters and glassmakers. Open daily 10-5. (B3) 01993 822371 www.saltgallery.com

Tolsey Museum. Burford's social and industrial history; charters, dolls house, objects of many rural trades. Open daily April to October Tu-F & Su 2-5, Sa & BHs 11-5. (B3) 01993 823238

Where to Eat & Drink...

Huffkins. Established in 1890. Cream teas a speciality. Traditional craft bakery, tea rooms and coffee shop. Open M-Sa 8-6, Su 10-6. (B3) 01993 822126

Lamb Inn

Where to Stay...

Bay Tree Hotel, Sheep Street.
This is Burford's most luxurious and smartest hostelry, for that is what they are on this old coaching route, hostelries. It is a traditional and charming inn with oak panelled rooms, stone fireplaces and tapestries. Dinner is quite a formal affair. There is a secluded walled garden for pre-prandials and intimate conversation. (B3) 01993 822791
www.cotswold-inns-hotels.co.uk/baytree

Cotland House B&B, Fulbrook Hill.
A substantial Cotswold house in elegant surroundings. A short walk from Burford. Single/double/twin and family rooms. (B2) 01993 822382
www.cotlandhouse.com

Highway Inn, 117 High Street.
A choice of 9 cosy bedrooms furnished in a mix of antique and modern styles. The Highway Inn has plenty of character and prides itself on offering an informal and individual experience akin to visiting friends in the country. Simple food made using local and seasonal produce. (B3) 01993 823661
www.thehighwayinn.co.uk

Lamb Inn, Sheep Street.
Your typical olde English hostelry: flagstone floors, low ceilings, nooks and crannies galore, fine ales (Hookie and 6X) and now with luxurious bedrooms and intimate lounges. Restaurant. Life can't get any better than this. More informal than its sister inn, The Bay Tree, just along the street. (B3) 01993 823155
www.cotswold-inns-hotels.co.uk/lamb

Burford House, 99 High Street.
Full of character and charm, and you'll never sleep alone in a 4-poster again; there's a teddy bear on every bed! Lunch M-Sa, Dinner Th, F & Sa evenings. No dogs.
(B3) 01993 823151
www.burfordhouse.co.uk

The Angel, 14 Witney Street.
Relaxed, stylish brasserie in C16 coaching inn provides mouth watering fare: mediterranean dishes and enormous breakfasts specifically cooked for the adventurous traveller.
(B3) 01993 822714
www.theangelatburford.co.uk

Bay Tree Hotel

One of the great Cotswold churches built in the C15 with proceeds earned by the local wool merchants. Hence the term 'Wool' church. It has a spacious interior more akin to a small cathedral. The porch and spire c.1450 are outstanding, as are the sculptured table tombs in the churchyard. Inside, don't miss the intricate medieval stained glass and the monuments (painted figures). Open daily 9-5 except during services. (B3)

Fettiplace Monument, Swinbrook Church

MINSTER LOVELL

Arguably the most beautiful village in the Windrush Valley. There is a fine C15 bridge leading to a street of pretty cottages and on to the C15 Church which rests beside the ancient Hall. The Manor House has been associated with the rhyme 'Mistletoe Bough'. (E3)

Special Places of Interest...

Minster Lovell Hall (EH). A picturesque C15 ruin beside the River Windrush. Reputed to be the haunted seat of the Lovell family. Open daily. Don't miss the Church next door. (E3)

WITNEY

The largest shopping centre in West Oxfordshire and a dormitory town to Oxford that has seen much rapid expansion in the past 20 years. A town of hustle and bustle with a good share of attractive limestone buildings. Note the C17 Butter Cross with gabled roof, clock turret and sundial, the Town Hall with room overhanging a piazza and across Church Green the unusually handsome spire to the Parish Church, visible from far and wide. Witney has a fair complement of ancient hostelries and the Angel Inn overlooking Church Green is steeped in history. Ethnic restaurants are plentiful and diverse in their culinary

Minster Lovell Hall

arts: The Witney Azis is highly recommended. For a trip to Italy and superb pasta, Café Messina is a local favourite. There have been signs of Iron Age and Roman settlements but the first records of any activity date from 969 AD. The Bishop of Westminster built a palace in 1044 which was eventually excavated in 1984. In 1277 the town's business centred on the fulling and cloth mills. In the Middle Ages gloves, blankets and brewing were the staple industries. Earlys of Witney, the blanket makers were in business for 300 years until quite recently. All of this has been ably recorded in the local Cogges Manor Farm Museum. (F4)

Special Places of Interest...

Bishop's Palace. The site of the Bishop's Palace situated near the Church on Church Green, is one of 24 luxurious residencies in the diocese and dates from the 12th century. The archaeological remains of the great hall and other features are exposed under a modern roof and were discovered in the early 1980s. (G4)

Cogges Manor Farm Museum, Church Lane. Historic buildings, exhibitions, traditional breeds of animals, daily demos and special weekends. Garden, orchard and riverside walk. Café. Open Apr to Oct Tu-F & BH Ms 10.30-5.30, W/Es 12-5.30. (G4) 01993 772602 www.cogges.org

Witney Museum, High Street. Situated in a traditional Cotswold stone building that was once the home of Malachi Bartlett, the proprietor of a well known local building firm. The museum shows the history of Witney and surrounding area featuring local industries such as Witney blankets, glove making and brewing together

with photographs and artefacts relating to Witney. Open Apr to Oct, W-Sa, 10-4. Children free. (G4) 01993 775915.

Where to Eat & Drink...

The Three Horseshoes, Corn Street. Stone built 16th century building, probably built originally as accommodation for Lord Weavers. Separate restaurant, providing quality food prepared by head chef Michel Loyeau. Beer garden. (G4) 01993 703086, and, across the road, the same family run the more traditional, Hollybush Inn.

The Fleece, 11 Church Green. A fine Georgian building, originally the home of Clinch's brewery and reputedly a favourite watering-hole of Dylan Thomas when he lived in South Leigh. Overlooking the beautiful Church Green with outside seating. En-suite bedrooms. (G4) 01993 892270. www.fleecewitney.co.uk

Bird in Hand Inn, Hailey, nr Witney. Grade II listed inn that has been totally renovated, but is still rich in charm and original features. Traditional British and European cuisine with a modern flair.

Restaurant open for breakfast, lunch and dinner. (G2) 01993 868321. www.birdinhandinn.co.uk

Where to Stay...

Fallowfields. An hotel with Edwardian-style elegance surrounded by 12 acres of trees and gardens. Food is English-French country cooking, and with the development of the owners' vegetable garden, the intention is to move the restaurant towards self-sufficiency. (J10) 01865 820416 www.fallowfields.com

Morris Clown, Bampton

COTSWOLD WOOLLEN WEAVERS, FILKINS

A former working, weaving mill in some splendid C18 buildings. Traditional machinery. Gallery - history of 'Wool in the Cotswolds'. Large mill shop & interiors gallery. Coffee shop. Picnic area. Masonry yard. Open daily M-Sa 10-6, Su 2-6. (A7) 01367 860491
www.naturalbest.co.uk

Special Places of Interest...

Aston Pottery. Working pottery, demonstrations, shop and tearoom. Open M-Sa 9-5, Su 10.30-4.30. (F7) 01993 852031. www.astonpottery.co.uk

Buscot Old Parsonage (NT). Early C18 house. Small garden. Open Apr to Oct W 2-6 by written appointment. (A10) 01793 762209 www.nationaltrust.org.uk

Buscot Park (NT). C18 house with park and superb water garden designed by Harold Peto. Collection of art: Italian, Dutch, Flemish, Spanish and English Schools. Chinese porcelain. Tea room. Open Apr to Sept W Th & F (including Good F, East W/Es) 2-6, and alternate W/Es in each month 2-6. Grounds also M & Tu 2-6. (A10) 01367 240786 www.buscot-park.com

Kelmscott Manor. The Elizabethan home of William Morris, the C19 poet, craftsman and socialist. Houses his furnishings which can be identified as examples from the Arts & Crafts Movement. Paintings by his fellow pre-Raphaelite, Dante Gabriel Rossetti. Open Apr to Sept W 11-5, and the 1st & 3rd Sa. Garden open Th June to Sept 2-5. Group bookings on Th & F by arrangement. (B9) 01367 252486 www.kelmscottmanor.co.uk

Kingston Bagpuize House. A beautiful early C18 manor house in parkland setting. The garden contains shrubs, bulbs and herbaceous borders. Teas. Small gift shop. Open all BH W/Es and various Su, Feb to Sept 2-5.30. See website or phone for details. (J10) 01865 820259 www.kingstonbagpuizehouse.org.uk

North Leigh Roman Villa (EH). This ruin was excavated in 1813 and 60 rooms were revealed surrounding the courtyard with a beautiful mosaic pavement. A charming spot beside the River Evenlode. Open daily in summer. (J1)

Stanton Harcourt Manor House & Gardens. A unique collection of medieval buildings. The house contains fine pictures, silver, furniture and porcelain. Moat and stew ponds. Pope's Tower. Open Apr

Kelmscott Manor

to Sept 2-6 Th, Su & BH Ms, as advertised. (K6) 01865 881928

Swinford Museum. Agricultural, craft and domestic bygones. Open May to Sept first Su 2-5, and by appointment. (A7)

Oxford Bus Museum, BR Station Goods Yard. 35 vehicles including the Morris Motors Museum. Open Su, W & BHs 10.30-4.30. (L2) 01993 883617 www.oxfordbusmuseum.org.uk

Churches of Interest...

Swinbrook. Fettiplace monuments. Mitford family memorials. (C3)

Kelmscott. Wall painting. William Morris tomb by Philip Webb. (B9)

Special Inns of Interest...

Lamb at Buckland, Lamb Lane. C18 Cotswold inn patronised by locals provides first class food. B&B. No dogs. Closed M. (F10) 01367 870484 www.thelambbuckland.co.uk

Masons Arms, South Leigh. Full of quirky old-fashioned spirit. Children, vegetarians, mobile phones and dogs are not welcome. Long meals are positively encouraged. Raymond Blanc's all-time favourite pub has a menu that is written up daily and reflects the place's individuality. Excellent if expensive food. (J4) 01993 702485

The Maytime, Asthall. The Maytime Inn is an authentic Cotswold stone building situated in a quiet country village. On a winter's day you can duck through the low door into the homely bar and imagine the pub as it was centuries ago. (C3) 01993 822068 www.themaytime.com

Morris Clown, High Street, Bampton. The headquarters of the Bampton Morris Men is a dark drinking man's boozer with a large open fire and an excellent selection of real ales. Operates a no food (only booze) policy. (E7) 01993 850217

Royal Oak, Ramsden. A listed Coaching Inn dating from the C17 that was used as a watering hole for the London to Hereford stagecoach. Traditional and rustic bar and restaurant with an excellent reputation for food. (G1) 01993 868213

Swan Inn, Swinbrook. Owned (and visited often) by the Dowager Duchess of Devonshire (the former Deborah Mitford, the last of the Mitford sisters). A beautiful pub, in a delightful location, with a good balance between traditional and modern cuisine. (C3) 01993 823339 www.theswanswinbrook.co.uk

The Trout, Tadpole Bridge. Remote location beside Thames footpath manages to be busy at lunchtime. Well worth a visit. Children & dogs welcome. B&B. (F9) 01367 870382 www.trout-inn.co.uk

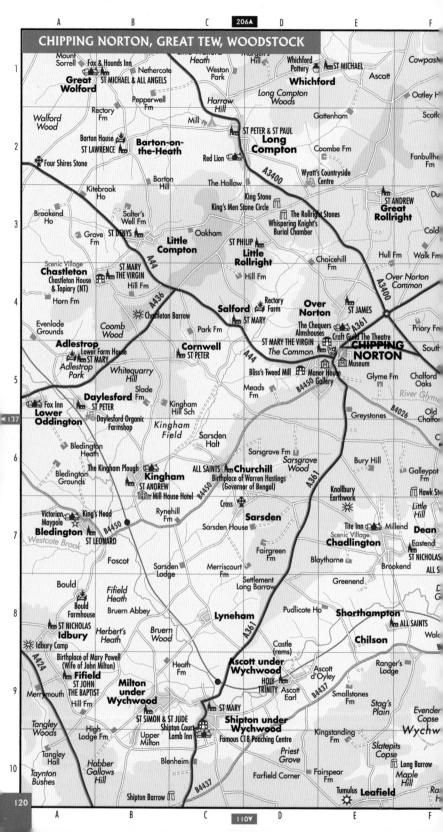

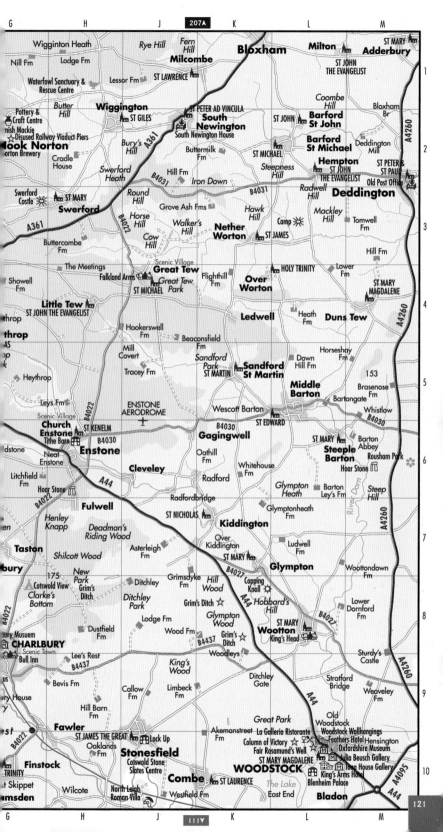

Wigginton Heath
Rye Hill
Fern Hill
Bloxham
Milton
ST MARY
Adderbury

Nill Fm
Lodge Fm
Milcombe
ST JOHN THE EVANGELIST

Waterfowl Sanctuary & Rescue Centre
Lessor Fm
ST LAWRENCE

Pottery & Craft Centre
Butter Hill
Wiggington
ST PETER AD VINCULA
South Newington
ST JOHN
Barford St John
Bloxham Br

nish Mackie
ST GILES
South Newington House
Barford St Michael
Deddington Mill
A4260

ook Norton
Disused Railway Viaduct Piers
Bury's Hill
Buttermilk Fm
ST MICHAEL
Hempton
ST PETER & ST PAUL

orton Brewery
Cradle House
Swerford Heath
B4031
Hill Fm
Iron Down
Steepness Hill
ST JOHN THE EVANGELIST
Old Post Office

Swerford Castle
ST MARY
B4031
Radwell Hill
Deddington

Swerford
Round Hill
Grove Ash Fms
Hawk Hill
Camp
Mackley Hill
Tomwell Fm

A361
B4022
Horse Hill
Walker's Hill
Nether Worton
ST JAMES
Hill Fm

Buttercombe Fm
Cow Hill
Scenic Village
Flighthill Fm
Over Worton
HOLY TRINITY
Lower Fm
ST MARY MAGDALENE

Showell Fm
Great Tew
Falkland Arms
Great Tew Park
ST MICHAEL
Ledwell
Heath Fm
Duns Tew
A4260

Little Tew
ST JOHN THE EVANGELIST
Hookerswell Fm
Beaconsfield Fm
Down Hill Fm
Horseshay Fm

hrop
AS
Mill Covert
Sandford Park
ST MARTIN
Sandford St Martin
153

p
Tracey Fm
Brasenose Fm

Heythrop
Whistlow
B4030

Leys Fm
Middle Barton
Bartongate

Scenic Village
B4022
ENSTONE AERODROME
Wescott Barton
ST EDWARD
Barton Abbey
Barton Abbey

Church Enstone
ST KENELM
B4030
Gagingwell
ST MARY
Steeple Barton
Rousham Park

Tithe Barn
Neat Enstone
B4030
Enstone
Oathill Fm
Whitehouse Fm
Hoar Stone
Steep Hill

dstone
Cleveley
Radford
Glympton Heath
Barton Ley's Fm
A4260

Litchfield Fm
Hoar Stone
A44
Radfordbridge
ST NICHOLAS
Glymptonheath Fm

Fulwell
Kiddington
Ludwell Fm

Henley Knapp
Deadman's Riding Wood
Asterleigh Fm
Over Kiddington
ST MARY
Glympton
Woottondown Fm

Taston
Shilcott Wood
Grimsdyke Fm
Hill Wood
B4027
Copping Knoll
Lower Dornford Fm

bury
175
New Park
Grim's Ditch
Ditchley
Grim's Ditch
Hobbard's Hill
ST MARY

Cotswold View
Clarke's Bottom
Ditchley Park
Glympton Wood
Wootton
King's Head
B4022

A4022
Dustfield Fm
Lodge Fm
Wood Fm
Grim's Ditch
Sturdy's Castle

bury Museum
B4437
Woodleys
CHARLBURY
Lee's Rest
King's Wood
Ditchley Gate
Stratford Bridge
Weaveley Fm

Bull Inn
B4437
Callow Fm
Limbeck Fm
A44

us
Bevis Fm
Hill Barn Fm
Old Woodstock
A4260

ry House
Great Park
Akemanstreet Fm
La Galleria Ristorante
Woodstock Wallhangings
Feathers Hotel Hensington

st
Fawler
ST JAMES THE GREAT
Lock Up
Column of Victory
Fair Rosamund's Well
Oxfordshire Museum
Julia Beusch Gallery

Finstock
Oaklands Fm
Stonesfield
Cotswold Stone Slates Centre
ST MARY MAGDALENE
King's Arms Hotel
Iona House Gallery

t Skippet
TRINITY
Wilcote
North Leigh Roman Villa
Combe
ST LAURENCE
WOODSTOCK
Blenheim Palace

msden
Westfield Fm
The Lake East End
Bladon
A44

Long Compton Camping, Mill Farm

CHIPPING NORTON

A well situated hill-top town affording spectacular views over the surrounding countryside. Mentioned in the Domesday Book. The new Market Place was built in 1205 and is today surrounded by elegant houses with Georgian facades. But it was the wool industry established in the C13 that brought wealth to this corner of Oxfordshire and, like so many before them and after, the wealthy merchants invested their coppers in the C15 'Wool' church in order to guarantee a place in heaven. The town's attraction is that it is very much a small market town responding to the demands of the local populace and is little affected by Cotswold tourism. It is home to some celebrities: Jeremy Clarkson, Susan Hill and, until his death, Ronnie Barker, who ran an antique emporium. Bookshop with coffee shop. Mop Fair in September. (E5)

Rollright Stones

Special Places of Interest...

Almshouses. A picturesque row of C17 houses still in use today. The occupants were to be 'Honest women of godly life and conversation'. (E5)

Bliss Tweed Mill. Built by William Bliss in 1872 to house his textile factory. He was instrumental in encouraging the railways to reach Chipping Norton. The mill closed as a factory in 1980 and was converted into domestic apartments. It is still quite a sight from the road and was apparently one of Sir John Betjeman's favourite buildings. (D5)

Chipping Norton Museum, 4 High Street. Agricultural equipment, a 30s kitchen and local 'Co-op'. Open East to Oct Tu-Su & BH Ms 2-4. (E5) 01608 641712

Manor House Gallery, West Street. Long established gallery with ever-changing exhibitions of 100 watercolours and oils specialising in the contemporary Scottish arts scene. Open M-Sa. (E5) 01608 642620 www.manorhousegallery.co.uk

Oxfordshire Craft Guild, Goddard Lane. Crafts supplied by co-operative of Guild Members. Pottery, textiles, fine metals, wood, glass and jewellery. Open M-Sa

10-5. (E5) 01608 641525 www.oxfordshirecraftguild.co.uk

Rollright Stones. The King's Men is a Bronze Age stone circle 100 feet in diameter, 2,000-1,800 BC and is easily accessible from the road. Just 400 yards east of this circle are The Whispering Knights, remains of a Bronze Age burial chamber. And, isolated in a field, the King's Stone. (D3)

The Theatre, Goddards Lane. Flourishing little theatre puts on dance, music, plays, films, workshops and is host to touring companies. (E5) 01608 642349 www.chippingnortontheatre.co.uk

Where to Eat & Drink...

The Chequers, Goddards Lane. Right next to the theatre - perfect for a pre-show tipple or a meal in the airy conservatory dining room. (E5) 01608 644717 www.chequers-pub.com

Almshouses, Chipping Norton

Where to Stay...

Barton House, Barton-on-the-Heath. Elegant Elizabethan manor house, extensively redesigned by Inigo Jones in 1636. The owners have great taste, and antique furnishings with an oriental bent grace the living and sleeping areas. 01608 674303

Bould Farm, Chipping Norton. 400 acre sheep and arable farm with C17 farmhouse in a large garden overlooking beautiful countryside. The owner breeds working sheep dogs. Comfortable bedrooms. 01608 658850 www.bouldfarm.co.uk

Long Compton Camping, Mill Farm. A small, simple site with only 11 units for pitching a tent. Set close to a good village pub, the Red Lion, and village shop. Ideal for cyclists and hardy campers. (C2) 01608 684663

1807 The Prince Regent visits Sezincote and demands the new
Brighton Pavilion design be copied, per se
1810 Kennet & Avon Canal opened
1813 Founding of Flower's Brewery in Stratford

Hamish Mackie Wildlife Sculpture ss

Adlestrop

Lower Farm House, Adlestrop.
This striking Grade II listed Georgian house makes an elegant retreat with comfort and good food awaiting you. Drawing Room with open log fire for cold days and a beautiful terrace for summer meals and drinks. 01608 658756 www.adlestrop-lowerfarm.com

Rectory Farm, Salford.
A 250 year old farm house in its own tranquil 450 acre valley of scenic farmland. The mature 2 acre garden leads down to two spring fed trout lakes (fishing is available for guests see www.salfordtroutlakes.co.uk). 01608 643209 www.rectoryfarm.info

CHARLBURY

A small town overlooking the Evenlode Valley towards Wychwood Forest. Group of stone-roof houses with 30-yard stretch of wisteria. (G8)

Cotswold View Campsite, Enstone Road. Spacious pitches set in rolling, wooded farmland. Well-signed trails where you can see a variety of farm animals

including Shetland ponies. Children's playgrounds. Tennis court. Skittle alley. Well-stocked shop and off-licence. Open late Mar to 31 Oct. (G8) 01608 810314 www.cotswoldview.co.uk

GREAT TEW

A sensationally beautiful village lined with ironstone cottages covered in thatch and stone tiles. Many fell into disrepair but are now undergoing renovation. Much of the village was designed by the Scottish architect, John Claudius London. The Falkland Arms is named after Lord Falkland who lived here, and who died fighting for Charles I at the Battle of Newbury. (J4)

Where to Eat, Drink & Stay...

The Falkland Arms. A traditional pub with flagstone floors, oak beams, inglenook fireplace, mugs and bric-a-brac hanging from the ceiling, and real ale in many potions to whet your senses. Garden. Accommodation with attractive bedrooms, two with 4-posters. (J4) 01608 683653 www.falklandarms.org.uk

The Old Post House, New Street, Deddington. Beautiful and luxurious accommodation. Guest sitting and dining rooms allow you to imagine it's all yours. The inner courtyard, walled gardens and swimming pool add a cherry to the top! 01869 338978 www.oldposthouse.co.uk

South Newington House, South Newington. Comfortable C17 house with a range of bedrooms as well as a separate cottage for B&B or self-catering. The organic kitchen garden and orchard provides produce for guests' meals. 01295 721207 www.southnewingtonhouse.co.uk

Special Places to Visit in Hook Norton...

Hamish Mackie Wildlife Sculptor, Manor Farm Barn. Hamish grew up on a livestock farm in Cornwall and his sculptures have benefited from this early exposure to English wildlife. 01608 737859 www.hamishmackie.com

Hook Norton Brewery. Visitor Centre displays brewing artefacts from 1849 to today. Two-hour tours M-F. Centre open all year M-F 9-5, Sa & BHs 9.30-4.30. (G2) 01608 737210 www.hooknortonbrewery.co.uk

Hook Norton Pottery & Craft Centre. Workshop and gallery open all year. Local crafts including paintings, basketware, woodcraft and cards. Open M-Sa 9-5. (G2) 01608 737414 www.hooknortonpottery.co.uk

Where To Stay...

Mill House Hotel, Station Road. If comfort and peace, with a touch of rustic charm, is your pleasure, and a restaurant to envy, then look no further. Family & dog friendly. (B6) 01608 658188 www.millhousehotel.co.uk

Great Tew Cottage

Daylesford Organic Farmshop

Chastleton House

Where To Eat...

The Kingham Plough. The quintessential Cotswold Inn. Yummy food served from the restaurant with a short crawl upstairs to 7 boutique en-suite bedrooms. 01608 658327 www.thekinghamplough.co.uk

Kings Head Inn, Wootton. Popular eating venue for local foodies and academics. High on personal service and exceptional ingredients. (L8) 01993 811340 www.kings-head.co.uk

Special Places To Visit...

Charlbury Museum. An exquisite little museum with Oxfordshire hay wagon, old photographs and domestic bric-a-brac from a bygone age. Open East to Oct Su & BH Ms 2.30-4.30. (G8) 01608 810060

Chastleton House & Topiary (NT). Jacobean Manor associated with the Gunpowder Plot retains its faded glory with a superb collection of tapestries, original furniture and ornamental topiary. Don't miss the church next door. Open Apr to Oct W-Sa 1-5 (4 in October). (B4) 01494 755560 www.nationaltrust.org.uk

Daylesford Organic Farmshop. The doyen of farm shops, and an expensive habit for those who can afford it. Takes the Waitrose experience onto another level. On display are the fine foods direct from their organic fields and pastures.

Kitchen and bakery. Café. Open daily M-Sa 9-6, Su 10-4. (A5) 01608 731700 www.daylesfordorganic.com

Enstone Tithe Barn, Rectory Farm. Dates from 1382 and is built with some magnificent timbers. Has been used for local functions such as craft fairs. Its future is uncertain as it has been put on the market along with the farm. (H6)

Rousham Park. Castellated house built c.1635 by Sir John Dormer. Remodelled by William Kent c.1773 to a Gothic style. Royal Garrison in Civil War. Beautiful garden with temples, dovecote and walled garden. No children under 15. Garden open all year, 10-4.30. House open May to Sept for groups only. (M6) 01869 347110 www.rousham.org

Waterfowl Sanctuary & Rescue Centre. A centre for rare breeds, with an emphasis on giving children a 'hands-on' experience with the farm animals. Baby barn. Open Tu-Su 10.30-dusk. (H1) 01608 730252 www.waterfowlsanctuary.co.uk

Wyatts Countryside Centre. Farm shop with ice cream parlour in organic conversion plus a garden nursery, animal and play area, and restaurant. Open daily. (D2) 01608 684835

Special Inns to Visit...

Bull Inn, Charlbury. Top quality B&B accommodation, with four en-suite bedrooms. Bar and

restaurant, using locally sourced produce. (G8) 01608 810689 www.bullinn-charlbury.com

The Fox and Hounds Inn, Great Wolford. A proper old-fashioned pub with hearty food and local ales, log fires and garden terrace. Children and pets welcome. Closed Mondays except East and Aug BHs. En-suite rooms. 01608 674220 www.thefoxandhoundsinn.com

Fox Inn, Lower Oddington. One of only 16 Pubs in the country to be Michelin Red Rated, the stone building is hidden behind a sea of Virginia creeper. A reputation for good food, wine and beer and a selection of awards under its belt. B&B. (A5) 01451 870555 www.foxinn.net

The Kings Head Inn, Bledington. A former C16 cider house, the Kings Head has a dreamlike setting on a village green by a meandering brook. 12 elegant en-suite bedrooms. There's substance under the beauty too with imaginative menus composed of locally produced and organic food. Sister pub to the Swan Inn Swinbrook (A7) 01608 658365 www.thekingsheadinn.net

Lamb Inn, Shipton-Under-Wychwood. Inviting C16 hostelry with a flourish of C21 interior design. Multi-ethnic bedrooms relive the proprietor's past travels. Food is eclectic, too. B&B. Family room. (C9) 01993 830465 www.lambinn.co.uk

The home of the Dukes of Marlborough was built as Queen Anne's gift to John Churchill, 1st Duke of Marlborough, for his defeat of Louis XIV in 1704, 'a monument to commemorate a military victory, and to glorify the Queen'. It is considered to be Vanburgh's C18 baroque masterpiece, although much of the detail was by Nicholas Hawksmoor. There are fine paintings, a Churchill Exhibition, tapestries, a 10,000 volume library and parkland designed by 'Capability' Brown. Plus, other attractions: the Butterfly House, Marlborough Maze, Adventure Play Area and Herb Garden. Restaurant. Palace open from mid-Feb to mid-Dec, daily to 1 Nov, then W-Su 10.30-5.30 (last admission 4.45pm), Park open daily all year (9-5) for rambling and dog walking. (L10) 08700 602080 www.blenheimpalace.com

Red Lion, Long Compton.
Built as a coaching inn in 1748,
The Red Lion has been modernised
but still retains the charm and
character of an 'olde' country
pub. Comfortable bedrooms.
Dog friendly. 01608 684221
www.redlion-longcompton.co.uk

Tite Inn, Chadlington.
Lovely outdoor patio. Specialises
in home reared South Devon
cross beef from fillet steak to beef
burgers all prepared in house. (E7)
01608 676475 www.titeinn.com

WOODSTOCK

A pretty town of stone built houses,
interesting shops and smart hotels,
and a practical centre for exploring
the eastern Cotswolds and Oxford.
Famous for glove-making in the
C16, and for Blenheim Palace, the
birthplace of Sir Winston Churchill
(1874-1965) who is buried nearby
in Bladon churchyard. There are
a number of antique shops, art
galleries and a fascinating
museum plus a melee of delis, inns,
restaurants, tearooms and coffee
shops. The foodaphile is spoilt for
choice, and below are listed a small
selection of what's on offer. (L10)

Special Places of Interest...

Combe Mill. A restored C19 beam
engine and a breast shot waterwheel.
Blacksmith's forge in operation.
Open days are advertised locally.
www.combemill.org

Grim's Ditch. Disconnected series of
ditches and banks built by Iron Age
tribes (Belgic) to defend their grazing
enclosures. Best sections in Blenheim
and Ditchley Parks. Grim is one of
the names of Woden - the masked
one, the god of victory, death and
magic power, the high god of the
Anglo-Saxons before their conversion
to Christianity in the C7. (K8)

**Iona House Gallery, 4 High
Street.** Paintings, etchings, prints,
sculpture, ceramics, glass, textiles,
silver and wood. Open M-Sa 10-5.30,
Su 11.30-5. (L10) 01993 811464
www.ionahousegallery.org.uk

**Julia Beusch Gallery, 21b
Oxford Street.** Gallery of modern
jewellery. Original and exquisite

The Feathers Hotel, Woodstock ss

designs. Open M-Sa. (L10)
01993 813445 www.juliabeusch.co.uk

**Oxfordshire Museum, Park
Street.** An exhibition of Oxfordshire,
and its people, from earliest times
to the present day. Changing
exhibitions. Coffee shop. TIC. Open
daily Tu-Sa 10-5, Su 2-5. (L10)
01993 811456
www.oxfordshire.gov.uk

**Woodstock Woolhangings,
Town Hall.** Story of Woodstock
from Norman times, told in thirteen
embroidered scenes. Open Apr to Oct,
W 1.30-5. (L10) 01993 812551

Where to Eat & Drink...

Chef Imperial, High Street. The
Chinese arrive here in coach loads
from far and wide, the locals will
queue patiently outside for a table. It
all adds up to a Chinese restaurant in
great demand. Need one add more?
01993 813593

**Hampers Food & Wine
Company, Oxford Street.**
A great deli and café provides a wide
range of sandwiches, paninis and
cakes whilst next door you can sit
down, relax and enjoy the ambience.
Open daily. 01993 811535
www.hampersfoodandwine.co.uk

**La Galleria Ristorante Italiano,
2 Market Place.** Sardinian Italian
with an emphasis on simplicity and
taste. (L10) 01993 813381
www.la-galleria.co.uk

Tea Rooms. You have a choice of
three: Harriets on the High Street, the

Iona House Gallery, Woodstock ss

Blenheim on Park Street just before
you enter the Palace, and Vickers
on Market Place.

Woodstock Arms, Market Street.
This is considered by many locals as
the best pub in Woodstock. It serves
great value pub-grub, most of the
day. (L10) 01993 811251
www.woodstockarms.co.uk

Where to Stay...

**The Feathers Hotel, Market
Street.** This romantic C17 top-notch
hotel is a labyrinth of rooms on all
levels. The bedrooms are plush and
intimate. The restaurant has been
producing superb food for many
years. Add the log fires and antique
furniture, and it makes for a winning
combination. (L10) 01993 812291
www.feathers.co.uk

**Kings Arms Hotel & Restaurant,
19 Market Street.** This has the
feel of a wine bar: leather chairs and
pine tables and a smart cocktail bar.
Upstairs the bedrooms are trendy
with low-slung, sexy beds to crawl
into. (L10) 01993 813636
www.kings-hotel-woodstock.co.uk

Tithe barns were built by the Church to store one-tenth of the peasant's (farmer's) produce, known as a tithe. This tax went to support the clergy and church. The estate barns belonged to the Manor or the Court House. Today, these buildings are either used as museums or have been left to gather dust and decay. Bredon Barn is a majestic building, but the aged design allows pigeons to merrily defecate over all below them, so its potential use as a venue for barn dances, parties and weddings has been overlooked. The Cotswolds has some of the finest examples in Britain.

The geological structure of the Cotswolds has had a profound and lasting effect on the landscape and 'look' of the area. The oolitic limestone that forms these hills has the appearance of 1000s of tiny balls, like fish roe, and is between 200 and 175 million years old. This material provides fine building matter. It is malleable and can be sculpted into beautiful shapes. When the sun shines on the stones the buildings exude a golden glow and the stone's colour is changeable, from the yellow Bath (Corsham) stone to the white stone of Painswick, to the golden stone of Broadway and Chipping Campden. Much of the best stone in Oxfordshire, known as Taynton limestone, has been worked out and is no longer commercially viable to quarry, so much so that the local builders import stone from Somerset and Dorset. As you travel north through the Cotswolds towards Banbury and the Northamptonshire villages the stone includes iron nuggets that darken the lustre of it, but makes it no less attractive. This is called Hornton Stone and is 20 million years older than Bath, Burford or Taynton Stone.

Galloping country, stonewalls, sheep pastures, hill top towns and villages, honey-pot villages, three Gloucestershire towns, Three Choirs Festival, racing stables.

If the Central Wolds are the centre of the Cotswolds, then Stow-On-The-Wold, sitting atop its hill, is the absolute heart of the region. This is due in part to the original route taken by the all important Fosse Way, a route which passes through Stow.

To the left of the Central Wolds lie three significant and interesting towns: Tewksbury, Cheltenham and Gloucester. The landscape is very flat here. As you move east, the terrain becomes more undulating and hilly. The Windrush river runs through the Wolds from east to west.

Cheltenham is a Georgian Spa town with interesting architecture and a range of decent places to stay and eat. Tewksbury and Gloucester are older, medieval towns with magnificent churches. Gloucester Cathedral is thought by some to be the birthplace of fan vaulting and Perpendicular architecture.

As well as the towns, there are also many pretty feeder villages to Cheltenham in the area including the Slaughters, the Swells, the Rissingtons and the twin villages of Stanton and Stanway.

This area is host to a number of festivals and cultural events including the Cheltenham Festivals, the Guiting Festival, and the Three Choirs Music Festival.

The Cloister's Fan Vaulting, Gloucester Cathedral

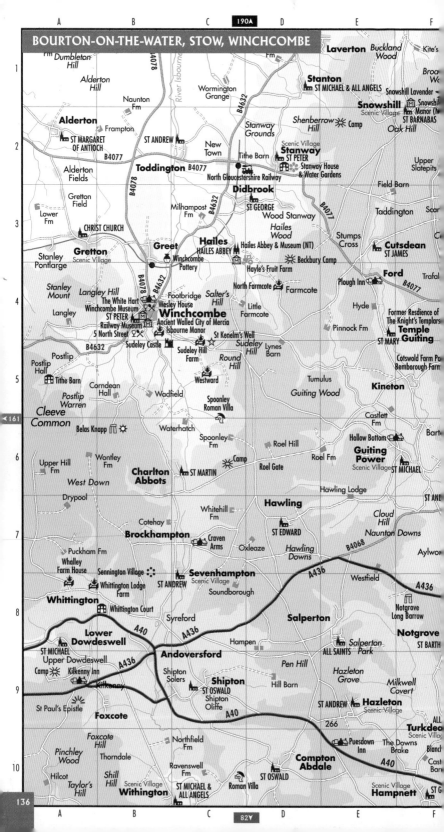

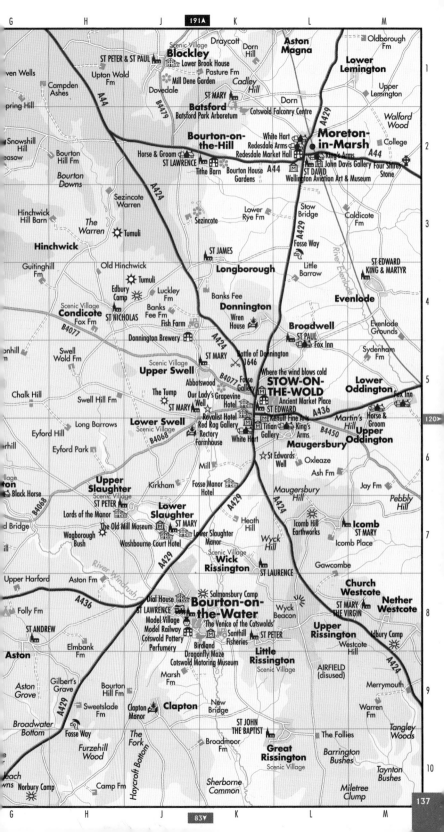

G

riven Wells
Campden
Ashes
pring Hill
Snowshill
Hill
easow

H

Upton Wold
ST PETER & PAUL
Bourton
Hill Fm

Horse & Groom
ST LAWRENCE

*Bourton
Downs*

Sezincote
Warren

Hinchwick
Hill Barn
*The
Warren*
☼ Tumuli

Hinchwick
Guitinghill
Fm
Old Hinchwick
☼ Tumuli
Edbury
Camp
Luckley
Fm

Condicote
Scenic Village
Fox Fm
ST NICHOLAS
Banks
Fee Fm
Fish Farm
Donnington Brewery

Chalk Hill
Swell Hill Fm
Swell
Wold Fm
Upper Swell
Scenic Village

Eyford Hill
Long Barrows
Eyford Park
Lower Swell
Scenic Village
Red Rag Gallery
Rectory
Farmhouse
White Hart

J

Blockley
Scenic Village
Lower Brook House
Mill Dene Garden
Dovedale
Pasture Fm
ST MARY
Batsford
Batsford Park Arboretum

**Bourton-on-
the-Hill**
Tithe Barn
Bourton House
Gardens

Sezincote

Lower
Rye Fm

ST JAMES

Longborough

Banks Fee

Donnington
Wren
House
Battle of Donnington
1646
ST MARY
Abbotswood
Fosse
Gallery
The Tump
Grapevine
Hotel
☼ **ST MARY**
Our Lady's
Well
Royalist Hotel

Kirkham
Mill

**Upper
Slaughter**
Scenic Village
ST PETER
Lords of the Manor
The Old Mill Museum
Wagborough
Bush
Washbourne Court Hotel

**Lower
Slaughter**
ST MARY
Lower Slaughter
Manor

K

Draycott
Dorn
Hill
Cadley
Hill
Dorn
Cotswold Falconry Centre

White Hart
Redesdale Arms
Redesdale Market Hall
Bourton House
Gardens
A44

Stow
Bridge
Fosse Way

Little
Barrow

Broadwell
ST PAUL
Fox Inn

Where the wind blows cold
**STOW-ON-
THE-WOLD**
Ancient Market Place
ST EDWARD
Kendall Fine Arts
Titian Gallery
King's
Arms
Maugersbury
☆ St Edwards
Well
Oxleaze
Ash Fm

*Maugersbury
Hill*

Icomb Hill
Earthworks

Heath
Hill
*Wyck
Hill*

L

**Aston
Magna**

**Moreton-
in-Marsh**
King's Arms
ST DAVID
John Davis Gallery
Wellington Aviation Art & Museum

Fosse Way

Evenlode

Evenlode
Grounds

Sydenham
Fm

**Lower
Oddington**
Fox Inn
Horse &
Groom
Martin's
Hill
**Upper
Oddington**

Jay Fm

Gawcombe

M

Oldborough
Fm

**Lower
Lemington**
Upper
Lemington

*Walford
Wood*
College

Four Shires
Stone

Caldicote
Fm

**ST EDWARD
KING & MARTYR**

Evenlode
Grounds

Sydenham
Fm

*Pebbly
Hill*

120 ►

Icomb
ST MARY
Icomb Place

**Church
Westcote**
**ST MARY
THE VIRGIN**
**Nether
Westcote**

1
2
3
4
5
6
7
8
9
10

Lower half

Folly Fm
☆ Black Horse
ton
rhill
B4068
d Bridge
il

Upper Harford
A436

Aston Fm
River Windrush

**Upper
Slaughter**

Dial House
ST LAWRENCE
Model Village
Model Railway
Cotswold Pottery
Perfumery

Salmonsbury Camp
**Bourton-on-
the-Water**
'The Venice of the Cotswolds'
Birdland
Dragonfly Maze
Cotswold Motoring Museum

Aston
Aston
Grove
Gilbert's
Grave
Sweetslade
Fm
Elmbank
Fm
Bourton
Hill Fm
Clapton
Manor
Clapton

*Broadwater
Bottom*
Fosse Way
*The
Fork*
*Furzehill
Wood*

New
Bridge
Broadmoor
Fm

each
wns
Norbury Camp
Camp Fm

Haycroft Bottom

*Sherborne
Common*

Marsh
Fm

**Wick
Rissington**
Scenic Village
ST LAWRENCE

Santhill
Fisheries
ST PETER

**Little
Rissington**
Scenic Village

Wyck
Beacon

**Upper
Rissington**

AIRFIELD
(disused)

**ST JOHN
THE BAPTIST**
**Great
Rissington**
Scenic Village

The Follies

Idbury Camp
Westcote
Hill
Merrymouth

Warren
Fm

*Tangley
Woods*

*Barrington
Bushes*

*Taynton
Bushes*

*Miletree
Clump*

Bourton-On-The-Water

BOURTON-ON-THE-WATER

One of the most popular beauty spots in the Cotswolds, but one that invites mixed opinions. It can be charming on a quiet, frostbitten morning when only the postman is out and about, but is best avoided on a busy bank holiday when the hordes arrive in coaches and charabancs. With ice cream in hand the visitors sit beside the river wetting their bare feet in the Windrush, and not a stitch of green grass is visible through all the paraphernalia. The tourist brochures describe it as 'The Venice of the Cotswolds', no doubt because the River Windrush is spanned with low graceful bridges - a poor description in my view. You must, however, look beyond the crowds and the tacky gift shops and wander the little streets for there are some beautiful houses to admire. Bourton may not thrill the jaded teenager or hard-bitten traveller, but it will delight small children - mine loved to run across the little bridges, paddle in the river and feed the ducks, and you have, of course, Birdland, the Model Village, the Motoring Museum and the Model Railway, all devised for family fun and rainy days. The village is built above Salmonsbury Camp, a Roman settlement, and also above a former underground reservoir. It is not an uncommon sight to see a sprightly pensioner move into the village, and within eighteen months, be seen wobbling along the lane, bent double by the damp. Bourton has its fair share of pubs that cater for the tourist. Perhaps the most traditional bar is in the Old New Inn. Tearooms are plentiful. July Carnival. Water Game - August bank holiday Saturday. (J8)

Special Places of Interest...

Birdland Park & Gardens.
Home to over 500 birds on banks of the River Windrush: penguins, tropical and sub-tropical birds. Feed the penguins and adopt a bird. Open daily, Apr to Oct 10-6, Nov to Mar 10-4. (J8) 01451 820480 www.birdland.co.uk

Cotswold Farm Park.
A unique survival centre for rare historic breeds of British farm animals including the Cotswold Lions (the Golden Fleece). High on the Central Wolds, three miles from Bourton. Pets and tots corner. Farm trail. Lambing, shearing and seasonal exhibitions. Café. Open daily Apr to Sept 10.30-5, & W/Es in Oct & Autumn 1/2 term, 10.30-4. (F5) 01451 850307 www.cotswoldfarmpark.co.uk

Cotswold Motoring Museum.
Motorcycles and vintage racing cars in C18 water mill. Collection of old advertising signs. Open daily mid-Feb to Oct 10-6. (J8) 01451 821255 www.cotswold-motor-museum.com

Cotswold Motoring Museum

1830   Edwin Budding of Stroud patents the first lawnmower   1835   William Henry Fox Talbot invents the negative process at Lacock Abbey

Cotswold Perfumery. Locally produced fragrances. Exhibition of perfumery. Factory tours. Open M-Sa 9.30-5, Su & BHs 10.30-5. (J8) 01451 820698
www.cotswold-perfumery.co.uk

Cotswold Pottery. Traditional rustic pots, hand-thrown using local materials. Bronze sculptures too. Open M-Sa 9.30-5, Su 10.30-5. (J8) 01451 820173
www.cotswoldpottery.co.uk

Dragonfly Maze, Rissington Road. Search for the Dragonfly within a traditional Yew Hedge Maze with a Rebus Puzzle and look upon the sculptures crafted by Kit Williams. Gift shop. Open daily from 10. (J8) 01451 822251

Model Railway. Over 400 sq.ft. of exhibits. Continental trains and British Railway trains in HO/OO and N Gauge. Open Apr to Sept 11-5.30, Oct to Mar W/Es 11-5. (J8) 01451 820686
www.bourtonmodelrailway.co.uk

Model Village, High Street. Bourton in miniature, at the scale of 1/9th of the original. Lovingly tended gardens. Open daily; summer 9-6, winter 10-4. (J8) 01451 820467
www.theoldnewinn.co.uk

Oxfordshire Way. A long distance footpath from Bourton-On-The-Water to Henley-On-Thames, linking the Cotswolds with the Chilterns. Follows the ancient tracks of the county through meadows and woods, along quiet river valleys and over windy escarpments through many a delightful village. Waymarked. (K8)

Salmonsbury Camp. The Romans' second legion of 5,000 soldiers was encamped here and built Lansdown Bridge to ford the Windrush on the Fosse Way. (K8)

Santhill Fisheries. Mature 26-acre lake stocked with rainbow and brown trout. Day, half-day, evening tickets and boat hire. Open Mar to 21 Dec. (K8) 01451 810291

The Lakes. These are flooded gravel pits from the 1960s and 70s. Now used for a carp farm, windsurfing centre and angling lake. There is a great abundance of wildlife: plants, insects and birds. (K8)

Windrush Valley. A slow, trickling stream in summer, with a tendency to flood in winter. The river snakes its way through quiet golden villages to create the idyllic Cotswold scene. (K10)

Where to Stay...

Blanche House, Turkdean. Almost 500 acres of farmland, meadows, woods and ponds surround this picturesque house. Guests are encouraged to explore on foot or horseback. Breakfast in the glass barn overlooking it all. 01451 861176
www.blanchehousebandb.co.uk

Clapton Manor, Clapton-on-the-Hill. Stunning Grade II listed Tudor house with a beautiful garden created by your host - a garden designer and historian. 01451 810202
www.claptonmanor.co.uk

Dial House. A sumptuous and small, intimate hotel with individually designed bedrooms. Informal lunches, candlelit dinners, roaring log fires and romantic rooms are all for your pleasure, and it's nicely tucked away within a large garden. (J8) 01451 822244
www.dialhousehotel.com

Folly Farm Campsite. Set high on an exposed plateau above Bourton. Ideal for tents and the simple life. Don't expect 5 star accommodation. (G8) 01451 820285
www.cotswoldcamping.net

The Curfew Tower, Moreton-in-Marsh

Cotswold Lion Sheep, Cotswold Farm Park

Cotswold Falconry Centre, Batsford Park

MORETON-IN-MARSH

Perhaps the first Cotswold town you'll visit if coming from the north along the ancient Fosse Way. And what an impressive site it is too. The wide main street built by the Abbot of Westminster in 1220 for the sheep and arable sales is today a lively scene on market day, every Tuesday since King Charles I granted the town a Charter in 1637. But its origins go back to the Romans who built a military camp around 43-50 AD whilst planning the construction of the Fosse Way. It remains the largest town in the Central Wolds and is dominated by the Market Hall built in 1887 by Lord Redesdale, father of the Mitford sisters. Look out for the Curfew Tower, an unusual phenomenon on the corner of Oxford Street, dated 1633, which rang until 1860. A fine centre given to a number of inns, art galleries and independent retailers. Associated with the English Civil War, for the Royalist Cavalry was based here. Just out of town on the Chipping Norton road is the Fire Services' College and HQ of the Institute of Fire Engineers. Moreton (Agricultural & Horse) Show - 1st Saturday in September. (L2)

Special Places of Interest...

Batsford Arboretum & Wild Garden. 56 acres of rare and beautiful trees are part of one of the largest private collection of trees in Britain. Open daily Feb to Nov 9-5, Dec and Jan daily except W, 9-4. (K2) 01386 701441 www.batsarb.co.uk

Cotswold Falconry Centre, Batsford Park. The Centre is dedicated to the conservation of eagles, hawks, falcons and owls, with many breeding pairs. Flying displays throughout the day. New parliament of owls. Open daily mid-Feb to mid-Nov, 10.30-5.30. (K2) 01386 701043 www.cotswold-falconry.co.uk

John Davies Gallery, The Old Dairy Plant. A much-respected Cotswold gallery established in 1977. Six fully catalogued annual exhibitions. Fine period, post Impressionist and contemporary paintings. Open daily. (L2) 01608 652255 www.johndaviesgallery.com

Mill Dene Garden, Blockley. A beautiful 2 1/2 acres set around an historic water mill. Rose terrace, grotto and trout stream. Lunches and teas. Open mid-Mar to Oct Tu-F 10-5. (J1) 01386 700457 www.milldenegarden.co.uk

Sezincote House & Garden. House designed in the Indian style (and inspiration for the Brighton Pavilion) is beautifully set in an oriental water garden. House open May to Sept Th F & BH Ms 2.30-5. Garden open Jan to Nov Th F & BH Ms 2-6. (J3) 01386 700444 www.sezincote.co.uk

Wellington Aviation Museum & Gallery. A funky, very personal collection of RAF memorabilia plus a choice of 250 aviation prints for sale. Open daily 10-12.30, 2-5. (L2) 01608 650323 www.wellingtonaviation.org

Where to Stay, Eat & Drink...

Horse & Groom, Bourton-on-the-Hill. A modern and airy feel permeates this Grade II listed Georgian inn which is peacefully set in a large garden on the hilltop. Bar, en-suite bedrooms and a blackboard menu that changes daily allowing great variety even for the most frequent visitors. 01386 700413 www.horseandgroom.info

Lower Brook House, Blockley. Inside this C17 house in the heart of the beautiful village of Blockley, you'll find a warm welcome, comfortable four-poster beds and a log fire. B&B and restaurant (guests and non-residents). 01386 700 286 www.lowerbrookhouse.co.uk

Redesdale Arms, High Street. An old coaching inn that mixes the traditional with contemporary designs. (L2) 01608 650308 www.redesdalearms.com

Snowshill Hill Estate B&B. Stay at the heart of a working farm in a comfortable, thoughtfully converted, self-contained dwelling within the extensive grounds of a prestigious and remote estate. 01386 853959

Sezincote House & Garden

1852   Emma Dent moves into Sudeley Castle   1852   Robert Dover's Olympick Games are banned due to drunken Birmingham yahoos

Bourton House Garden has 3 acres of intense planting: topiary, knot garden, potager and a profusion of herbaceous borders and exotic plants. The wonderful tithe barn is host to a gallery of contemporary arts and crafts. Lunches and teas. Pre-booked groups only. Open late May to Aug 31, W-Sa & BHs 10-5. Sept to Oct Th & F 10-5. (K2) 01386 700754 www.bourtonhouse.com

Old Mill Museum, Lower Slaughter

Washbourne Court ss

Wren House, Donnington. Wren House accommodation comprises two en-suite bedrooms in the C15 house, recently renovated to a high standard, and the C17 Grade II listed Cotswold stone cottage - an old Granary - which has been converted into a surprisingly spacious one bedroom self-catering cottage. 01451 831787 www.wrenhouse.net

Special Places of Interest...

Old Mill Museum, Lower Slaughter. This iconic C19 flour mill has been lovingly restored into a small museum with ice cream parlour, tea room and mill shop. The proprietor is the lead singer in a Jazz band, hence the funky music. Open daily (W/Es January to February), 10-6. (J7) 01451 820052 www.oldmill-lowerslaughter.com

Where to Stay...

Lower Slaughter Manor. Perfectly proportioned C17 Cotswold manor. Large, spacious rooms furnished with antiques. No children U-12. No dogs. (J7) 01451 820456 www.lowerslaughter.co.uk

Lords of the Manor, Upper Slaughter. Classy, well-established Country House Hotel with C17 origins set in eight acres of parkland. Child friendly. No dogs. The former home of the Reverend F E B Witts, Rector of this parish who wrote his famous chronicle of the C18, The Diary of a Cotswold Parson. (H7) 01451 820243 www.lordsofthemanor.com

Washbourne Court, Lower Slaughter. This C17 hotel, once an Eton cramming school, stands in four acres of beautiful grounds alongside the River Eye. A Country House Hotel with a pleasing mix of contemporary and historic features and a reputation for fine food. (J7) 01451 822143 www.washbournecourt.co.uk

Lower Slaughter Manor

| 1854 | Death of the Reverend F E Witts author of Diary of a Cotswold Parson | 1854 1854 | Founding of Cheltenham Ladies College Woodchester Mansion is designed by Pugin |

Lower Slaughter is one of the most popular villages in the Cotswolds. Little bridges cross the Eye Stream which runs beside rows of golden cottages. The much painted C19 red-brick Corn Mill stands on the western edge of the village. Upper Slaughter is a couple of miles upstream and has an old Manor House once lived in by the Slaughter family, an old Post Office with a beautiful kitchen garden and, along a lane past the church, a ford crosses the stream hidden beneath lush greenery. (J7)

Snowshill

NAUNTON

A pretty village surrounded by rolling sheep pastures and overlooked by some steep gallops. The handsome Church has some interesting gargoyles and a stone pulpit. (G6)

Naunton Church. Idyllic country setting on edge of village below rolling pastures. Gargoyles. (F6)

SNOWSHILL

(Pronounced Snosill). This charming and unspoilt hilltop village is a short distance by car from Broadway. There's a striking church, a pub and a row of much photographed cottages opposite Snowshill Manor. (F1)

STANTON

Charming village with houses of warm honey-coloured stone. Restored by Sir Philip Scott, 1903-37. Centre for equine excellence in the Vine, a popular horse riding centre. The Mount Inn is a welcome refuge if one's tackling the Cotswold Way. (D1)

Stanton Church of St Michael. Impressive Perpendicular tower. Much is C12 -15 with wall paintings, Jacobean pulpit, but its fame was associated with the many visits of John Wesley, the Methodist preacher. (D1

Naunton

Stanton

A Cotswold manor house containing Charles Paget Wade's extraordinary collection of craftsmanship and design amounting to some 22,000 items from toys to musical instruments, Samurai armour to clocks and bicycles. Open W-Su mid-Mar to 1 Nov 12-5, grounds, restaurant and shop from 11. (F1) 01386 852410 www.nationaltrust.org.uk

STANWAY & STANWAY HOUSE

This village is dominated by the outstanding Manor House. In its grounds stands one of the country's finest tithe barns designed with the Golden Proportion in mind and across the road a thatched cricket pavilion, set on staddle stones. The beautiful Gatehouse is C17, and was probably built by Timothy Strong of Little Barrington. It bears the arms of the Tracy family. The little Church of St Peter has C14 origins and some amusing gargoyles. (D2)

Stanway House & Water Garden
This exquisite Jacobean Manor House and Gatehouse is built from the local stone known as Guiting Yellow which lights up when the sun touches it. All is set within an enchanting and ancient parkland designed by a numerologist, the home of the Earl of Wemyss and March. The partially restored C18 Cascade and Canal was designed by the highly respected Charles Bridgman, and is now open June to Aug, Tu & Th 2-5. (D2) 01386 584469
www.stanwayfountain.co.uk

STOW-ON-THE-WOLD

With a name like this it is bound to attract visitors, and it has, and does so to this day, for with its exposed position at the intersection of eight roads (one being the Fosse Way) Stow has been party to some momentous events in history. The Romans used Stow as an encampment and route centre. The Viking merchants traded down the Fosse Way, but it was the Saxon hill farmers who laid the foundations for the fleece which created wealth for the wool merchants who used the great Market Place for sheep sales of 20,000, or more. The Kings Arms is

Stow-On-The-Wold

pleasing place to be. It still has free parking and you may wander freely about and admire the art galleries and many antique shops. 'Where the wind blows cold' so the song goes. (K5)

Fosse Gallery, The Square. Well-established gallery displaying paintings; contemporary and modern. Most artists are RA, RAI, ROI members. Open Tu-Sa 10.30-5. (K5) 01451 831319 www.fossegallery.com

Abbotswood

Donnington Brewery

named after Charles Stuart who stayed here in 1645 before the Battle of Naseby. In March 1646 the Battle of Stow was the last skirmish or battle of the English Civil War. Stow has a number of historic hostelries and is thus an agreeable place in which to succumb to fine ales and wine, and the comfort of a four-poster bed. Today the town is a busy and

Special Places of Interest...

Abbotswood, Upper Swell. Manor house altered by Sir Edwin Lutyens. Extensive heather and stream gardens. Formal terraced gardens. Plantings of spring bulbs. Open for National Gardens Scheme. (K5) 01451 830173

Donnington Brewery. Established in 1865 by Thomas Arkell who used the spring water to concoct his delicious potions. The brewery remains independent and supplies 15 tied houses and a number of free trade outlets. (J4) www.donnington-brewery.com

Donnington Fish Farm. Spring-fed fresh trout, smoked trout and paté. Open Tu-Sa 10-5.30. (J4) 01451 830873 www.go-fish.co.uk

Kenulf Fine Arts, Digbeth Street. Conservative mix of C18/20 oils and watercolours and contemporary art. Antiques. Open daily. (K5) 01451 870878 www.kenulf-fine-arts.com

Market Cross. The lantern head represents four meanings: 'A Rood', St Edward, The Wool Trade and The Civil War. (K5)

Parish Church of St Edward (The Confessor). Set behind the Market Place in the centre of town. The building is a mix of the C11 and C15. Originally of Saxon origins, it has an impressive tower of 88 feet that was built in 1447. Modern stained glass is of interest. (K5)

This is held twice a year, in the spring and autumn. Its origins have been lost in time but today it is very much a Romany get-together. They come from far and wide to trade in ponies, tack and odds and sods. It's quite a sight but one visit will probably suffice and satisfy your curiosity. On arriving in Stow one can't help but notice that the police (and RSPCA) presence is considerable and that most of the shops, tearooms and inns are closed. No doubt the matrons of the town have also locked up their daughters! As you make your way towards the site, gaggles of young girls showing more flesh than common sense, often in freezing conditions due to the time of year, strut their stuff. All apparently (according to a 10-year old Romany boy) to attract members of the opposite sex. I can't imagine that they were very successful because the only males I saw were well into their 40s, and possibly older, and only intent on doing a deal, often clasping wodges of £50 notes. The elderly female Romanies were fun to talk to and were there to meet up with old friends and to experience the camaraderie of times past. What did impress me (and left me envious) was their stack of brand new motors: black Golf GTis for the women folk, and spanking new, black Land Rover Discoveries for the men folk. (K5)

Belas Knap Long Barrow

Red Rag Gallery, Church Street.
Original paintings from living artists.
Sculpture. Scottish art. Open daily.
(K5) 01451 832563
www.redraggallery.co.uk

Titian Gallery, Sheep Street.
C18 and C19 British and European
oil paintings and watercolours.
Changing exhibitions. Open Tu-Sa
10-5. (K5) 01451 830004
www.titiangallery.co.uk

Where to Eat & Drink...

**Horse & Groom, Upper
Oddington.** The inn dates back to
1580 and has retained some original
features since its early days as a
simple hostelry. Set in a beautiful
conservation village, this freehouse
provides sustenance and comfort.
B&B. 01451 830584
www.horseandgroom.uk.com

Kings Arms, The Square.
Fine pub in Market Square set on
two levels. Lively and comfortable
matched by well prepared
ingredients. Greene King and Hook
Norton beers. Children & dogs
welcome. B&B. (K5) 01451 830364
www.thekingsarmsstow.co.uk

The White Hart, The Square.
The Inn boasts two cosy bars and
a comfortable dining room. The food

is recommended by one and all. (K5)
01451 830674.
www.whitehartstow.com

Where to Stay...

Fosse Manor Hotel.
Refurbished into a sleek, friendly,
stylishly simple and traditional
country house hotel. Local suppliers
provide for the restaurant. Croquet
lawn. (K6) 01451 830354
www.fossemanor.co.uk

Grapevine Hotel, Sheep Street.
The Conservatory Restaurant serves
imaginative food and fine wines. 22
beautifully furnished and decorated
bedrooms. Relaxing ambience. (K5)
01451 830344 www.vines.co.uk

**Rectory Farmhouse,
Lower Swell.** This fully renovated
and comfortable B&B with en-suite
bedrooms has had several historical
incarnations. Once a monastery
whose cellars date back to the C14.
Once a home confiscated from its
owner by Henry VIII. And, before
its incarnation as a B&B, the
Rectory was a working farmhouse.
01451 832351

Royalist Hotel, Digbeth Street.
Claims to be the oldest Inn in
England dating from 947 AD.
Seasonal menu, lunch and dinner.

Eight bedrooms. Adjacent, the Eagle
& Child pub. (K5) 01451 830670
www.theroyalisthotel.com

WINCHCOMBE

This small Cotswold town lies cradled
in the Isbourne Valley. It was an
ancient Saxon burh (small holding)
and famous medieval centre visited
from far and wide for the market,
horse fair and monastery which was
destroyed in the C16. You can still
walk the narrow streets beside the C16
and C18 cottages, but do look up and
admire the many fine gables above
the shop fronts. There's a
local saying: Were you born in
Winchcombe? which is directed at
those of us who leave doors open. It
can be a wee bit drafty. (B4)

Special Places of Interest...

Belas Knap Long Barrow.
In Old English translates 'beacon
mound'. A burial chamber, 4,000
years old. Opened in 1863 to reveal
38 skeletons. In superb condition
and good viewpoint. Steep footpath
from road. (B6)

**Folk & Police Museum, Town
Hall.** History of the town, police and
weapons. TIC. Open East/Apr-Oct M-
Sa 10-1, 2-4.30. (B4) 01242 609151

| 1865 | Chedworth's Roman Villa is discovered by rabbiters seeking a lost ferret | 1865 1866 | Donnington Brewery established by Thomas Arkell Vulliamy designs the neo-Baroque Westonbirt (school) |

A Tudor house and the original home of the Seymour family. Katherine Parr, widow of Henry VIII, lived here and lies buried in the chapel. There is a fine collection of needlework, furniture and tapestries plus paintings by Van Dyck, Rubens and Turner. All surrounded by award-winning gardens and open parkland. The Castle is open daily Apr to 1 Nov 10.30-5. (B5) 01242 602308 www.sudeleycastle.co.uk

WINCHCOMBE'S GARGOYLES

The word gargoyle is a derivation from the French word gargouille meaning throat or pipe. The carved gargoyles were invented to channel water off, or away, from the roofs of buildings in Egypt and Ancient Greece. Their popularity became almost endemic in Europe during the Middle Ages. Fine examples are to be seen on Notre Dame in Paris, and on Rouen's Cathedral in northern France. In Britain, the Cotswold churches, especially Winchcombe's, have some fine, amusing examples, as illustrated. The reason for these strange and often ugly designs is open to conjecture. Some believe they are caricatures of the clergy, or that they are there to ward off evil spirits. Perhaps to protect the church's building from the devil. Others believe they are transformed into ghosts and ghoulies at night! They were certainly a popular architectural ornament during the dark days of the superstitious Middle Ages.

Winchcombe Pottery

Wesley House ss

Hailes Abbey (EH/NT). Built in 1246 by Richard, Earl of Cornwall, brother of Henry III, having vowed he would found a religious house if he survived a storm at sea. Museum. The Abbey became a popular place of pilgrimage in the Middle Ages until Henry VIII closed it down. It remains an attractive ruin with many surviving artefacts on display in the museum. Open daily Apr to Oct 31 10-dusk. (C3) 01242 602398
www.nationaltrust.org.uk

Hayles Fruit Farm. Wide range of locally produced fruit, cider and home-cured hams. Tea room. Two nature trails. Open daily June to Oct 9-6, Nov to Mar 9 5. (D3) 01242 602123
www.hayles-fruit-farm.co.uk

Parish Church of St Peter. One of the great 'Wool' churches. It is of a C15 Perpendicular design but is strangely plain, yet dignified. Not as elaborate as some of the other 'Wool' churches. For example, it has no chancel arch. The gargoyles are

the one notable feature, and a circumnavigation of the exterior is advised. The weathercock is the county's finest. (B4)

Postlip Hall & Tithe Barn. A former Jacobean Manor House set in fifteen acres, Postlip Hall has been for the past 40 years a co-housing idyll. Eight families live in separate dwellings, working the organic kitchen garden and grounds, and pursuing their own creative pleasures, be it writing, painting, sculpting or inventing. The original tithe barn is also in continual use except when it is hired out as a venue for weddings, parties and beer festivals. (A5)

Railway Museum, 23 Gloucester Street. Relics and bygones including operating exhibits in a peaceful Cotswold garden. Open daily East to Oct 1.30-6. Winter W/Es & BHs 1.30-dusk. (B4) 01242 609305

Salt Way. This prehistoric track runs east of Winchcombe from Hailes, south towards Hawling along Sudeley Hill. It was used in medieval times to carry salt from Droitwich and coastal salt towns, salt being the essential meat preservative. (D6)

Winchcombe Pottery. One of the country's most respected potteries, known throughout the ceramic world. A large variety of hand-made domestic ware on sale

in the shop. Open daily M-F 8-5, Sa 10-4 (& Su May to Sept 12-4). (B3) 01242 602462
www.winchcombepottery.co.uk

Where to Eat & Drink...

5 North Street. Has gained a healthy respect from fellow restaurateurs in the Cotswolds. A small and well-run restaurant with low-beamed ceiling in a quaint C17 building providing a relaxed and friendly atmosphere. (B4) 01242 604566

Wesley House, High Street. Deserved reputation for excellent food. Locals travel miles to this gastronomic oasis, and no wonder. Now, with a chic, new wine bar for the local lovelies. Five bedrooms. (B4) 01242 602366
www.wesleyhouse.co.uk

White Hart, High Street. Variously viewed as a pub or a hotel, the White Hart offers quality in both departments. This C16 inn has eight en-suite bedrooms and a bar, restaurant and wine shop. (B4) 01242 602359
www.wineandsausage.co.uk

Hailes Abbey

Westward

View from Sudeley Hill

Where to Stay...

Isbourne Manor B&B.
Castle Street. Elizabethan/Georgian house beside the grounds of Sudeley Castle. Your host's warm hospitality will tempt you back, again and again. No dogs. (B4) 01242 602281
www.isbourne-manor.co.uk

North Farmcote. A working family farm producing sheep and cereals situated high on the Cotswold escarpment. Built around 1840 as a dower house for Lord Sudeley's mother, the house is surrounded by a large garden where guests can have afternoon tea. Visit their specialist herb garden (open May to Oct). (C4) 01242 602304

Sudeley Hill Farm. Comfortable C15 listed farmhouse with panoramic views over a working sheep and arable farm of 800 acres. Three en-suite bedrooms. (C4) 01242 602344

Westward B&B. Sudeley Lodge was built in 1730 as the hunting lodge of Sudeley Castle and guests have included many notable persons such as George III in 1788. The house sits in 550 acres including a beautiful garden with small orchid

house and ornamental pond and 80 acres of woodland and a lake. Three en-suite bedrooms. 01242 604372
www.westward-sudeley.co.uk

Just Outside Cheltenham, What to See...

Whittington Court. An impressive, statuesque Cotswold stone house beside a pretty church. Open Easter fortnight, then mid to end Aug, 2-5. (B8) 01242 820556

Where to Stay...

Whalley Farm House, Whittington. Grade II listed farmhouse on a large working farm just four miles from Cheltenham. Help milk the cows or learn about the hand-reared Holstein Friesian calves. Have a game of tennis or simply read a book in one of the quiet corners in the garden. (B8) 01242 820213
www.whalleyfarm.co.uk

Whittington Lodge Farm, Whittington. Your hostess takes your comfort and enjoyment very seriously and the bedrooms are perfect down to the smallest details. The farm has a special emphasis on conservation and wildlife and you

can take farm wildlife tours and walks. (B8) 01242 820603
www.whittingtonlodgefarm.com

Special Inns to Visit...

Black Horse, Naunton.
A Donnington Brewery tied house so naturally there is an excellent selection of beers on offer. A little off the beaten track so ideal for those wishing to avoid the crowds. B&B (G6) 01451 850565

Fox Inn, Broadwell. Very picturesque inn with a large beer garden situated opposite the village green thus making it an ideal pit stop for families. Real ales from the local Donnington Brewery, and tasty pub-grub from the kitchens. Jus Purrfik, Ma Larkin! (L5) 01451 870909

Craven Arms, Brockhampton.
An attractive C17 inn noted for its fine food and lovely views tucked away on the edge of this hillside village. Some years ago it had but a hole in the wall and served only beer. I remember watching the stunned expression on a visiting gin drinkers face when told "O no Sir, we don't av that ere...will lemonade do?" (C7) 01242 820 410

Fox Inn, Oddington.
Origins are C11 with flagstone floors, open fireplaces and wooden beams. Wholesome pub grub. (M5) 01451 870555 www.foxinn.net

Hollow Bottom. Friendly pub popular with the racing fraternity. Traditional pub grub plus more ambitious delights. (E6) 01451 850392
www.hollowbottom.com

Plough Inn, Ford. The first pub my 90-year old Grandmother entered, and surprisingly, she was impressed at how civil and well behaved everyone was. It's all flagstone floors, beams and old-world charm. (E4) 01386 584215
www.theploughinnatford.co.uk

Sudeley Hill Farm

A hidden, somnolent estate village that surprisingly manages to support two pubs, a village shop and bakery, a nursery school and an active village hall. The blue-grey cottages belong to the Cochrane Estate (or Guiting Manor Amenity Trust) that has thankfully saved this village from greedy developers and second homers. The Church of St Michael & All Angels lies on the edge of the village and has some Norman features, a beautiful Tympanum and some weather-beaten tombstones. It was an early Anglo-Saxon settlement called Gyting Broc. A classical and jazz music festival is held in late July for the past 38 years and attracts many artists of international renown. www.guitingfestival.org

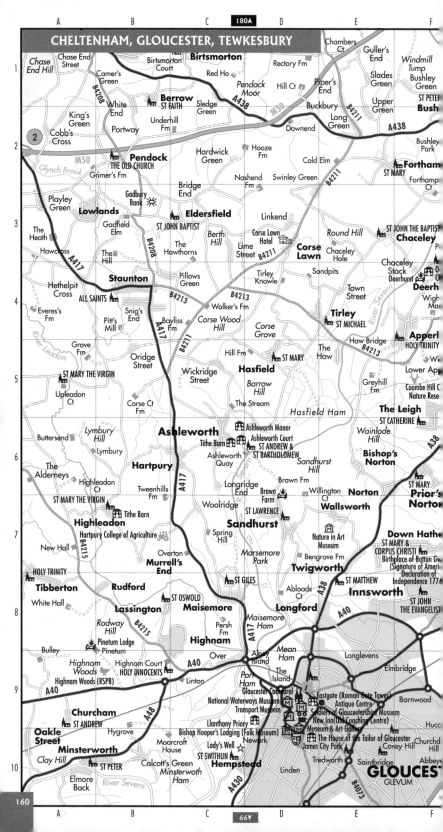

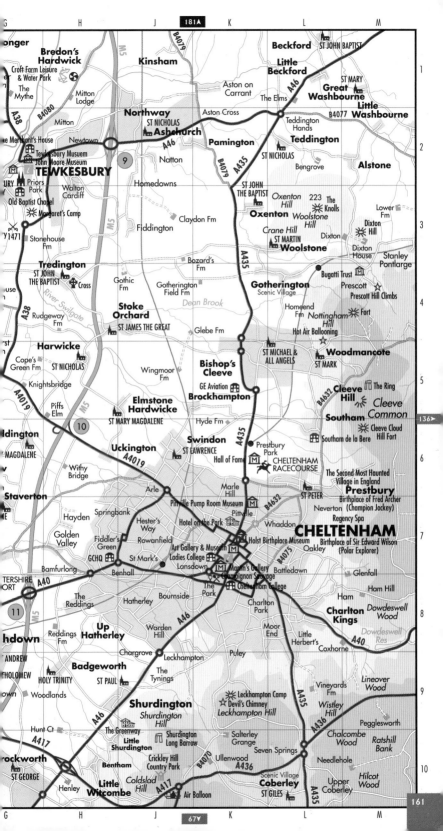

CHELTENHAM

A smaller version of Bath, often described as 'the most complete Regency town in England'. Elegant Regency buildings overlook the crescents, squares, tree-lined avenues and spacious parks. Cheltenham remains, in historic terms, a young town of a mere 300 years. It grew as a spa after George III had approved the waters in 1788. Thereafter, distinguished visitors such as George Handel and Samuel Johnson came to be revitalised. The Promenade is one of the most attractive shopping streets in England which becomes progressively more independent and up-market as you trudge with heavy bags and depleted purse west towards Montpelier. Style and fashion epitomise this smart town. Youth and hedonism a-plenty. Cheltenham has seen a phenomenal explosion of new nightclubs, bars and restaurants patronised by the ever-increasing student population and, come the evening, by an influx of visitors from Birmingham, Bristol and Gloucester and not least from the surrounding villages and small towns. It is no longer the home of Colonel Blimps and tweedy ladies of means. Cheltenham is proud of its calendar of festivals: Antique, Folk, Greenbelt,

Jazz, Literature, Music, Science, Wychwood...but it is during the Cheltenham Festival of National Hunt Racing which takes place in March that the town takes on a carnival atmosphere. The Irish arrive in thousands and this brings out the Cheltonians hospitality. Hotel rooms are like gold dust so many of Cheltenham's citizens open their homes and do a brisk and highly profitable B&B trade for three or four nights. A centre of administration, commerce, education, high-tech industries and secret surveillance. The Countryside Commission and UCAS have their headquarters here. So do a number of large organisations: the Chelsea Building Society, Dowty, Endsleigh Insurance, GE Aviation, Kraft Foods and Zurich Insurance. The University of Gloucestershire has expanded its faculties to countenance the weight of the highly regarded private

schools. What stands out for those who arrive from the Gloucester side is the large circular building known as GCHQ, locally known as the Puzzle Palace. This was established after WWII as a secret surveillance centre for the Foreign Office.

It is a most congenial town that could well be described as the centre for the Cotswolds. Its motto is: Salubritas et Eruditio 'Health and Education'. If you can achieve either of these then your luck is in. (L7)

Cheltenham Art Gallery & Museum ss

Special Places of Interest...

Art Gallery & Museum, Clarence Street.

World-renowned Arts & Crafts Movement collection inspired by William Morris. Rare Chinese and English ceramics. Social history of Cheltenham. C17 Dutch and C17-20 British paintings. Open M-Sa 10-5.20. (K7) 01242 237431 www.cheltenhammuseum.org.uk

Bugatti Trust, Prescott Hill.

A small exhibition illustrates the work of Ettore Bugatti the genius of industrial design and invention. Study Centre with drawings, photos and some cars. Open M-F 10.30-3.30, and during Hill Climb days. (M4) 01242 673136 www.bugatti.co.uk

Cheltenham College.

An independent Public School of architectural renown distinguished by the superb Chapel and Refectory. The ground for the oldest cricket festival in the world (first staged in 1872) which takes place every August. (K8) To visit contact 01242 522697 www.cheltcoll.gloucs.sch.uk

Cheltenham Gallery, 4 Regent Street.

Collection of original oil paintings in a variety of styles. Open Tu-Sa 10-5. (K7) 01242 573990 www.cheltenhamgallery.com

Cheltenham Ladies College, Bayshill Road.

If you see young ladies dressed in green apparel walking at pace through the streets of Cheltenham (in twos and threes) you can be sure they are educated at this the most elitist of academies. Its buildings are undistinguished, modern and rarely favourably commented upon. However, the aesthetics of the buildings have no effect on the school's academic achievements for it usually comes in the top 3 of all A Level results. (K7)

Cheltenham Racecourse Hall of Fame.

The story of steeple chasing and its immortals, in sight and sound, from Cheltenham's first Gold Cup in 1818 to Desert Orchid's heart-stopping win in 1989. Open M-F and Racedays 9-5. Free. (L6) 01242 513014 www.cheltenham.co.uk

Cheltenham College

Montpelier by Michael Edwards, Martin's Gallery, Cheltenham ss

Gustav Holst Birthplace Museum, Clarence Road, Pittville. Memorabilia of composer's life. Period furnished rooms. Open all year Tu-Sa 10-4, some BHs. (K7) 01242 524846 www.holstmuseum.org.uk

Hot Air Ballooning, Woodmancote. Daily flights (at dawn, or two hours before sunset) over the Cotswolds. Single or group bookings/gift vouchers. Office open M-F 9-5. (L4) 01242 675003 www.hot-air-ballooning.ltd.uk

Martin's Gallery, Montpellier Parade. Bright gallery with an interest in Asian art. Open W-Sa 11-6. (K7) 01242 526044 www.martinsgallery.co.uk

Pittville Pump Room. A masterpiece of C19 Greek Revivalism adorned with colonnaded facades, portico, pillared and balconied hall. Open daily except during private functions. (K7) 01242 264231 www.pittvillepumproom.org.uk

Seven Springs. One of the sources of the River Thames. There is a stone plaque here with a Latin inscription which reads, roughly translated: 'Here thou, O Father Thames, hast thy sevenfold beginning'. (L10)

Where to Eat & Drink...

Brosh, 8 Suffolk Parade. Eastern Mediterranean restaurant where everything is made on the premises. The chef was brought up on an Israeli Kibbutz where he learnt different culinary traditions from the other residents. Open W-Sa from 7pm 01242 227277 www.broshrestaurant.co.uk

Champignon Sauvage, 24-26 Suffolk Road. A two Michelin starred restaurant with a reputation for their original approach on serving fine cuisine. (K7) 01242 573449 www.lechampignonsauvage.co.uk

Daffodil, 18-20 Suffolk Parade. Converted from a 1920s art deco cinema to a restaurant and mezzanine Circle Bar and full of original features such as posters advertising films and even the original projectors. (K7) 01242 700 055. www.thedaffodil.com

Pittville Pump Room

Thirty Two Imperial Square, Cheltenham ss

The Beehive, 1-3 Montpelier Villas. Relaxed, busy, laid-back pub with great food. Upstairs restaurant. Lunch and dinner. (K7) 01242 579443

Morans Eating House, 123-129 Bath Road. Family-owned restaurant and wine bar that has been popular and busy since its inception 20 years ago. Squeeze amongst the regulars for a glass of wine or good value, unpretentious fare from brunch to a bedtime snack. (K8) 01242 581411 www.moranseatinghouse.co.uk

Where to Stay...

Hanover House B&B, 65 St George's Road. An attractive Grade II listed house built in a mix of Italian and Georgian architecture. The B&B is beautifully light and airy inside and the books, flowers and pictures adorning the rooms make you feel at home. Edward Elgar and his wife Alice once lived here. 01242 541297 www.hanoverhouse.org

Hotel On The Park, 38 Evesham Road. Sumptuously decorated bedrooms and bathrooms. Impressive Baccanalian restaurant serves modern British fare. (K7) 01242 518898 www.hotelonthepark.com

5 Ewlyn Road. A simple red brick villa in a bustling suburb of Cheltenham. Unmodernised

and unpretentious. Old-fashioned simplicity reigns supeme. 01242 261243

Georgian House, 77 Montpelier Terrace. Georgian house amidst elegant terrace close to many antique shops. Superb breakfasts. No children U-16. (K7) 01242 515577 www.georgianhouse.net

Thirty Two, Imperial Square. This is luxury, boutique-style

B&B, par excellence. Your hosts are interior designers of exuberance. Just live the dream and treat yourself. (K7) 01242 771110 www.thirtytwoltd.com

The Greenway, Shurdington. Elizabethan manor house provides elegance, peace and self-indulgent comfort with easy access to the M5 motorway. (J9) 01242 862352 www.thegreenway.co.uk

The Greenway, Shurdington ss

GLOUCESTER

The county town of Gloucestershire and its administrative centre is set to the west of the Cotswold Hills, south of the Malvern Hills, and to the east of the Forest of Dean. Originally a port connected to the tidal Bristol Channel and a strategic point developed by the Romans into the fort Glevum. This ancient city is today dominated by the magnificent Cathedral. One of the great attractions are the Old Docks where the spectacular C19 warehouses have been restored for commercial and leisure use. It is not unknown to spy tall ships, and ships in the dry dock for renovation. The city is undergoing a great deal of new development on the south side just off the Bristol road. The history of Gloucester is immense and this is well covered in the many museums listed below. (E10)

The Royal Gloucestershire Hussars Yeomanry First World War Memorial, College Green

Special Places of Interest...

City Museum & Art Gallery, Brunswick Road.
Roman relics, dinosaurs, aquarium, art exhibitions. Open Tu-Sa 10-5. (D9) 01452 396131
www.gloucester.gov.uk/citymuseum

Eastgate.
Roman and Medieval Gate. Towers and medieval stone-lined Horse Pool (Moat). Open May to Sept Sa 10-12, 2.15-5. (D9)

Folk Museum, 99-103 Westgate Street.
Medieval timber-framed buildings associated with martyrdom of Bishop Hooper in 1555. Social history, folklore, crafts and industries of city and county. Herb garden. Open Tu-Sa 10-5. (D9) 01452 396868
www.gloucester.gov.uk/folkmuseum

Glevum, Gloucester.
Occupied since Neolithic times. Became of strategic importance to Early Man and the Roman legions. Fort at Kingsholm beside the River Severn. Lost out to Corinium (Cirencester) in importance in the C3 AD. (D9)

Gloucester & Sharpness Canal.
Opened in 1827 and built above the River Severn. It's 16 miles long and was originally used by ocean-going ships in transit to Gloucester. (D9)

National Waterways Museum, Llanthony Warehouse.
A major national exhibition about the history of the inland waterways. Historic boats and leisure cruises on hand: 01452 318200. Café. Open Sa, Su, & BHs 11-4 and daily during school holidays. (D9) 01452 318200
www.nwm.org.uk

Nature In Art Museum, Wallsworth Hall.
World's first museum dedicated exclusively to Art inspired by Nature. Life-size sculptures in the garden. Artists at work (Feb-Nov). Coffee shop. Play area. Open all year Tu-Su & BHs 10-5. (E7) 01452 731422
www.nature-in-art.org.uk

Soldiers of Gloucestershire Museum, The Docks.
300 years' service portrayed by sound effects and life-size models, weapons and uniforms. Open Mar to Sept, daily 10-5, Oct to Feb Tu-Su & BH Ms, 10-5. (D9) 01452 522682
www.glosters.org.uk

Where to Stay...

Pinetum Lodge, Churcham.
A Victorian hunting lodge situated in 13 acres of woodland garden planted by Thomas Gambier Parry in 1844, The owners encourage you to surround yourself with nature. 01452 750554
www.pinetumlodge.ik.com

Nature In Art Museum

GLOUCESTER CATHEDRAL

The Cathedral Church of St Peter and the Holy and Undivided Trinity. Without exception the most magnificent building in Gloucestershire and one of the finest of all English cathedrals. The building's foundation stone was laid down by Abbot Serlo in 1089 on the site of a religious house founded by Osric, an Anglo-Saxon prince living here in about 678-9 AD. The Nave was completed in 1130. Its architecture is Romanesque, with some early Perpendicular. The reconstruction of the Quire followed the burial in 1327 of Edward II. The East Window behind the altar had at its installation the largest display of medieval stained glass in the world and dates from 1350. The same year, fan vaulting was invented here at Gloucester and its intricate design covers the roof of the cloisters. Some would argue that Gloucester also saw the birth of Perpendicular architecture. In the South Transept survives the oldest of all Perpendicular windows. Allow a couple of hours to wander around this spiritual hot house. There are tours of the crypt and tower. You will also be shown the location used for part of Hogwarts in the Harry Potter films. Evensong is a most magical experience not to be missed, as is the Christmas Carol service.

Restaurant. Open daily 7.30am to 6pm. (D9) 01452 528095 www.gloucestercathedral.org.uk

One of England's finest medieval towns set at the confluence of the rivers Avon and Severn. Just look up at the gables of the many ancient buildings and admire (or venture into) one of the 30 narrow alleyways that make up this historic place so magnificently brought to life in John Moore's Brensham Trilogy. In the Middle Ages Tewkesbury was a flourishing centre of commerce: flour milling, mustard, brewing, malting and shipping. Today, it has its flourmills and is a centre for boating and tourism. It is still a busy market town of half-timbered buildings, overhanging upper storeys and carved doorways. Following

the recent floods the town has a new energy and purpose. Note the new Tourist Information Centre and Out of the Hat Museum which symbolises the ambitions of the Town's elders. (G2)

TEWKESBURY ABBEY

Founded in 1087 by the nobleman Robert Fitzhamon. However, the present building was started in 1102 to house Benedictine monks. The Norman abbey was consecrated in 1121. The Nave and roof finished in the C14 in the Decorated style. Much is Early English and Perpendicular, although it is larger than many cathedrals and has according to Pevsner 'the finest Romanesque Tower in England'. The Abbey opens its doors to three major music festivals: Musica Deo Sacra, the Three Choirs Festival and the Cheltenham Music Festival. You can park opposite and take a tour. Info on 01684 850959. Shop and refectory. Open daily 7.30am to 5pm. (G2) www.tewkesburyabbey.org.uk

Odda's Chapel, Deerhurst

Special Places of Interest...

Old Baptist Chapel. Reputed to be the first Baptist Chapel in southern England. Restored in 1976. Open daily 9-dusk. (G3)

John Moore Countryside Museum, 41 Church Street. Dedicated to children and all aspects of nature conservation, displayed in a C15 timber framed house. Open Apr to Oct Tu-Sa & BHs, 10-1 & 2-5. (G2) 01684 297174

Merchant's House, 45 Church Street. Restored medieval merchant's house. Open Apr to Oct Tu-Sa & BHs 10-1 & 2-5. (G2) 01684 297174

Tewkesbury Museum, Barton Street. Local folk history and heritage centre. Open Mar to Aug Tu-Fri 1-4.30, Sa 11-4, Sept to Oct Tu-Fri 12-3, Sa 11-3, Nov to Mar, Sa & for special events. (G2) 01684 292901 www.tewkesburymuseum.org

Where to Stay...

Corse Lawn Hotel. Elegant Queen Anne house run enthusiastically by the Hine family. Noted for fine cuisine. 19 attractive bedrooms. Bistro for informal meals. Pool. 01452 780771 www.corselawn.com

Brawn Farm, Sandhurst. Historic farmhouse set in a beautiful landscaped garden with far-reaching views. Three en-suite guest bedrooms. 01452 731010 www.brawnfarmbandb.co.uk

Deerhurst B&B. Deerhurst Priory is a solid working farm adjoining the ancient Saxon Priory Church of St Mary. Pets welcome. 01684 293358 www.deerhurstbandb.co.uk

Natural Places of Interest...

Coombe Hill Canal Nature Reserve. Two-mile stretch of canal closed in 1876. Habitat of birds, dragonflies, aquatic and bankside plants. Open all year. (F5)

Crickley Hill Country Park. Nature trails, geological and archaeological trails are signposted, as is the Cotswold Way. There are traces of Stone Age and Iron Age settlements. Fine views. Open daily. (J10)

Devil's Chimney. A 50 foot high limestone rock which according to local superstition 'rises from hell.' Its origins resulted from quarrying the surrounding stone. (K9)

Highham Woods Nature Reserve. 300 acres of broad-leafed woodland, with bluebells in spring. Nightingales call (if you are listening). Open daily. (A9) 01594 562852 www.rspb.org.uk

Leckhampton Hill. A popular dog walking area for Cheltonians providing superb views towards the Malvern Hills and Wales. The golden stone of 'Regency' Cheltenham was quarried here. Iron Age and Roman camps. (K9)

Special Places of Interest Beside the River Severn...

Ashleworth Court. C15 limestone manor with a notable stone newel staircase. Closed to the public. All is overlooked by the tithe barn, next door which can be visited. (D6) 01452 700241

Ashleworth Manor. C15 timber framed and E-shaped. Open by written appointment for parties of eight or more. (C6) 01452 700350

Ashleworth Tithe Barn (NT). This C15 barn has an impressive stone-tile roof and two projecting porch bays. The roof timbers are held together by Queenposts. Open daily, all year 9-6. (C6) 01452 814213 www.nationaltrust.org.uk

Deerhurst (St Mary). C9 Saxon church with superb font. (F4)

Deerhurst (Odda's Chapel). One of the few surviving Saxon chapels left in England. Earl Odda dedicated this rare chapel to the Holy Trinity on the 12th April 1056 in memory of his brother. Open daily. (F4)

Cheese Rolling, Cooper's Hill

CLEEVE HILL & COMMON

Cleeve Hill. At 1,083 feet this is the highest point in the Cotswolds and thus a superb viewpoint across to the Malvern Hills, Welsh Mountains, and northwards across the Cotswold landscape. A popular dog walking area and, in winter snow, ideal for tobaggan runs. In 1901 a tramway was built from Cheltenham to Cleeve Cloud but sadly closed in 1930. Cleeve Cloud is the site of an Iron Age hill fort and just below the scarp is The Ring, a site of religious/pagan rituals, 100 feet in diameter. Castle Rock is popular with novice rock climbers. (M5)

Cleeve Common. A vast expanse of common land where you are free to roam, with dog and friends. It is more like a piece of wild moorland with its extensive horizons, and you may be forgiven for believing you are in the midst of a National Park. There are wild flowers, the Gallops (for exercising race horses) and tracks that lead off in all directions. Park in the golf course, or in the lay-byes, on the B4632. (M5)

Devil's Chimney, Leckhampton Hill

Theatre, festivals, Elgar and Shakespeare, Bredon Hill, poets' laments, Cotswold jewels and the Blossom Trail.

The Northern Cotswolds incorporates Stratford-Upon-Avon, the birthplace of England's greatest poet, William Shakespeare, and site of many Shakespearian locations of interest. The area was also the birthplace of England's finest composer, Edward Elgar who hailed from Lower Broadheath on the outskirts of Worcester. Perhaps there was, and still is, something in the water!

This area also contains a pair of villages of note which are the jewels in the Cotswold crown: Chipping Campden and Broadway. Chipping Campden is an outstanding example of medieval architecture whilst behind the high walls and hedges of Broadway stand the very epitome of Cotswold domestic architecture

Just off the North Cotswold escarpment, the Evesham Vale, a verdant and productive fruit and vegetable farming area with many farm produce stores beside the road. And, in late May you can follow the annual Blossom Trail, a bonanza of colour and new growth.

Bredon Hill is in the centre of the region and is a very beautiful spot. So beautiful, that poets and writers have been moved to describe it in verse and prose. A E Houseman and John Moore wrote poems and novels about this area. The Gloucestershire composer Ralph Vaughan Williams' 'Lark Ascending' could have been inspired from a field atop this hill, for from the peak are stunning views across to the Cotswolds, the Malverns and the distant Welsh hills

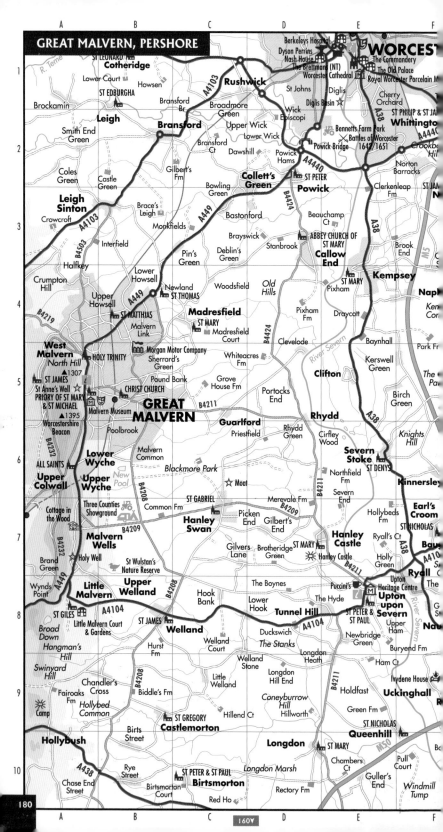

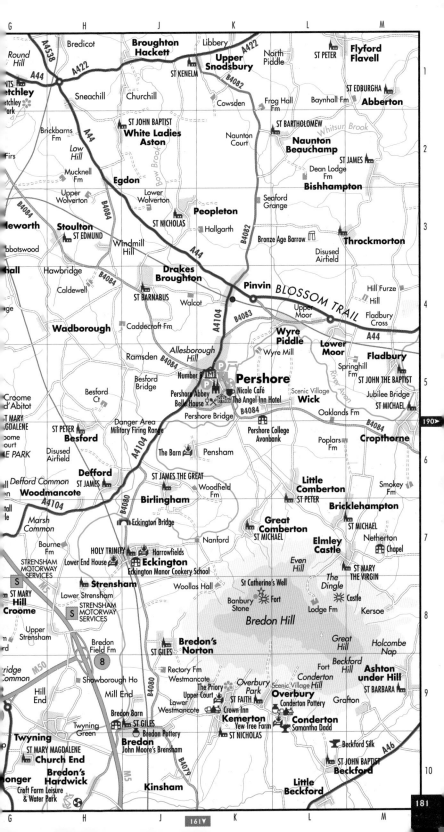

GREAT MALVERN

Pull the word Malvern out of a hat and what does its name conjure up? Edward Elgar, education, festivals, open-top sports cars, spring water, stained glass, walking holidays...quite a diverse spectrum of interests. There has been a settlement here since Iron Age man built forts at the British Camp on Herefordshire Beacon and on the southern tip at Midsummer Hill. Work began on the Priory in the C11 and continued well into the C16. But it was not until a Dr Wall promoted 'Taking The Waters' that Malvern developed as a spa town in 1756. The town's true popularity took shape when the Baths and Pump Room opened in the 1820s. It even attracted the desperate Charles Darwin to bring his beloved ten-year old daughter Annie here for a cure. She had developed scarlet fever and possibly tuberculosis. She died and was buried in the Priory's churchyard. Her death had a profound and lasting effect on Darwin's attitude and philosophy. Worth a quiet moment of reflection, in this bicentennial year of his birth. It remains a popular walking centre and once up on the hill there are fine views across to Wales, the Severn Vale and the Cotswolds. The healthy rigour of the town encouraged the Victorians to open schools for both sexes. Even George Bernard Shaw visited and help co-found the Theatre. The busy calendar of events is made up of various arts festivals: Elgar, Fringe, Music, Three Counties. The show goes on. Be prepared for some steep climbs - take comfy footwear. There are a number of coffee shops and delis on the main street below the Elgar statue. C15 Priory Church with famous medieval stained glass and tiles. (B5)

Special Places of Interest...

Croome Park (NT). 'Capability' Brown's first significant landscape project. A restoration plan has begun by dredging and replanting the Lake Garden. Open Mar, Sept & Oct W-Su, daily Apr to Aug, Xmas & Jan W/Es, 11-5. (G6) 01905 371006 www.nationaltrust.org.uk

St Anne's Chapel, Malern Priory

Little Malvern Court & Gardens. Former Benedictine monastery. Home of the Russell and Berington families since the Dissolution. Priors Hall with needlework, family and European furniture and paintings. 10 acre garden: spring bulbs, rose garden and views. Open mid-Apr to mid-July W & Th only 2.15-5. (A8) 01684 892988

Malvern Hills. A superb viewpoint. 6 paths and more criss-cross these hills. The highest point is Worcestershire Beacon at 1,394 feet. (A5)

Malvern Hill's Ancient Settlements. A natural location for Early Man, the Herefordshire Beacon is the site of the Iron Age, British Camp. At the southern end is the monument and fort, Midsummer Hill. Superb views. (A5)

Spetchley Park. 25 acres of rare and unusual trees, shrubs and plants. Red and fallow deer in park. Open mid-Mar to Sept W-Su & BH Ms 11-6, Oct W/Es 11-4. (G1) 01453 810303 www.spetchleygardens.co.uk

The Priory of St Mary & St Michael. The Abbot of Westminster Abbey decreed that work begin in 1085 on a church to cater for 30 monks. Extensions to this Norman church were added between 1440 and 1500. The Tower was built by the self-same masons at work on nearby

Gloucester Cathedral. There are two quite outstanding subjects to savour here. The first is the great East window that in its day was the largest piece of stained glass in England. The second is the collection of bells that some consider to be the Priory's finest possessions. These were built in Gloucester. The oldest built between 1350 and 1380 weighs some 8 cwt. The others were made in 1611, 1706 and 1707. Look at the Victorian glass in the North Aisle, modern glass in the Millennium window and another magnificent window in the North Transept given by Henry VII portraying scenes from Mary's life. A good deal of restoration was carried out by Sir Gilbert Scott in 1860. (A5)

Where To Stay...

Cottage in The Wood, Holywell Rd. Superb hillside location with panoramic views across the Severn Vale towards the Cotswold Hills. Walks from hotel onto the Malvern Hills. Child friendly. (A7) 01684 588860 www.cottageinthewood.co.uk

Ivydene House, Uckinghall. A special B&B for garden lovers, so before settling in to your sumptuous bedroom with all the luxuries to hand, you must take a stroll in their beautiful garden that has plenty of nooks and crannies, ideal for a quiet read. 01684 592453 www.ivydenehouse.net

1904   Baker's the Jewellers (Gloucester) shop front is built featuring Father Time and John Bull   1907   Major Laurence Johnstone begins the construction of Hidcote Manor Gardens

THE MORGAN MOTOR COMPANY

This is the Centenary Year of Celebration for this most British of car manufacturers. Founded by HFS Morgan in 1909 whose first vehicle was a Three-Wheeler converted from a 7 hp Peugeot. The company specialised in three-wheelers up to the First World War and managed to win the French Grand Prix at Amiens in 1913. During the First World War the factory built ammunition and machinery for the war effort. Thereafter in 1918 the company moved to its present factory at Madresfield, known as the "Works". The company has become synonymous with the halcyon days of British motoring. Producing hand-built, custom-made sports cars for the enthusiast.

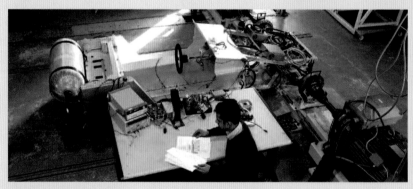

Plans are afoot to produce green,
high tech cars for the eco-aware
market, and the new stable of high
performance machines bears witness
to this ambition. You can take a
factory tour from the new Visitor
Centre in Spring Lane from late
Apr through to Dec. (B4)
Pre-book on 01684 800040
www.morgan-motor.co.uk

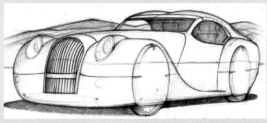

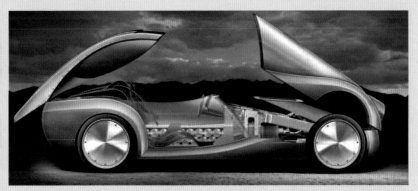

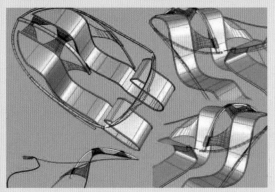

Pershore Abbey

Belle House Restaurant

Angel Inn Hotel

PERSHORE

A market town well known for its plums and elegant Georgian buildings. The Abbey was founded c.689 and established in the late C10 by the Benedictine monks who later built the six-arched bridge across the River Avon. (K5)

Special Places of Interest...

Number 8, High Street.
This is Pershore's new community centre for the arts, cinema and theatre. It holds live events and creative courses. Coffee shop. Open daily. (K5) Box office 01386 555488
www.number8.org

Pershore Abbey. Established in the late C10 by Benedictines. C14 tower and the superb vaulting of the Prestbytery remain. Beautiful Early English Choir, but sadly much was destroyed by Henry VIII. Visitor Centre summer weekends. Look out for the intricate wooden sculpture in the grounds. Open daily 9-5.30. (K5) 01386 552071
www.pershoreabbey.fsnet.co.uk

Eckington Manor Cookery School, Manor Road, Eckington. This cookery school with state of the art facilities and a team of passionate tutors uses fresh, locally sourced seasonal ingredients. (J7) 01386 751600
www.eckingtonmanorcookeryschool.co.uk

Where to Eat, Drink & Sleep...

Belle House Restaurant, Bar & Traiteur, Bridge Street.
There are a number of good reasons to visit Belle House: the exterior and interior architecture, the adjacent deli, the aroma of newly ground coffee and the mouth-watering restaurant run with enthusiasm. Ideal for morning coffee, lunch or dinner. (K5) 01386 555055
www.belle-house.co.uk

Nicole Café, 4 High Street.
Breakfast is served from 8.30am. All day sandwiches, baguettes, paninis and jacket potatoes. A friendly, little town café open daily. (K5) 01386 555005

The Angel Inn Hotel, High Street. Refurbished inn marries period detail with contemporary décor in a stylish format. Weekend breaks, coffee, lunch and dinner for two. (K5) 01386 552581
www.theangelinnpershore.co.uk

Outside Pershore...

Harrowfields, Cotheridge Lane, Eckington. This picturesque black-and-white timbered country cottage nestles peacefully in the Cotswold landscape. Fine attention to detail and guests' needs. 01386 751053
www.harrowfields.co.uk

Lower End House, Manor Road, Eckington. Believed to be one of the oldest houses in Worcestershire. A period house full of character that has been renovated with emphasis on quality and style. Perfectly located for walking on the nearby Bredon or Malvern Hills. 01386 751600
www.lowerendhouse.co.uk

The Barn B&B, Pensham. A large and spacious barn ideally suited for a large family or group. No dogs or children U-12. (J6) 01386 555270
www.pensham-barn.co.uk

Riverside Walk, Upton-Upon-Severn

UPTON-UPON-SEVERN

An attractive town beside the River Severn that has been an important river crossing and route centre for centuries, thus the profusion of medieval buildings and hostelries. The 2007 floods left a devastating mark on the town, so much so that many inns were closed for 12 months. The rush to generate cash has encouraged cheaper beer, binge drinking and unsavoury behaviour at night. Not the venue for a quiet pint or romantic evening. Better to visit during the day and enjoy the riverside walk and views, a visit to the international Map Shop to plan further adventures. For a coffee and some antipasta or pizza and a piece of Italy, try Puccini's at 20 Church Street, opposite the Heritage Centre. (E8)

Upton Heritage Centre.
History of the town, and the River Severn's activities. Civil War connections. Open daily East to Sept 1.30-4.30. (E8) 01684 592679

BREDON HILL & VILLAGES

A circumnavigation of Bredon Hill is a fine introduction to the beautiful villages of Kemerton, Overbury, Conderton, Ashton-under-Hill and Elmley Castle. A lovely mixture of Cotswold stone and black-and-white timbered buildings with many fine inns and peaceful churchyards. Various footpaths lead up to the summit from Elmley and Kemerton. Superb views from this isolated limestone hill at 961 ft. (K8)

Beckford Silk.
Hand printers of silk. Gallery of textiles. Tours of factory. Coffee shop 10-4. Open M-Sa 9-5.30. (L10) 01386 881507
www.beckfordsilk.co.uk

Bredon Barn (NT). A beautifully constructed large medieval threshing barn extending to 132 feet. Expertly restored after fire. Open mid-Mar to end Oct W Th & W/Es 10-6. (H9) 01451 844257
www.nationaltrust.org.uk

Bredon Hill Fort.
Iron Age fort with two ramparts. Scene of great battle at time of Christ, possibly against the Belgic invaders. The hacked remains of 50 men were found near entrance. Superb views over to Wales, Vale of Evesham, the rivers Severn and Avon, and to the Cotswolds. (K8)

Bredon Pottery, High Street.
Slipped decorative earthenware. Plant pots. Functional, ovenproof and dish-washer safe. Open daily Tu-Sa 10-6. (H10) 01684 773417
www.bredonpottery.co.uk

Conderton Pottery.
Distinctive stoneware pots by specialist saltglazed country potter, Toff Milway. Open M-Sa 9-5. (L9) 01386 725387.
www.toffmilway.co.uk

Croft Farm Leisure & Water Park, Bredons Hardwick.
Lake and river fishing, camping, windsurfing tuition, and supervised health centre. Open daily Mar to Dec. (H10) 01684 772321
www.croftfarmleisure.co.uk

Eckington Bridge

Eckington Bridge. Built between the C16 and C17s. A car park beside the river with map board detailing a circular walk. (H7)

Samantha Dadd. Artist in situ inspired by flowers and the local landscape. Holds art classes. Open Tu-F 10-6, W/Es by appointment. (L9) 01386 725679
www.samanthadadd.com

The Priory Garden.
Long herbaceous borders in colour groups. Stream and water garden. 4 acres. Redesigned walled garden. Unusual plants for sale. Open every Th July to Sept 2-6 and various Su (Teas). (K9) 01386 725258

Where to Eat, Drink & Be Merry...

Yew Tree Inn, Conderton.
One of the most popular local pubs around Bredon Hill. Conveniently situated for pre- or post-walk drinks. Basic pub grub. (L9)
01386 725364

Upper Court, Kemerton.
Self-catering within a very grand house. Minimum stay for 2 nights. 01386 725351 www.uppercourt.co.uk

1912   Death of Edward Wilson on Scott's ill-fated Antarctic expedition
1914   Birth of Laurie Lee
1919   Charles Paget Wade moves into Snowshill Manor
189

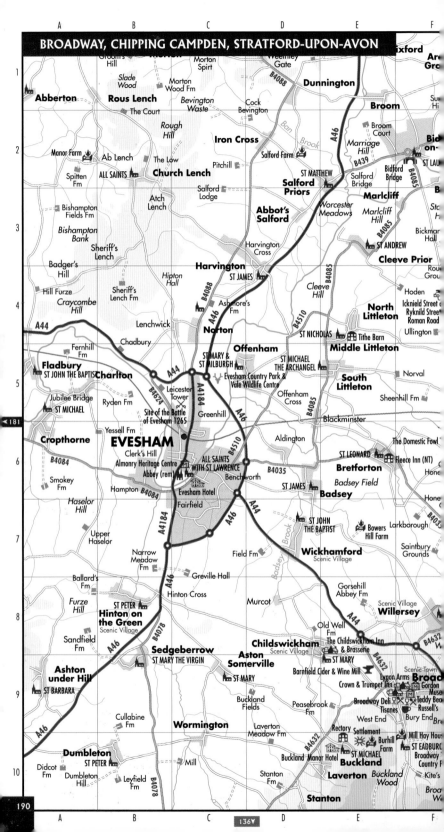

Groom's Hill
Slade Wood
Abberton
Rous Lench
The Court
Rough Hill
Morton Spirt
Morton Wood Fm
Bevington Waste
Cock Bevington
Weethley Gate
B4088
Dunnington
ixford
Are
Gro

Broom
Sur
Hi

Manor Farm
Spitten Fm
Ab Lench
ALL SAINTS
The Low
Church Lench
Iron Cross
Pitchill
Salford Farm
Salford Lodge
ST MATTHEW
Salford Priors
Abbot's Salford
Marriage Hill
B439
Salford Bridge
Broom Court
Bidford Bridge
Marlcliff
Bid
on-
ST LAU
B4085
B

Bishampton Fields Fm
Bishampton Bank
Atch Lench
Worcester Meadows
Marlcliff Hill
B4085
Sto
H

Badger's Hill
Sheriff's Lench
Hill Furze
Craycombe Hill
A44
Sheriff's Lench Fm
Hipton Hall
Harvington
ST JAMES
Harvington Cross
Cleeve Hill
ST ANDREW
B4085
Cleeve Prior
Hoden
Rou
Grou

Fernhill Fm
Fladbury
ST JOHN THE BAPTIST
Lenchwick
Chadbury
Norton
Ashmore's Fm
B4088
A46
Offenham
ST NICHOLAS
North Littleton
Tithe Barn
Middle Littleton
Icknield Street
Ryknild Street
Roman Road
Ullington

Jubilee Bridge
ST MICHAEL
Charlton
Ryden Fm
Leicester Tower
B4624
A44
A4184
ST MARY & ST MILBURGH
Evesham Country Park & Vale Wildlife Centre
Greenhill
A46
ST MICHAEL THE ARCHANGEL
Offenham Cross
B4085
South Littleton
Sheenhill Fm
Norval

Cropthorne
B4084
Yessell Fm
Clerk's Hill
Almonry Heritage Centre
Abbey (rem)
EVESHAM
Site of the Battle of Evesham 1265
ALL SAINTS WITH ST LAWRENCE
Benchworth
Blackminster
Aldington
B4510
B4035
ST JAMES
ST LEONARD
Bretforton
Badsey Field
Badsey
The Domestic Fowl
Fleece Inn (NT)
Hone
181

Smokey Fm
Haselor Hill
Hampton
B4084
A4184
Evesham Hotel
Fairfield
A46
A44
ST JOHN THE BAPTIST
Bowers Hill Farm
Larkborough
Saintbury Grounds
Hone
C
B403

Upper Haselor
Narrow Meadow Fm
Greville Hall
Field Fm
Wickhamford
Scenic Village
B4632

Ballard's Fm
Furze Hill
Sandfield Fm
ST PETER
Hinton on the Green
Scenic Village
A46
Hinton Cross
B4078
Murcot
Gorsehill Abbey Fm
Scenic Village
Willersey
B463

Ashton under Hill
ST BARBARA
A46
Sedgeberrow
ST MARY THE VIRGIN
Aston Somerville
Childswickham
Scenic Village
ST MARY
Barnfield Cider & Wine Mill
ST MARY
Old Well Fm
The Childswickham Inn & Brasserie
Crown & Trumpet Inn
Lygon Arms
Broadway Deli
Tisanes
West End
Scenic Town
Broad
Gordon
Muse
Teddy Bea
Russell's
Bury End
Br

Cullabine Fm
Wormington
Buckland Fields
Peasebrook Fm
Laverton Meadow Fm
Rectory
Settlement
Burhill Farm
Mill Hay Hou
ST EADBUR
Broadway
Country F
Kite's

Dumbleton
ST PETER
Didcot Fm
Dumbleton Hill
Leyfield Fm
B4078
Mill
Buckland Manor Hotel
Stanton Fm
ST MICHAEL
Buckland
Laverton
Stanton
Buckland Wood
B4632
A46

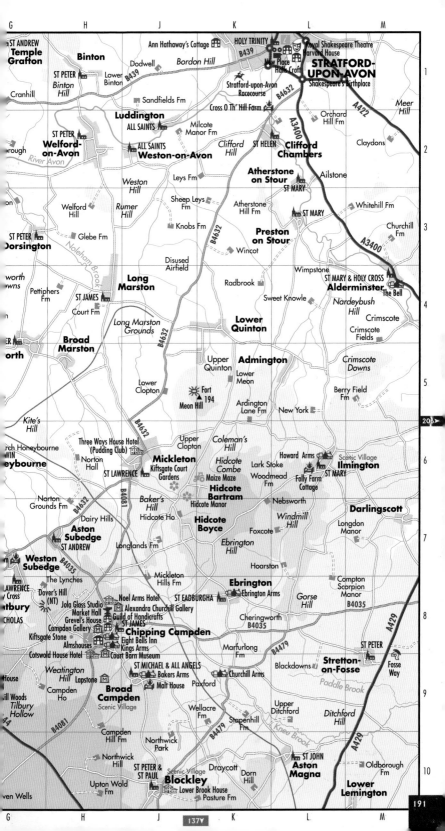

'The Painted Lady of the Cotswolds' is a term often used to describe this beautiful village. The honey-coloured stone captivates the visitor today as it did in the C19 when William Morris and his pre-Raphaelite friends settled here. A slow walk up the High Street will reveal some large and impressive houses that have been homes to Edward Elgar, JM Barrie (Peter Pan), Ralph Vaughan Williams, Sir Gerald Navarro MP and Laura Ashley. These great houses with bow windows, dormers and finely graduated stone roofs are usually hidden behind statuesque gates. There are a number of fine hotels, restaurants, tearooms, art galleries and a splendid bookshop. (F9)

Broadway Tower

Special Places of Interest...

Barnfield Cider & Wine Mill, Childswickham Road.
Famous cider and country wines. Museum. Open daily from 10, all year. (E9) 01386 853145
www.barnfieldcidermill.co.uk

Broadway Tower Country Park.
A unique Cotswold attraction: an C18 folly tower with historical and geographical exhibitions. Country retreat of the pre-Raphaelite, William Morris. Breeders of red deer with adventure playground, nature walks, barbecue and restaurant. Superb views from the top of the Tower - a clear day gives a view of 12 counties. Open Apr to Oct 10.30-5, Nov to Mar W/Es 11-3. (F10) 01386 852390
www.broadwaytower.co.uk

Buckland Church, St Michaels.
An exquisite church preserved with an almost undisturbed history from the C13 to the C17. Beautiful roof, painted and wood panelled. C14 tower with gargoyles. C15 stained glass in East window restored by William Morris. Not to be missed, the wainscotting: medieval wooden benches along the far wall as you enter, the Hazel Bowl made in 1607 of Dutch maple with a silver rim, the

Buckland Pall and C15 embroidered vestments from the V&A Museum, London. Sadly, the medieval frescoes were removed by the restorer FS Waller in 1885. (E10)

Buckland Rectory.
The oldest and most complete rectory in the county. Notable Great Hall with timbered roof. Open occasionally for village events. (E10)

Fish Hill Woods.
Attractive woodland providing superb views. (G9)

Gordon Russell Museum, 15 Russell Square.
A collection spanning 60 years that is dedicated to one of the C20's finest furniture designers. With original design drawings and furniture embracing the 'Arts & Crafts' movement. Open Tu-Su 11-4 and BH Ms. (F9) 01386 854695
www.gordonrussellmuseum.org

St Eadburgh's Church.
A rare architectural gem of almost perfect proportions with a mix of C12-C18 additions. Superb brass work, topiary in churchyard, interesting tombstones and a welcome retreat from the hustle and bustle of Broadway. (F10)

Where to Eat, Drink & Be Merry...

Crown & Trumpet Inn.
A necessary pit stop as you enter Broadway from the Cotswold Way. Music Sa evenings. Monthly jazz and blues nights. (F9) 01386 853202

Broadway deli, 16 High Street.
For those who are self-catering, treat yourself to a trip to this excellent deli with a passion for organic and ethically produced food. (F9) 01386 853040

St Eadburgh's Church

Buckland Manor Hotel ss

Russell's ss

Tisanes, 21 The Green.
A friendly tea room set in a C17 Cotswold stone building full of charm. Homemade cakes. (F9) 01386 853296

The Childswickham Inn and Brasserie, Broadway Road, Childswickham. Bar and restaurant that successfully combines the contemporary with the classic resulting in a pleasing venue for a drink or meal. Large secluded beer garden for those sunny afternoons. (D8) 01386 852461 www.childswickhaminn.co.uk

Where to Stay...

Barn House, High Street.
Fabulous gardens surround large barn conversion. Chintz and pine bedrooms. Indoor pool. (F9) 01386 854858

Buckland Manor Hotel. The benchmark for the Country House Hotel: quiet, understated luxury, and

so relaxing and soothing. Formal dress code for dinner - the exquisite cuisine deserves your respect. Open all year. (E10) 01386 852626 www.bucklandmanor.co.uk

Burhill Farm, Buckland.
Peaceful setting. Two en-suite bedrooms. 01386 858171 www.burhillfarm.co.uk

Dormy House Hotel, Willersey Hill. C17 farmhouse converted into a comfortable hotel with ample leisure facilities. Adjacent 18 hole golf course. Popular dining room and barn owl bar. (G9) 01386 852711 www.dormyhouse.co.uk

Luggers Hall, Springfield Lane.
Built by the Victorian Royal Academy artist Alfred Parsons, this listed building is set in two acres of landscaped gardens. Peaceful and tranquil setting, yet less than two minutes walk from Broadway Village centre. B&B. Also Dove cottage - self catering two bedroom period cottage on Upper High Street available for holiday lets. (F9) 01386 852040 www.luggershall.com

Lygon Arms. This former coaching inn of renown has been converted into a luxurious Spa and Country House Hotel. The centrepiece is the Great Hall with imposing barrel-vaulted ceiling, C17 Minstrels' Gallery and oak panels. Off the hall are cosy lounges with log fires and deep armchairs. (F9) 01386 852255 www.barcelo-hotels.co.uk/lygonarms

Mill Hay House. Imposing Queen Anne house provides luxurious B&B on the outskirts of Broadway. No children U-12. No dogs. (F9) 01386 852498 www.millhay.co.uk

Mount Pleasant Farm, Childswickham. 900 acre family farm in a quiet rural area with stunning views from all of the en-suite bedrooms. Traditional farmhouse English breakfast. B&B and holiday cottages. 01386 853424

Russell's, 20 High Street.
Gaining quite a reputation as a great place to eat in the North Cotswolds. So feast on their food, then settle into one of their contemporary, comfy bedrooms with all the latest mod cons. (F9) 01386 853555 www.russellsofbroadway.co.uk

Lygon Arms

1929 Campden Trust set up to protect Chipping Campden from development and destruction

1932 New Shakespeare Theatre opens designed by Elizabeth Scott

Bennetts
FINE WINES

www.bennettsfinewines.com
t. 01386 840392

INTERESTED
IN WINE?
DO YOU WANT
TO LEARN MORE?
JOIN THE
CELLAR CLUB
GREAT RANGE
OF BENEFITS.
BI-MONTHLY DELIVERIES
WITH TASTING NOTES,
FOOD & WINE MATCHING
ADVICE.
JOIN NOW!

Bennetts Fine Wines, High Street, Chipping Campden

William Grevel's House

If you choose to visit just one Cotswold village make sure it's this one. There is no better introduction. The harmony of Cotswold stone mirrors the town's prosperity in the Middle Ages. The Gabled Market Hall was built in 1627 by the wealthy landowner Sir Baptist Hicks whose mansion was burnt down in the Civil War, and the remains are the two lodges beside the Church. The Church of St James is a tall and statuesque 'Wool' church. William

Grevel, one of the wealthiest wool merchants, is remembered in the church on a brass transcription which reads: 'the flower of the wool merchants of all England'. Opposite his house (Grevel's House, now a Doctor's Surgery) on the High Street is the Woolstaplers Hall, the meeting place for the fleece (staple) merchants. Dovers Cotswold Olympick Games & Scuttlebrook Wake, June. (H8)

Campden Gallery

Special Places of Interest...

Alexandra Churchill Gallery, High Street. Artist in situ painting flowers, wildlife and hot-air balloon scenes. Open daily. (H8) 01386 841600
www.alexandrachurchill.co.uk

Almshouses. You will pass these on your left as you make your way toward the parish church. Built about the same time as the Market Hall (in 1627) by the town's wealthy benefactor, Sir Baptist Hicks. (H8)

Campden Gallery, High Street. One of the most respected of Cotswold galleries has constant changing exhibitions of paintings, sculpture and prints. Open daily. (H8) 01386 841555
www.campdengallery.co.uk

Court Barn Museum. A celebration of the town's association with the Arts & Crafts Movement. An exhibition of silver, jewellery, ceramics, sculpture, industrial design and more, all beautifully set up by the Guild of Handicraft Trust. Open Apr to Sept Tu-Sa 10.30-5.30, Su 11.30-5.30, Oct to Mar Tu-Sa 11-4, Su 11.30-4. (H8)
www.courtbarn.org.uk

Cotswold Way. A long distance footpath covering 97 miles from Chipping Campden to Bath. It follows the edge of the escarpment, meanders through picturesque villages, past prehistoric sites and provides spectacular views. It is signposted. For short excursions set out from Cleeve Hill, Winchcombe, Broadway, Painswick, Coaley Peak or Brackenbury Ditches. (H8)
www.cotswold-way.co.uk

Dover's Hill. A natural amphitheatre on a spur of the Cotswolds with magnificent views over the Vale of Evesham. The 'Olympick Games & Scuttlebrook Wake' have been held here since 1612, and take place the Friday and Saturday following the Spring Bank Holiday. (G8)

Grevel's House. Built by the wealthy wool merchant, William Grevel: 'The flower of the Wool Merchants of England'. The house has intricately decorated windows, gargoyles and a sundial. Today it is a doctor's surgery. (H8)

Guild of Handicraft and The Gallery @ The Guild - The Old Silk Mill. Founded in 1888 as part of the 'Arts & Crafts' movement. The Harts gold and silversmith workshops (open Tu-Su) remain in situ and the Gallery @ The Guild is a co-operative of artists and craftspeople, open daily, all year. Coffee shop. (H8) 01386 841100
www.hartsilversmiths.co.uk
07870 417144
www.thegalleryattheguild.co.uk

Hidcote Manor Farm Maize Maze. As the title suggests it's corn on the cob in 'Lost' mode. Open late July to Sept 10-6. (K6) 01386 430178
www.hidcotemaze.co.uk

Jola Glass Studio, High Street. Glass forms in all shapes, designs and colours. Open daily. (H8) 01386 841199 www.jolaglass.com

Kiftsgate Court Garden

HIDCOTE MANOR GARDEN (NT)

One of the finest gardens of the C20 designed by Major Lawrence Johnston in the Arts & Crafts style. It is made up of garden rooms with rare trees, shrubs, herbaceous borders and 'old' roses. The all-weather court has recently been restored. Barn café, plant sales and restaurant. Open mid-Mar to Oct M Tu W & W/Es, 10-6. (J6) For other (more complex) times phone 01386 438333 www.nationaltrust.org.uk

Parish Church of St James

Kiftsgate Court Garden. Rare shrubs, plants, and an exceptional collection of roses in a magnificent situation. Water Garden. Plants for sale. Open Days. Open Mar to Apr & Aug to Sept Su, M & W 2-6, May to July Sa-W 12-6. (J6) 01386 438777 www.kiftsgate.co.uk

Lapstone, Westington Hill. A different shopping experience for the design conscious. Shop, Café, hairdresser and beauty salon in a contemporary barn conversion set in the middle of a Cotswold field. (H9) 01386 841611. www.lapstone.net

Market Hall. This iconic image of Chipping Campden was funded by Sir Baptist Hicks (merchant banker) in 1627 for the cheese and butter markets. It is Jacobean with pointed gables. (H8)

Meon Hill. Iron-age hillfort. The locals keep well away from this spot for fear of the spookery of witchcraft. (J5)

Parish Church of St James. A fine old 'Wool' church, of Norman origin, restored in the C15, with a tall and elegant tower and large Perpendicular nave. 'Brilliant' in late summer afternoons. C15 cope, and a unique pair of C15 altar hangings. Brasses of woolstaplers. C15 falcon lectern. Open daily. (H8)

Where to Eat, Drink & Be Merry...

Bakers Arms, Broad Campden. Good old-fashioned, traditional Cotswold pub with no jarring modernities serving fine ales. (J9) 01386 840515

Churchill Arms, Paxford. Popular and busy local provides sophisticated fare. Local beers. One of the earliest examples of a gastro-pub. Child friendly. B&B. (K9) 01386 594000 www.thechurchillarms.com

Ebrington Arms, Ebrington. A C17 traditional inn full of charm and character and popular with both locals and visitors to the area. Luxurious en-suite bedrooms. Home cooked English breakfast. Closed M except BH Ms. (K8) 01386 593223 www.theebringtonarms.co.uk

Eight Bells Inn. Church Street. C14 inn full of rustic charm contrasts well with modern cuisine and bright bedrooms. Fresh fare. B&B. (H8) 01386 840371 www.eightbellsinn.co.uk

Market Hall

The birthplace of William Shakespeare, home to the Royal Shakespeare Company and one of the great tourist destinations in England. The town was established as a Romano-British settlement beside the river crossing on the busy Exeter to Lincoln route. In 1086 during the Domesday survey Stratford was a manor house belonging to Wulstan, Bishop of Worcester. In 1196 Richard I granted permission for a weekly market thereby establishing Stratford's early days as a market town. This instigated the annual Mop Fair on October 12 where local labourers sought employment. The tradesman's society, the Guild of the Holy Cross, was later formed to promote the crafts and local industries. During Shakespeare's time Stratford was home to 1,500 persons and was a bustling centre for the marketing of corn, malt and livestock, as well as being a centre for local government, and proud to foster one of the country's finest grammar schools. The town's buildings were predominantly Elizabethan and Jacobean. Today, there are C15 half-timbered buildings on Church Street, and C16 to C17 timber-framed houses in Chapel Street, the High Street and Wood Street plus a number of C18 period buildings of re-frontings with brick and stucco. Sheep Street has the best restaurants in town: Lambs, The Vintner (also teas and coffees) and The Opposition. Just around the corner, The Shakespeare Hotel where you can have morning coffee and afternoon teas in the hotel or next door at Othello's Bar Brasserie, or perhaps stay the night. Down by the Waterside is Carluccios, an ideal spot for coffee and sandwiches, and people watching. Most, or all, eating places cater for pre-Theatre suppers. (L1) Abbreviation in the following text: WS William Shakespeare

Shakespeare's Birthplace

Anne Hathaway's Cottage

PROPERTIES OF THE SHAKESPEARE BIRTHPLACE TRUST

The Shakespeare Birthplace Trust was established in 1847 and is probably the oldest conservation society in Britain. Its purpose is to promote the appreciation and study of William Shakespeare's plays and prose to an international audience and to protect and care for the buildings associated with the poet for future generations. 01789 204016 www.shakespeare.org.uk

Anne Hathaway's Cottage, Shottery. This is the picturesque home of Anne before her marriage to WS in 1582. A large 12-room farm house surrounded by a colourful and charming garden of perennial shrubs, box hedges and apple orchard. This cottage belonged to descendants of the Hathaway family until 1892. Open daily. (K1)

Hall's Croft, Old Town. A fine Tudor house beautifully furnished with a walled garden. It was the home of WS's daughter

Susanna and her husband Dr John Hall who in his day was considered an advanced medical practitioner. Open daily. (L1)

Mary Arden's House, Wilmcote. Mary Arden was WS's mother and she lived in this beautiful C16 farmhouse with Jacobean furniture and bygones from a former time. There is a farm museum exhibiting carts, carriages and a 650-hole dovecote. Open daily. (North of map)

New Place & Nash's House, Chapel Street. Sir Hugh Clopton built New Place in 1483. In 1597 it was bought by WS and was one of the finest and most prestigious houses in Stratford. WS retired here in 1610, and it was where he died on 23rd April 1616 whilst celebrating his 52nd birthday. In 1702 it was almost completely rebuilt was demolished by the Reverend Francis Gastrell in 1759 following a dispute with the corporation about his rates. The foundations of New Place remain in the garden adjoining Nash's House, formerly the home of

Thomas Nash, husband of Elizabeth Hall, who was WS's granddaughter. It remains half-timbered with an ancient interior and is a museum of local history. The Great Garden of New Place has the original orchard and kitchen garden with a mulberry tree raised from a cutting of WS's tree. Adjoining, the Knot Garden, a replica of an enclosed Elizabethan garden with old English flowers and herbs. Open daily. (L1)

Shakespeare's Birthplace, Henley Street. WS was born here on 23rd April, 1564. The house was originally divided into two buildings and used as a home and a workshop for his father, a wool-dealer and glove maker. It is half-timbered with strong oak framing, leaded windows and wide sills. The building was restored in the C18 by the actor and manager David Garrick. There is a comprehensive collection of Shakespeariana and the garden displays flowers named in his plays and poems: daisies, violets, pansies, lady smocks and mary buds. Open daily. (L1)

Harvard House & Pewter Museum, High Street. Harvard House was built in 1596 by a wealthy townsman, Alderman Thomas Rogers, who had twice served as High Bailiff. His initials are carved on the front of the house (with a bull's head to denote his trade as a butcher) together with those of his wife Alice and his eldest son, William, and the date 1596. The elaborately carved facade, by far the richest example in the town, is testimony to Rogers's wealth and standing. From the mid C17, there was a succession of owners until the Shakespeare Birthplace Trust assumed responsibility for the building and, in 1996, it became the Museum of British Pewter. (L1)

Mary Arden's House

1953 Chipping Campden's Almshouses restored
1959 Laurie Lee's novel Cider With Rosie is published
1960 The Shakespeare Theatre is renamed the Royal Shakespeare Theatre
203

WILLIAM SHAKESPEARE

Statue of William Shakespeare, Holy Trinity Church

"The Swan of Avon", as Ben Jonson described his friend, was born in Henley Street on 23rd April, 1564. His father, John Shakespeare was the son of a yeoman farmer from nearby Snitterfield who traded as a glover and wool-dealer and who later was to become the town's mayor. His mother, Mary Arden, married John Shakespeare in 1557 and was the daughter of a prosperous gentleman farmer from an old Warwickshire family. Although we know little of William's early life we know that he attended the local Grammar School where he took a close interest in the touring actors who performed in the Guildhall below the Grammar School. In 1582 he married Ann Hathaway, a farmer's daughter from Shottery and six years older than him. Shottery is still today linked to Stratford by a footpath that the courting William must have trod. One wonders at the success of their marriage for he soon fled to London in 1587 after having been caught poaching Sir Thomas Lucy's deer in Charlecote Park. The more likely reason was to pursue his ambitions in the theatre. In London he joined the Leicester Players and later the King's Company which was patronised by the Elizabethan court and men of the Inns of Court. Despite his success in London he retained a close association with Stratford. In 1597 he bought New Place, the finest house in Stratford and took up permanent residence in 1611. He died in 1616 on his 52nd birthday following a merry meeting with his fellow poets Ben Jonson and Michael Drayton. He is buried in Holy Trinity Church beside members of his family. The statue which overlooks his grave was placed there seven years after his death.

Gower Memorial

Special Places to Visit...

Brass Rubbing Centre, Avon Bank Gardens. Learn how to make brass rubbings using some of the best national and local brasses. All materials and instruction included in the price. Open daily summer 10-6, winter 11-4. (L1) 01789 297671 www.stratfordbrassrubbing.co.uk

Butterfly Farm & Jungle Safari, Tramway Walk. Europe's largest butterfly farm where you can wander through a jungle of exotic plants, fish filled pools, and waterfalls amid hundreds of tropical butterflies. (L1) 01789 299288

Clopton Bridge. Built in late C15 by Sir Hugh Clopton who became the Lord Mayor of London, and who died circa 1496. (L1)

Falstaff's Experience, 40 Sheep Street. A waxworks museum recreates Stratford's darkest hours. Ghost tours from 6pm. Open daily 10.30-5.30. 0870 3502770 (L1) www.falstaffsexperience.co.uk

Gower Memorial (Shakespeare Statue). This was presented to the town in 1888 by Lord Gower. The statue is made up of figures depicting Hamlet, Lady Macbeth, Falstaff and Prince Hal which in turn symbolizes philosophy, tragedy, comedy and history. (L1)

Guild Buildings. Guild Chapel, Guildhall, Grammar School and Almshouses, Chapel Street. (L1)

Holy Trinity Church, Southern Lane. The burial place of WS, and his family, and a magnificent building too. Note the Clopton Chapel, C15 vestry screen, C15 misericords, C15 font, The Bible c. 1611, the stained glass windows and the Chapel of Thomas a Becket. Open daily. (L1) 01789 290128 www.shakespeareschurch.org

Mason's Court, Rother Street. A beautifully preserved C15 domestic building of red brick and timber-framing. Views of exterior only. (L1)

Mason Croft, Church Street. C18 property of the Shakespeare Institute of Birmingham University. The home, until 1921, of Marie Corelli, the Victorian novelist. Open for academic studies. (L1) 0121 4149500

Open Top Bus tours. Travel to 14 stops including all the Shakespeare landmarks. Tickets are valid for 24 hours and passengers can hop on and off. Main departure point outside the TIC. (L1) 01789 294 466

River Cruises, Waterside. A number of companies operate cruises. Contact TIC for details on 0870 1607930. (L1)

Royal Shakespeare Theatre, Waterside. The home of the Royal Shakespeare Company was built in 1932 to Elizabeth Smith's design, following the fire of 1926. Closed until 2010 for rebuilding. Until then, performances take place at the Courtyard Theatre in Southern Lane. (L1) 01789 403 444 for information and bookings.

Shakespearience, The Waterside. A hi-tech show full of special effects and the latest developments in show technology takes you through the life and legacy of WS. Open daily (except Christmas). Shows on the hour from 10. (L1) 01789 290111 www.shakespearience.co.uk

Town Hall, Sheep Street. Originally built in the reign of Charles I, and throughout its chequered history has seen calamitous events including being extensively damaged from a gunpowder explosion in 1643. Currently available for hire. (L1)

Where to Stay...

Cross O' Th' Hill Farm, Clifford Road. Just a short walk from the centre of Stratford and a thousand miles from the plethora of tourists is this C19 farmhouse. The comfy beds, enormous pillows, top-notch bathrooms, contemporary art, communal breakfasts and local knowledge make for a real treat. (K1) 01789 204738 www.cross-o-th-hill-farm.com

Three Ways House Hotel, Mickleton. Home of the Pudding Club since 1985. Walking tours arranged (to burn off the calories!). Special themed 'Pudding Club' bedrooms. (J6) 01386 438429 www.puddingclub.com

Cross O' Th' Hill Farm ss

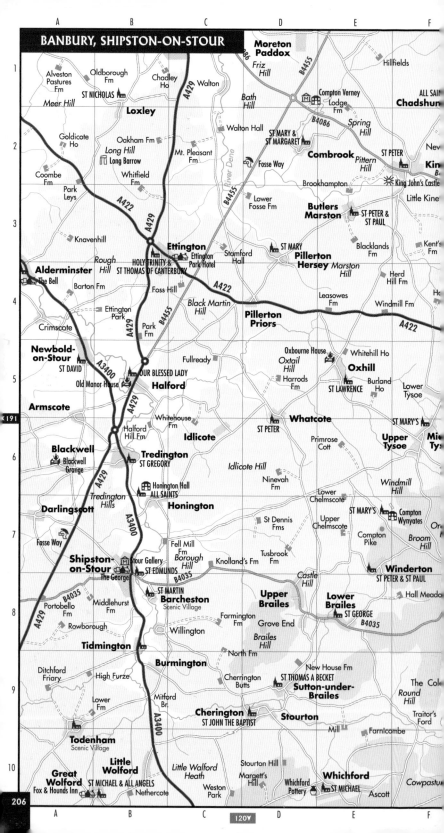

A   B   C   D   E   F

1

Alveston Pastures Fm
Oldborough Fm
ST NICHOLAS
Chadley Ho
Walton
Moreton Paddox
Friz Hill
Hillfields
Meer Hill
Loxley
Bath Hill
Compton Verney Lodge Fm
ALL SAIN
Chadshun

2

Goldicote Ho
Oakham Fm
Long Hill
Long Barrow
Mt. Pleasant Fm
Walton Hall
ST MARY & ST MARGARET
Spring Hill
ST PETER
Nev
Combrook
Pittern Hill
Kin
King John's Castle
Coombe Fm
Park Leys
Whitfield Fm
Brookhampton
Little Kine

3

Knavenhill
A422
A429
River Dene
Fosse Way
Lower Fosse Fm
Butlers Marston
ST PETER & ST PAUL
Blacklands Fm
Herd Hill Fm
Kent's Fm

Alderminster
The Bell
Rough Hill
HOLY TRINITY & ST THOMAS OF CANTERBURY
Ettington
Ettington Park Hotel
Stamford Hall
ST MARY
Pillerton Hersey
Marston Hill

4

Barton Fm
Foss Hill
Black Martin Hill
Leasowes Fm
Windmill Fm
Ho
Ettington Park
Pillerton Priors
A422
Crimscote
Park Fm

5

Newbold-on-Stour
ST DAVID
Old Manor House
OUR BLESSED LADY
Fullready
Oxbourne House
Oxtail Hill
Whitehill Ho
Oxhill
ST LAWRENCE
Burland Ho
Lower Tysoe
Halford
Harrods Fm

Armscote
Whitehouse Fm
Idlicote
ST PETER
Whatcote
ST MARY'S
Primrose Cott
Upper Tysoe
Mid Ty

6

Blackwell
Blackwell Grange
Halford Hill Fm
Tredington
ST GREGORY
Idlicote Hill
Ninevah Fm
Windmill Hill

Darlingscott
Tredington Hills
Honington Hall
ALL SAINTS
Honington
Lower Chelmscote
ST MARY'S
Compton Wynyates
Or

7

Fosse Way
Upper Chelmscote
Compton Pike
Broom Hill
St Dennis Fms
Shipston-on-Stour
Stour Gallery
ST EDMUNDS
The George
Fell Mill Fm
Borough Hill
Knolland's Fm
Tusbrook Fm
Castle Hill
Winderton
ST PETER & ST PAUL

8

ST MARTIN
Barcheston
Scenic Village
Upper Brailes
Lower Brailes
ST GEORGE
Hall Meado
Portobello Fm
Middlehurst Fm
Farmington Fm
Grove End
B4035
B4035
A429
Rowborough
Willington
Braile s Hill

Tidmington

9

Ditchford Friary
High Furze
Burmington
North Fm
New House Fm
The Cole
Round Hill
Lower Fm
Mitford Br.
Cherrington Butts
ST THOMAS A BECKET
Sutton-under-Brailes
Traitor's Ford
Cherington
ST JOHN THE BAPTIST
Stourton
Mill
Farnicombe

10

Todenham
Scenic Village
Little Wolford
Little Walford Heath
Stourton Hill
Margett's Hill
Whichford
Cowpastur
Great Wolford
ST MICHAEL & ALL ANGELS
Nethercote
Weston Park
Whichford Pottery
ST MICHAEL
Ascott
Fox & Hounds Inn

◄191

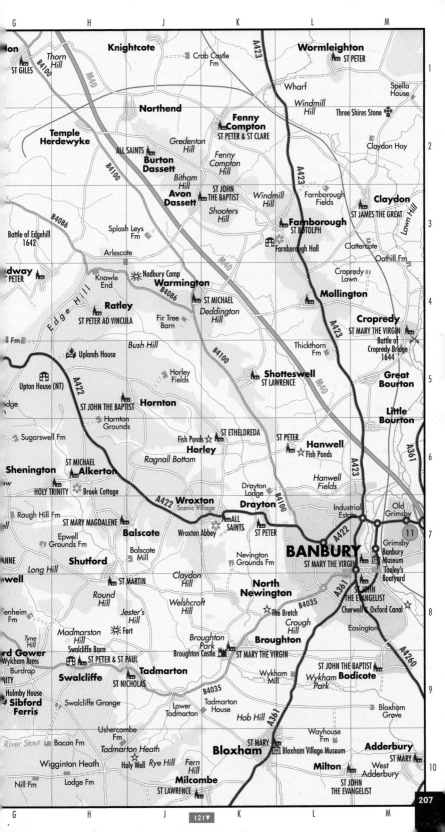

Grid references (top): G H J K L M
Grid references (side): 1 2 3 4 5 6 7 8 9 10

- Thorn Hill
- ST GILES
- Knightcote
- Crab Castle Fm
- A423
- M40
- Wormleighton
- ST PETER
- Wharf
- Spella House
- Northend
- Windmill Hill
- Three Shires Stone
- B4100
- Temple Herdewyke
- Fenny Compton
- ST PETER & ST CLARE
- Claydon Hay
- ALL SAINTS
- Burton Dassett
- Gredenton Hill
- Fenny Compton Hill
- Claydon
- ST JAMES THE GREAT
- Lawn Hill
- Bitham Hill
- B4100
- Avon Dassett
- ST JOHN THE BAPTIST
- Windmill Hill
- Farnborough Fields
- A423
- Shooters Hill
- Farnborough
- ST BOTOLPH
- Clattercote
- B4086
- Battle of Edgehill 1642
- Farnborough Hall
- Oathill Fm
- dway
- PETER
- Knowle End
- Nadbury Camp
- Warmington
- B4086
- Cropredy Lawn
- Mollington
- Edge Hill
- Ratley
- ST PETER AD VINCULA
- Fir Tree Barn
- ST MICHAEL
- Deddington Hill
- Cropredy
- ST MARY THE VIRGIN
- Battle of Cropredy Bridge 1644
- ll Fm
- Uplands House
- Bush Hill
- B4100
- Thickthorn Fm
- A423
- Upton House (NT)
- A422
- Horley Fields
- Shotteswell
- ST LAWRENCE
- M40
- Great Bourton
- dge
- ST JOHN THE BAPTIST
- Hornton
- Hornton Grounds
- A361
- Sugarswell Fm
- Fish Ponds
- ST ETHELDREDA
- ST PETER
- Hanwell
- Fish Ponds
- Little Bourton
- Shenington
- ST MICHAEL
- Alkerton
- Horley
- Ragnall Bottom
- Hanwell Fields
- ow
- HOLY TRINITY
- Brook Cottage
- Drayton Lodge
- Rough Hill Fm
- ST MARY MAGDALENE
- Wroxton
- Scenic Village
- Drayton
- B4100
- Industrial Estate
- Old Grimsby
- ANNE
- Epwell Grounds Fm
- Balscote
- ALL SAINTS
- Wroxton Abbey
- ST PETER
- 11
- ell
- Shutford
- Balscote Mill
- Nevington Grounds Fm
- BANBURY
- ST MARY THE VIRGIN
- Grimsby
- Banbury Museum
- Tooley's Boatyard
- Long Hill
- ST MARTIN
- Claydon Hill
- North Newington
- A422
- A361
- well
- Round Hill
- Welshcroft Hill
- B4035
- ST JOHN THE EVANGELIST
- enheim Fm
- Jester's Hill
- Fort
- Crough Hill
- Cherwell & Oxford Canal
- Easington
- Tyne Hill
- Madmarston Hill
- Broughton Park
- Broughton
- rd Gower
- Swalcliffe Barn
- Broughton Castle
- ST MARY THE VIRGIN
- Wykham Mill
- A4260
- Wykham Arms
- ST PETER & ST PAUL
- Tadmarton
- ST JOHN THE BAPTIST
- Bodicote
- Burdrop
- NITY
- Swalcliffe
- ST NICHOLAS
- Wykham Park
- Holmby House
- Sibford Ferris
- Swalcliffe Grange
- Lower Tadmarton
- Tadmarton House
- Hob Hill
- A361
- Bloxham Grove
- River Stour
- Bacon Fm
- Ushercombe Fm
- Wayhouse Fm
- Adderbury
- ST MARY
- Wigginton Heath
- Tadmarton Heath
- Holy Well
- Rye Hill
- Fern Hill
- Bloxham
- ST MARY
- Bloxham Village Museum
- Milton
- West Adderbury
- Nill Fm
- Lodge Fm
- Milcombe
- ST LAWRENCE
- ST JOHN THE EVANGELIST

The Fyne Lady's Statue, Banbury Cross

Oxford Canal

BANBURY

A prosperous commercial and retail centre situated on the northern edge of the Cotswold escarpment. The extension of the M40 in 1991 has provided access to Birmingham, London and Oxford and thus given Banbury infinite opportunities. Since 2005 a massive influx of Polish immigrants has boosted the local economy and the congregation in the Catholic churches. Kraft Foods has the largest coffee processing plant in the world here. Famous for Banbury Cakes (similar to Eccles cakes), and the celebrated 'Banbury Cross'. Man has lived here since an Iron Age settlement of 200 BC, a Roman villa at Wykeham Park around 250 AD and a Saxon stronghold in the C5. The Danes developed trade routes and the Salt Way came through Banbury. A focus of Civil War hostilities in the C17 - the first battle

took place at Edgehill in 1642. Shortly after Banbury became a centre of Puritanism. From about 1700-1800 cloth-making took a hold on the local economy producing shag, then plush. With the expansion of the Oxford Canal in 1790 Banbury again prospered. The Cattle Market was once the largest in Europe but sadly closed in 1998. You can follow a Town Trail around all the historic buildings. (M10)

Ride a cock horse to
Banbury Cross,

To see a Fyne lady ride on
a white horse.

With rings on her fingers and
bells on her toes,

She shall have music wherever
she goes.

Special Places to Visit...

Banbury Museum. The new canal side location features interactive art and historic exhibitions with some fabulous displays of clothes, bicycles, a timeline of events and changing exhibitions. Café Quay. Open daily 9.30-5, Su and BHs 10.30-4.30. (M7) 01295 259855

Oxford Canal. Built by James Brindley in 1769 to connect the industrial Midlands with London via the River Thames. Financial

problems delayed the construction but it was eventually to reach Oxford in 1789. Today it runs for 77 miles from Hawkesbury Junction, south of Coventry to Oxford. You can enjoy a multitude of leisure activities from solitary walks to boating, canoeing, cycling, fishing and the wildlife. (M7) www.waterscape.com

Tooley's Boatyard & Tours, Spiceball Park Road. This is the oldest working dry dock boatyard on the inland waterways of Britain. Established in 1790 to build and repair the wooden horse-drawn narrow boats. 200-year old forge, chandlery and gift shop. Self drive hire and private boat trips. (M7) 01295 272917 www.tooleysboatyard.co.uk

Where to Eat, Drink & Sleep...

S H Jones Wine Merchants, 27 High Street. Enjoy a coffee or snack in one of Banbury's oldest buildings, or sample a soupçon of fine wine. Open daily. (M7) 01295 251179 www.shjoneswines.com

Ye Olde Reindeer Inn, behind Parson Street. Visit this inn for its Civil War associations and superb C17 panelling, and gate. (M7) 01295 264031 www.yeoldereindeer.co.uk

Whately Hall Hotel, Horse Fair. A pragmatic destination for morning coffee, business meetings and lunch. The building is impressive from the exterior, and once inside look to the superb Jacobean staircase. It is an old fashioned hostelry with a long history of ghosts, regal visits and town functions. Sadly, let down by the modern additions. (M7) 01295 253261 www.mercure.com

Market Square

1968   Kelmscott Manor restored
1969   Death of the Rolling Stone, Brian Jones born in Cheltenham in 1942

1970   The Cotswold Way designated a long distance footpath
1970   Joe Henson opens the Cotswold Farm Park, HQ of the Rare Breeds Survival Trust

SHIPSTON-ON-STOUR

A working town with some attractive Georgian inns and houses amidst some rich pastoral farmland. In the C16, a prosperous weaving centre holding one of the great sheep markets. (B7)

Special Places to Visit...

Stour Gallery, 10 High Street.
A popular and long running gallery displaying contemporary paintings, studios ceramics and sculpture, all set on three floors. Open M-Sa 10-5.30 (B7) 01608 664411
www.thestourgallery.co.uk

Where to Eat, Drink & Be Merry...

The George, High Street.
A handsome building given a contemporary makeover. Downstairs has a pleasing ambience. Upstairs, the 16 bedrooms have been designed with a food theme: chocolate, strawberry, meringue, fig, lobster. You can chose a savoury, a fruit or a dessert. Chocolate is apparently the most digestible. (B7) 01608 661453
www.georgehotelshipston.com

The Horseshoe Inn, 6 Church Street. This is where the locals go for a pint and some conversation. It is pretty basic. Curry nights and unpretentious pub grub for those seeking the simple life.
(B7) 01608 661225
www.horseshoe-shipston.com

Special Places of Interest...

Adderbury Church.
Early C13 cruciform. C14 West tower with massive carvings. Superb chancel and vestry. (M10)

Bloxham Church. C14 spire. Carvings. C15 wall paintings. East window by William Morris and Edward Burne-Jones. (K10)

Batttle of Edgehill site. The battle of Edgehill on Sunday 23rd October, 1642 was the first major battle of the English Civil War. It was fought in the open fields around the villages of Radway and Kineton in Warwickshire between the army of the Earl of Essex, the parliamentarian Lord General, and the King's army. The outcome was deemed indecisive. (G3)

Brook Cottage. Four acre hillside garden surrounding C17 house (closed). Over 200 shrubs, colour co-ordinated borders, climbing roses, clematis, alpine and water gardens. Plant stall/teas. Open East M-Oct M-F 9-6. (H6) 01295 670303
www.brookcottagegarden.co.uk

Compton Verney.
Art Gallery in C18 Robert Adam mansion set in parkland by 'Capability' Brown. Naples School, British portraits, folk art. Open mid-Mar to mid-Dec Tu-Su & BHs 11-5. (D1) 01926 645500
www.comptonverney.org.uk

Compton Wynyates. A Tudor dream house built in 1460 with multi-coloured bricks: pale rose, crimson, blood red, shades of orange and bluish brown. Twisted chimneys. Panelled rooms. Plaster ceilings. Perhaps the most romantic of all England's country houses. Sadly, no longer open. May be glimpsed through the trees from the nearby road. (F7)

Farnborough Hall (NT).
A beautiful honey-coloured stone house sits in parkland crated in the 1740s. Noted for the exquisite C18 plasterwork. Parkland walks and lake views. Open Apr to Sept, W & Sa 2-5.30. (L3) 01295 690002
www.nationaltrust.org.uk

Honington Hall. Small house c.1680 with fine plasterwork. Open W in June, July & Aug (also BH Ms) 2.30-5, and by appointment. (B6) 01608 661434

Portrait of Mrs Baldwin by Joshua Reynolds, Compton Verney ss

Moated medieval manor house, substantially enlarged in the C16. Magnificent plaster ceilings, fine panelling and fireplaces. Interesting Civil War connections. In the family of the Lords Saye and Sele for over 600 years. Multi-coloured borders. The location for much of the film Shakespeare in Love. Open East & BHs, then W & Su May to mid-Sept, also Th in July & Aug 2-5. (K9) 01295 262624 www.broughtoncastle.com

Swalcliffe Barn. Early C15 tithe barn with fascinating displays of Oxfordshire's agricultural and trade vehicles. Exhibition of 2,500 years of the area. Open East Su to Oct Su & BH Ms 2-5. (H9) 01295 788278

Upton House & Gardens (NT). This house exhibits the lifestyle of a 1930s millionaire. It also has an outstanding display of English and Continental Old Masters paintings plus a wealth of herbaceous borders, terraces and tranquil water gardens. Open most days. See website for details. (G5) 01295 670266 www.nationaltrust.org.uk

Whichford Pottery. Hand-made English terracotta flowerpots of immense size. Thirty craftsmen and women. Shop. Open daily. (E10) 01608 684416 www.whichfordpottery.com

Where to Eat, Drink & Be Merry...

The Bell, Alderminster. Former C18 coaching inn now run by the Alscot Estate. It is spacious, comfortable, and serves good, solid food. Perhaps more restaurant, than inn. (A4) 01789 450414 www.thebellald.co.uk

Wykham Arms, Sibford Gower. Thatched inn set in pretty North Oxford village. The proprietors, Damian and Debbie, are chefs so expect pub food of the highest order. Open for coffee and pastries, lunch and dinner. Sundays are special. (G9) 01295 788808 www.wykhamarms.co.uk

Where to Stay...

Blackwell Grange. C17 Working farm with charming cottage garden. Beams, inglenook fireplaces and flagstones conjure up a relaxing hideaway. Suppers (of local produce). Stabling for horses. Two self-catering cottages. 01608 682357 www.blackwellgrange.co.uk

Ettington Park Hotel. Flamboyant Victorian Gothic hotel with rococo plasterwork and many leisure activities. Open all year. (C3) 01789 450123 www.ettingtonpark.co.uk

Holmby House, Sibford Ferris. An elegant wisteria-clad Victorian house set in fragrant gardens complete with heated outdoor pool and tennis and croquet equipment for the restless. The en-suite bedrooms are spacious and light. Dinner available if pre-booked. 01295 780104 www.holmbyhouse.com

Old Manor House, Halford. English country house style B&B at its finest. From lounging black

| 1996 | Bath's city council abolished | 2000 | Gloucester Cathedral becomes a film location for Harry Potter and the Sorcerer's Stone |
| 1996 | The Cotswolds are designated an 'Area of Outstanding Natural Beauty' | | |

Swalcliffe Barn

Labradors to chintz, marmalade and family antiques. Anyone for tennis? (B5) 01789 740264
www.oldmanor-halford.co.uk

Oxbourne House, Oxhill.
Only 15 minutes from Stratford, set on the edge of the village of Oxhill, Oxbourne House is a tranquil oasis. Choose from the comfortable en-suite bedrooms or the self-contained Annexe with bedroom, sitting/dining room, kitchen and shower room. 01295 688202
www.oxbournehouse.com

Uplands House, Upton.
The owners of this Country House B&B are former Olympic fencers with interesting stories aplenty, as well as detailed, rapier-like knowledge to help you plan your break. A comfortable and welcoming home-from-home. 01295 678663
www.cotswolds-uplands.co.uk

Upton House

Banbury
Spiceball Park Road
OX16 2PQ
banbury.tic@cherwell-dc.gov.uk
01295 259855

Bath
Abbey Chambers
Abbey Church Yard
BA1 1LY
tourism@bathtourism.co.uk
0906 711 2000

Bourton-On-The-Water
Victoria Street
GL54 2BU
bourtonvic@btconnect.com
01451 820 211

Bradford-On-Avon
The Greenhouse
50 St. Margaret's Street
BA15 1DE
tic@bradfordonavon.co.uk
01225 865797

Broadway
Unit 14 Russell Square
High Street
WR12 7AP
01386 852 937

Burford
The Brewery
Sheep Street
OX18 4LP
burford.vic@westoxon.gov.uk
01993 823 558

Cheltenham
Municipal Offices
77 Promenade
GL50 1PJ
info@cheltenham.gov.uk
01242 522 878

Chippenham
Yelde Hall
Market Place
SN15 3HL
tourism@chippenham.gov.uk
01249 665 970

Chipping Campden
The Old Police Station
High Street
GL55 6HB
visitchippingcampden@lineone.net
01386 841 206

Cirencester
Corinium Museum
Park Street
GL7 2BX
cirencestervic@cotswold.gov.uk
01285 655 611

Corsham
Arnold House
31 High Street
SN13 0EZ
enquiries@corshamheritage.org.uk
01249 714 660

Evesham
The Almonry
Abbey Gate
WR11 4BG
tic@almonry.ndo.co.uk
01386 446 944

Gloucester
28 Southgate Street
GL1 2DP
tourism@gloucester.gov.uk
01452 396 572

Malvern
21 Church Street
WR14 2AA
malvern.tic@malvernhills.gov.uk
01684 892 289

Moreton-In-Marsh
Moreton Area Centre
High Street
GL56 0AZ
moreton@cotswold.gov.uk
01608 650 881

Nailsworth
The Old George
George Street
GL6 0AQ
01453 839222

Painswick
The Library
Stroud Road
GL6 6UT
01452 813552

Pershore
Town Hall
34 High Street
WR10 1DS
tourism@pershore-tc.gov.uk
01386 556 591

Stratford-Upon-Avon
Bridgefoot
CV37 6GW
stratfordtic@shakespeare-country.co.uk
0870 1607930

Stroud
Subscription Rooms
George Street
GL5 1AE
tic@stroud.gov.uk
01453 760 960

Tetbury
Shop 1
33 Church Street
GL8 8JG
tourism@tetbury.org
01666 503 552
Seasonal opening

Tewkesbury
Out of the Hat Tewkesbury Heritage
and Visitor Centre.
100 Church Street
GL20 5AB
tewkesburytic@tewkesbury.gov.uk
01684 855 040

Upton-Upon-Severn
4 High Street
WR8 0HB
upton.tic@malvernhills.gov.uk
01684 594200

Winchcombe
Town Hall
High Street
GL54 5LJ
winchcombetic@tewkesbury.gov.uk
01242 602 925
Seasonal opening

Witney
26a Market Square
OX28 6BB
witney.vic@westoxon.gov.uk
01993 775802

Woodstock
Oxfordshire Museum
Park Street
OX20 1SN
woodstock.vic@westoxon.gov.uk
01993 813 276

Worcester
The Guildhall
High Street
WR1 2EY
touristinfo@cityofworcester.gov.uk
01905 726 311

Wotton-Under-Edge
The Heritage Centre
The Chipping
GL12 7AD
01453 521541

For specific dates please contact the local Tourist Information Centre

January
Gloucester Cajun & Zydeco Festival
Royal Shakespeare season ends

February
Snowdrops at Colesbourne Park
Snowdrops at Rococo Gardens, Painswick

March
Cheltenham National Hunt Festival
Chipping Norton Music Festival
Evesham Spring Regatta
Lambing, Cotswold Farm Park
Royal Shakespeare Theatre season begins
West Country Game Fair, Royal Bath & West Showground

April
Adderbury Day of (Morris) Dance www.adderbury.org
Broadway Spring point-to-point
Cheltenham International Jazz Festival
Cirencester Beer Festival
Evesham Vintage Easter Gathering
Great Blenheim Palace Easter Egg Challenge
GWR Toddington Spring Diesel Gala
Nailsworth Festival
Highnam Court Spring Fair
Shakespeare Birthday celebrations, Stratford
Stratford-Upon-Avon Literary Festival

May
Badminton Horse Trials
Banbury Beer Festival
Bath International Music Festival
Burford Levellers Day
Chipping Campden Music Festival
Clipping the yews, Painswick
Coopers Hill Cheese Rolling
Dover's Olympick Games, Chipping Campden
Gloucester Tall Ships Festival
Kemble Great Vintage Flying Weekend
Malvern Arts Festival
Malvern Spring Gardening Show
Pershore Carnival
Prescott Hill Classic Car Event
Randwick Cheese Rolling
South Cerney Street Fair BH M
Stow Horse Fair
Tetbury Woolsack Races BH M
Tewkesbury Festival of Food & Drink (&Merriment)
Tortworth Vintage Rally
Upton Folk Festival
Wychwood Music Festival, Cheltenham Racecourse

June
Banbury Show
Bledington Music Festival
Bloxham Steam Rally
Cheltenham Science Festival
Deddington Festival
Gloucester Medieval Fayre
Kemble Air Day
Longborough Festival Opera
Pershore Festival of Arts
Severn Project
Sudeley Castle Rose Week
Three Counties Agricultural Show, Malvern

July
Banbury Hobby Horse Festival
Cornbury Music Festival, Charlbury
Cotswold Show, Cirencester Park
Fairford Air Tattoo
Fairport Convention, Cropredy
Gloucester Festival
Gloucester Rhythm & Blues Festival
Hook Norton Fetsival of Fine Ales
Music Deo Sacra, Tewkesbury Abbey
Music At The Crossroads, Hook Norton

August
Bourton Water Games BH M
Evesham Flower Show
Prescott Vintage Hill Climb
Three Choirs Festival
Winchcombe Flower Show

September
Banbury Cavalcade of Sport
Battle of Britain Weekend, Kemble Airfield
Cheltenham Carnival
Chipping Norton Mop Fair
Moreton-in-Marsh Show

October
Banbury Canal Day
Cheltenham Literary Festival
Shipston Medieval Fun Fair
Stratford Mop Fair
Tewkesbury Mop Fair
Westonbirt Arboretum's Autumn Colours

November
Bonfire Show, Cheltenham Racecourse

December
Christmas Carol Service, Gloucester Cathedral

I would like to thank my darling wife, Caroline, for her constant support and encouragement, and for helping me choose the final images. Thank you Mike Taffinder, for reading my first and second drafts, and for your impeccable proof reading skills, encouragement and advice. Thank you to my parents, Margaret and Derek, for their open hospitality, often at a moments notice, and for their constant support over the years. Thank you to Richard Martin for allowing me to print extracts from his essay on the Golden Fleece. Not to be forgotten, all the kind persons at the many attractions, places to stay and eat, for showing me around their establishments and for putting up with my endless questions. Finally, I must thank Chris Dyer (Book Designer), Caroline Patterson (Editor) and David Cox (Cartographer) for maintaining a passion for this project. And, thank you, to Sebastian Faulks for permitting me to quote your praiseworthy comments on the cover of this book.

Photography

Until the introduction of digital photography most of my images were taken with a Nikon FE, a brilliantly robust and simple manual SLR, ably assisted by my trusty Manfrotto tripod. I must have got through at least six bodies over a twenty-year period. I was a little hesitant, at first, to be fully sold into the use of digital machines but I have been truly bowled over by the flexibility and practicality of this medium for my type of work. I started using a Fuji S1 Pro because of its compatibility with my lenses and because of its wonderful range of colour. Its slowness was a complete bore. I now use a Nikon D300 and despite its 450 page manual. I am just about coping with it. Its speed and quality of tone is awesome. I am not a techno freak and have little knowledge of other cameras and their multitudinous effects. I am a firm believer in getting up early and staying out late. If you have the patience you never know what light will unfold, or what may befall before you. These images have taken a good few years to muster. And, it can often be an incredibly frustrating business. I had been working on a book of Cotswold Gardens. It all went well the first year. The weather was kind and temperate. But, in the following year the whole of June was struck by constant rain and bitter winds. The same happened in the third year. The project is on-going and has yet to be completed. This book has a fair few of the first year's successes. I am loath to give advice about what I consider to be an incredibly difficult medium.I will just say get to know your subject well, and snap, snap-away, get closer, and be ruthless with your editing. For example, to achieve some decent images of surfers I had to learn to anticipate the curling wave and the carving surfer. I had to learn to surf and I am still learning but regrettably know that I will never really master it.

William Fricker

Loan of Images

Goldeneye would like to thank the following for allowing us to photograph their property, or for providing us with an image to illustrate their property. It is now not uncommon for a tourist attraction or charitable organisation to charge a fee for photographing their property. Goldeneye makes it a policy not to pay a fee given that a) we are promoting these properties (free of charge) and b) the cumulative expense would make this book an unfeasible production. We would hope that this policy may change and that a more mutually beneficial outcome may arise. A good number of illustrations used in this book were shot with permission before these organisations had a policy change at head office. Goldeneye would therefore prefer to illustrate a lesser-known property rather than the expected. Therefore, if you wonder why we have not illustrated the obvious key attraction in a town (a rare occurrence) that is the reason. So, again, thank you:

32 Imperial Square, Abbey House Gardens, Abbotswood, Andrew Dawkes Custodian of The Glebe, Barnsley House, Bath Priory Hotel, Beaufort Polo Club, Bell at Sapperton, Bennetts Fine Wines, Bibury Trout Farm, Blenheim Palace, Bliss Tweed Mill, Bradford Old Mill, Browns, Buckland Manor Hotel, Burford Parish Church, Calcot Manor & Spa, Campden Gallery, Celia Wet Paint Gallery, Cerney House Gardens, Cheltenham Art Gallery, Chipping Campden, Parish Church, Colin Carruther Martin's Gallery, Compton Verney Trust, Corsham Court, Cotswold Inns, Cotswold Motoring Museum, Cotswold Woollen Weavers, Cowley Manor, Cross O' Th' Hill Farm, Dalton Cotswold Falconry Centre, Daylesford Organic Farm, Demutha Vegetarian Restaurant, Donnington Brewery, Dorian House, Dyson, Earl of Wemyss & March, Stanway, Fairford Parish Church, Frocester Estate Barn, Gallery Pangolin, Gerald Harris Old Mill Museum, Gloucester Cathedral, Great Tew Estate, Guiting Power Parish Church, Hamish Mackie, Henson, Cotswold Farm Park, Hole in the Wall, Holy Trinity Church, Iona Gallery Woodstock, Jack Russell Gallery, Jake Sutton, Jane Bury, Jeremy George of The Glebe, John Davies Gallery, Keith Harding, Kelmscott Manor Trust, Kiftgate Court Gardens, Lords of the Manor Hotel, Lords Saye & Sele Broughton Castle, Lower Slaughter Manor, Lowsley-Williams Chavenage, Malvern Priory, Mike Finch Winchcombe Pottery, Mill Farm Long Compton, Misarden Park Garden, Morgan Motor Company, Mrs Paice Bourton House Garden, National Trust Ltd, Nature In Art Museum, New Inn Coln St Aldwyn, No 1 Royal Crescent, No 12 Park Street Cirencester, Owlpen Manor, Oxford Canal Trust, Oxfordshire Museums Trust, Painswick Rococo Garden, Pershore Abbey, Phil Adler, Rectory Kitchen, Royal Crescent Hotel, Russell's of Broadway, Sezincote, Shakespeare Birthplace Trust, Sudeley Castle, Sudeley Hill Farm, Tewkesbury Abbey, The Feathers, The Old Passage, The Rectory Crudwell, The Wheatsheaf, Trouble House Inn, Washbourne Court, Wesley House, Westonbirt Arboretum, Westward B&B, Wild Garlic, Wildfowl & Wetlands Trust, William Grevel's House, Winchcombe Parish Church, WM Ski, Woodchester Mansion

INDEX

MAP SYMBOLS EXPLAINED

♠ Abbey/Cathedral	♣ Pottery		Inshore Rescue Boat
✕ Battle Site	Pub/Inn		Leisure/Sports Centre
Bed & Breakfast Accomodation	Railway Interest		Lifeboat
Café	Restaurant		Parking
Castle	Standing Stone/Barrow		Picnic Site
Church/Chapel of Interest	Theatre/Concert Hall		Tents & Caravans
Cinema	Tourist Information		Sailing
Craft Interest	Tumulus/Tumuli		Surfing
Cross	Viewpoint		Tourist Information
Cycleway	Windmill/Wind Farm		Windsurfing
Fun Park/Leisure Park	Airfield		Youth Hostel
Hill Fort/Ancient Settlement	Aquarium		Agricultural Interest
Historic Building	Boat Trips		Arboretum
Hotel	Camping Site (Tents)		Bird Reserve
Industrial Interest	Caravan Site		Garden of Interest
Karting	Ferry (Pedestrians)		Vineyard
Lighthouse	Ferry (Vehicles)		Walks/Nature Trails
Mining Interest/Engine Houses	Fishing Trips		Wildlife Park
Miscellaneous/Natural Attraction	9/18 Hole Golf Course		Zoo
Museum/Art Gallery	Harbour		National Trust Car Park

381m.
305m.
229m.
152m.
76m.

A Road

B Road

Minor Road

Other Road or Track
(not necessarily with public
or vehicular access)

Railway

Cycleway

Open Space owned
by the National Trust

Built-up Area

Scale 1:100,000

0   1   (miles)   2

0   (km)

Barrow Wake, Birdlip Hill